# A practical guide to
# package holiday law and contracts

Fourmat Publishing

# A practical guide to Package Holiday Law and Contracts

by
John Nelson-Jones and Peter Stewart
both of Field Fisher Waterhouse, Solicitors

Second edition

*Foreword to the first edition by A. G. Kennedy,*
*Deputy Chairman & Chief Executive*
*of the Thomas Cook Group Ltd.*

London
**Fourmat Publishing**
1989

ISBN 1 85190 041 1


First published January 1985
Second edition June 1989

© 1989 Fourmat Publishing
27 & 28 St Albans Place, London N1 0NX

Printed in England by
Billing & Sons Limited, Worcester

# Foreword to the first edition

*by A. G. Kennedy, Deputy Chairman & Chief Executive of the Thomas Cook Group Ltd.*

In the last two decades the inclusive tour holiday business has shown dramatic growth. In any developing industry mistakes will always be made and in the case of the travel industry the collapse of Court Line in 1974 and more recently the demise of Laker have focused attention on the legal aspects of those involved in the travel industry, be they tour operators, airlines or travel agents.

During this period of growth, consumerism has come to the fore with members of the public questioning their rights in regard to contracts with tour operators and the role of travel agents.

As far as I know, this book is the first to deal solely with package holiday law and contracts; it is certainly timely and, more importantly, I believe it is readable both by those engaged in the holiday and travel industries and others who are connected with it in their capacity as journalists or legal advisers.

The authors have had considerable practical experience on this subject and the book will be a most useful reference work, dealing as it does with relatively new statutes and the increasing volume of case law which has now arisen.

AGK
November 1984

# Preface

The package holiday industry is affected by a wide range of common and statute law. This includes the common law of contract, agency, misrepresentation and tort; general legislation such as the Misrepresentation Act 1967, the Trade Descriptions Act 1968, the Unfair Contract Terms Act 1977, and Part III of the Consumer Protection Act 1987; specific holiday industry legislation such as the Air Travel Reserve Fund Act 1975 and certain provisions of the Civil Aviation Act 1982; and much else beside. In addition there are the Articles of Association and codes of conduct of the Association of British Travel Agents, and various codes of advertising and sales promotion practice.

This book aims to explain the relevant law and regulations in a concise and practical manner, and to describe and analyse the contracts which tour operators enter into with customers, travel agents, and the hoteliers, airlines etc whose services are featured in package holidays. In pursuing these aims, the authors seek to provide guidance both to holiday makers and their legal advisers and to those engaged in the holiday industry and their legal advisers.

Before examining the law relating to package holidays in detail, it would be beneficial for those readers who are not already familiar with it to have a general idea of how the holiday industry works and of the roles of its various trade associations and regulatory bodies. Chapter 1 is devoted to this.

It is critically important for readers to appreciate the essential difference between tour operators and travel agents. It is the tour operator who actually arranges the component facilities, such as hotels and flights, which comprise a package holiday. It is the travel agent who sells, as agent for the tour operator, the operator's package holiday. The holiday-maker's contract is with the tour operator, and allegations of breach of contract should usually be directed against the tour operator, not the travel agent. Chapter 2 deals in some detail with the nature of the contract between a holiday-maker and a tour operator and discusses the extent of the tour operator's contractual responsibility for the acts and omissions of hotels, airlines etc which he does not own and over which he has no control.

Travel agents have a dual role in relation to package holidays. The first is that of sales or booking agent for the tour operator. It involves displaying brochures, taking bookings, the subsequent servicing of bookings, and dealing with cancellations. The second is that of travel consultant to the customer, especially when a customer asks questions to try to establish whether a particular holiday will meet his requirements. Chapter 3 considers both these roles, and their attendant duties in law.

Allegations of misrepresentation can arise through, for example, the failure of a hotel to live up to its description, or through an inaccurate oral representation made by a travel agent about particular facilities offered by a tour operator. Misrepresentation can result not only in civil proceedings but also in proceedings under section 14 of the Trade Descriptions Act 1968 and under Part III of the Consumer Protection Act 1987. Chapter 4 examines the law relating to misrepresentation and misleading descriptions.

The landmark decisions in *Jarvis* v *Swan Tours* and *Jackson* v *Horizon Holidays* established that disappointment and vexation form a legitimate head of damages when, in breach of contract, a holiday goes wrong. Chapter 5 surveys the damages which a wronged holiday-maker might expect to receive in view of recent case law. It also deals with a holiday-maker's duty to mitigate his loss.

Chapter 6 seeks to summarise the position when a holiday-maker has a complaint about his holiday. Should he use the ABTA Arbitration Scheme, or should he issue proceedings? What difficulties does a tour operator face in defending claims and how can they be minimised?

In creating a package holiday the tour operator enters into a range of contracts with, for example, airlines, coach companies and hoteliers. Chapter 7 examines these contracts, and also the international conventions which limit the liabilities of carriers.

The travel industry has seen some spectacular crashes—Laker being just one example. Such crashes leave some holiday makers stranded and others having paid for holidays which will never take place. No book on package holidays would be complete without a chapter (Chapter 8) which discusses this problem and the bonding schemes and legislation which have been introduced to cope with it.

This book concentrates on the primary legislation, common law and ABTA regulations affecting the package holiday industry but the reader should also be aware of the following statutes which can be relevant:

(a) The Restrictive Practices Act 1976 requires trade associations, such as ABTA, to register restrictive provisions in their articles of association etc for approval, and reduces the scope for certain restrictive practices which might otherwise be adopted by tour operators and travel agents.

(b) The Resale Prices Act 1976 contains, *inter alia,* provisions prohibiting trade associations from imposing minimum price requirements upon their members.

(c) The Fair Trading Act 1973 contains various provisions for protecting consumers.

(d) The Competition Act 1980 enables the Office of Fair Trading to take action against anti-competitive practices.

(e) The Consumer Credit Act 1974 is applicable if a travel company provides consumer credit facilities for the purchase of holidays etc.

(f) The Transport Act 1980 lays down various requirements concerning, for example, the operation of coach services.

Because so little has been written about UK package holiday law this book would not have been possible without advice and assistance from many sources. The authors take this opportunity of thanking all of them.

The law is stated as at 1 March 1989.

John Nelson-Jones and Peter Stewart
Field Fisher Waterhouse
Lincoln House
296-302 High Holborn
London WC1V 7JL

# Contents

# Table of cases

# Chapter 1

# The structure of the holiday industry

## 1. Package holidays

Package holidays are holidays the elements of which are packaged together to form a whole which is sold at an inclusive price. The creator of the package is the tour operator who makes arrangements for transport companies, hotels etc to provide the travel, accommodation, meals and other items which together constitute a particular holiday. In some cases the tour operator, or companies under common ownership and control, will own the airlines and hotels which feature in the package. But many substantial operators do not own any airplanes or hotels and are not members of a group of companies which does. And even operators who own hotels and planes will often use some which they do not own.

People normally think of package holidays as involving a flight to some sunny resort, a comfortable hotel by the sea and a few excursions. But the range of package holidays is truly astonishing: ski holidays, cruise and coach holidays, self-catering holidays, sporting and adventure holidays, Holy Land and other special interest holidays and many more.

A tour operator normally sets out the package holidays which he is offering for a particular season in a brochure. As well as containing the basic factual information regarding each holiday, and items such as the operator's booking conditions and booking form, the brochure contains a battery of photographs and titillating prose—"the stuff that dreams are made of".

Most tour operators sell their holidays through travel

agents. Travel agents are the retailers of the travel industry. Between them they man travel shops in virtually every high street in the land. An agent will stock the brochures of the operators for whom he acts, answer questions about them, assist customers to complete the booking form and forward it to the operator for acceptance. Thereafter he performs a number of administrative functions. His role is totally different from that of the tour operator and an awareness of this is essential to a proper understanding of the legal responsibilities of each.

It is the tour operator who arranges the various facilities and services which make up the package holiday. For example, the tour operator who puts together a two week package holiday at the Hotel Luxury, Utopia, will normally:

(a) arrange for a representative to be at the airport from which the holiday makers depart to deal with any queries or problems on check-in;

(b) arrange with the carrying airline that either a whole plane or a certain number of seats on a plane will be available for his customers on the given departure date;

(c) arrange for representatives to meet the plane on arrival at its destination and assist the holiday makers in assembling on the coach that is to take them from the airport to the hotel;

(d) arrange for the coach to attend the airport on the given date;

(e) arrange for the hotel to make available the appropriate number of rooms and the appropriate meals for the two week period;

(f) arrange for his representatives to be available during the two week period to deal with any queries, sell excursions etc;

(g) arrange for a coach to collect the holiday makers and take them to the airport on the date of return to the UK;

(h) arrange the required number of seats on the airplane returning to the UK on the appropriate day.

Normally the cost of the package holiday will include all the above facilities and services (with the possible exception of the cost of excursions) and sometimes more, such as travel insurance.

A travel agent has no part in arranging or providing the facilities and services set out above. He is concerned solely with the business of selling package holidays, train tickets, airplane tickets, traveller's cheques, holiday insurance etc. It must be borne in mind that a travel agent sells not only package holidays but, in his capacity as booking agent for airlines, coach companies, hotels etc, sells the individual components which can provide a tailor-made holiday for those who do not like their holidays in packages. A travel agent will also give advice about which holiday to choose or the facilities available on a particular holiday.

The roles and responsibilities of tour operators and travel agents are totally separate and the public usually deal exclusively with travel agents. Many of the large travel companies are both tour operators and travel agents but proper consideration must always be given to the capacity in which such a company acts on a particular occasion. It frequently happens that, in its capacity as travel agent, a travel company will sell a package holiday provided by itself as tour operator, in which event its respective functions and responsibilities should be analysed separately.

Certain companies sell their own package holidays direct to the public without the services of a travel agent. In theory, they can provide holidays at a lower cost by avoiding having to pay sales commission to travel agents. They will, though, not be travel agents unless they also sell to the public holidays provided by other tour operators. Article 10(4) of the Articles of Association of ABTA (The Association of British Travel Agents) states that a tour operator member of ABTA who also carries on business as a travel agent must inform ABTA of this straight away and apply to be a travel agent member of ABTA as well as a tour operator member, unless its agency business is limited to the sale of its own holidays.

Most tour operators and travel agents are members of ABTA, and the leading ABTA operators are also members of the Tour Operators' Study Group. In addition the Civil Aviation Authority and the Air Travel Trust play important roles in relation to the holiday industry.

## 2. ABTA

The Association of British Travel Agents is a company limited by guarantee but not having a share capital which was incorporated in 1955. Its members comprise tour operators and travel agents all of whom pay annual subscription fees. As well as the rules laid down in its Articles of Association, ABTA also has codes of conduct for its operator and agent members (see Appendix).

### (a) ABTA travel agents

Article 4(1) of ABTA's Articles of Association provides that an applicant for membership of the Travel Agent's Class of ABTA must satisfy the ABTA's Travel Agent's Council that:

(i) he is engaged in the business of a travel agent; and

(ii) he employs at least one staff member who has two years' practical experience; or 18 months' practical experience plus COTAC Level 1 (COTAC is the industry's system of internal examinations); or 12 months' practical experience plus COTAC Level 2 (this follows the decision of Mr. Justice Lincoln in the Restrictive Trade Practices Court in January 1984 which relaxed the more stringent requirements which ABTA had previously imposed upon its retail members); and

(iii) his financial position is sound; none of the directors, partners or persons concerned with the management of the company is an undischarged bankrupt or has been involved with a business which has failed to meet its liabilities (for example, after the collapse of Laker Holidays, Sir Freddie Laker's subsequent application for membership of ABTA was rejected), or has been guilty of conduct which had he been a member of ABTA would have rendered him unfit for membership; and

(iv) he is not save at the discretion of the Travel Agents Council trading under the name of a previous member of ABTA which has failed to meet its liabilities.

Article 6 details the subscription fees which increase in proportion to a member's annual turnover. In addition an entrance fee is payable, details of which are contained in Article 5.

Every ABTA travel agent is required to contribute to the ABTA Travel Agent's Fund ("the Fund") such amount, not exceeding in any year half the amount of his annual subscription, as ABTA's Travel Agent's Council may determine. The primary purpose of the Fund is to indemnify "members of the travelling public" against losses sustained by them as a result of the insolvency of an ABTA travel agent. The Fund may also be used to indemnify ABTA tour operators against such losses sustained by them (Article 7(2)).

Article 7(4) enables ABTA to require any travel agent member to provide security for the protection of the Fund in such form and for such amount as the Travel Agent's Council shall in its discretion think necessary. ABTA's current policy is to require a new travel agent member to put up a £7,500 bond for each travel shop it operates, to be obtained from a bank or other financial institution acceptable to ABTA. This requirement is reviewed after the second and subsequent years of trading. Further protection for the Fund is currently provided by an indemnity insurance policy taken out by ABTA.

The need for the Fund and its supporting protection arrangements arises because in the course of their business travel agents hold significant sums of money which have been paid to them for onward transmission to tour operators, airlines and others. The problems which this creates when a travel agent ceases trading are discussed in Chapter 8.

ABTA travel agents who are also tour operators and whose annual tour operating turnover (as defined) exceeds £200,000 are required to become tour operating members of ABTA as well as travel agent members (Article 10(1)). If their annual tour operating turnover is £200,000 or less but more than £15,000, they are required to provide such bond or other security to protect the Fund as ABTA may consider necessary (Article 10(2)).

An ABTA travel agent is not permitted to sell package holidays organised by an operator who is not a member of ABTA without obtaining a dispensation from ABTA. He is bound by ABTA's published code of conduct for travel agents, copies of which can be obtained from ABTA on request. Certain provisions of the code of conduct are considered in Chapters 2 and 3 but at this stage it should be noted that:

(i) all advertising must comply with the Codes or Regulations of recognised bodies such as the Advertising Standards Authority, the Code of Advertising Practice Committee, the Independent Broadcasting Authority, the Independent Television Companies Authority and the Association of Independent Radio Companies (regulation 2.2);

(ii) to allow tour operators to contact the agent as a matter of urgency outside normal office hours an appropriate telephone number should be supplied (regulation 3.4).

If any infringement of the Code of Conduct is alleged against a member, the facts should be reported to ABTA for investigation during the course of which the member is under an obligation to supply as much documentation

and assistance as is sought by ABTA. The member will
be given an opportunity to put his case either orally or in
writing with or without the assistance of legal advisers.
The investigation is conducted by the Code of Conduct
Committee of the Travel Agents Council. A member who
is dissatisfied with its decision can appeal to an Appeal
Board, set up by the National Council (Article 16(3) of
ABTA's Articles of Association).

A member who is found guilty of a breach of the Code of
Conduct or of contravention of the Articles of Association
is liable to a reprimand, fine, suspension, or termination
of membership, depending upon the gravity of the
infringement (Article 16). Alternatively it may be
required to give suitable undertakings.

## (b) ABTA tour operators

Article 8 of ABTA's Articles of Association provides that
a tour operator will be admitted as a member of ABTA
provided that it can satisfy the Tour Operators' Council
that:

(i) it is engaged in the business of tour operator
(tour operator is defined as someone who as
principal organises and offers for sale to the
public, at an inclusive price, tours, holidays or
other travel arrangements comprising at least
transport and accommodation);

(ii) it publishes promotional literature to market
its tours or holidays;

(iii) its financial position is sound;

(iv) none of the directors, partners or persons concerned with the management of the company is
(or has been) an undischarged bankrupt; has
been involved with a business which has failed
to meet its liabilities or has been guilty of
conduct which had he been a member of ABTA
would have rendered him unfit for membership;

(v) it is not (save with the consent of the Tour
Operators' Council) trading under the name of

a previous member of ABTA which has failed to meet its liabilities; and

(vi) there is in force a bond or guarantee or other security in such form and amount as is acceptable to the Tour Operators' Council for securing the operator's liabilities.

A bond is an irrevocable guarantee to pay a specified amount, or sums not exceeding a specified amount, given by a third party such as a bank or insurance company which can be called upon in specified circumstances such as the insolvency of the company in respect of which the bond is provided. Under the ABTA bonding system the bonds are given in favour of ABTA except where the ABTA member is also a member of the Tour Operators' Study Group (see page 10), in which event it is given in favour of the TOSG Trust Fund Limited. In the event of the collapse of an ABTA member, ABTA or TOSG as the case may be calls in the member's bond and applies the bond monies in repatriating stranded holiday makers and thereafter in reimbursing customers of the failed operator whose holidays "never got off the ground".

The ABTA bonding arrangements are discussed in some detail in Chapter 8. The bonding levels are set by the Civil Aviation Authority which (as explained in Part 4 of this chapter) accepts bonds granted in favour of ABTA as satisfying its bonding requirements.

To supplement the bonding system, ABTA imposes upon its tour operator (and travel agent) members an obligation in the event of a financial collapse by a fellow member to assist in transporting back to the United Kingdom stranded customers of that member (Article 13(12)). Accordingly they must accede to any reasonable request by ABTA to make available unsold seats on aircraft or other forms of transport for use by ABTA to return a passenger to any point in the UK or elsewhere in fulfilment of the contractual obligations of a member who has ceased trading. Unsold accommodation is to be made available on the basis that it shall be paid for if the funds available under the bond of the defaulting member shall suffice for the purpose after satisfying all liabilities to members of the public properly payable thereout, but that otherwise it shall be made available free of charge.

The subscription rates payable by tour operator members are the same as those payable by travel agent members. As mentioned previously, it is possible for a travel company to be a member of the Association as a travel agent and as a tour operator. This does not necessarily mean that it would be liable to double subscription fees because Article 10(5) imposes a maximum combined subscription fee of £12,480 (increasing to £30,000 on 1 July 1989).

Tour operators are also subject to an ABTA code of conduct (copies can be obtained from ABTA on request). Its guidelines for booking conditions are considered in Chapter 2. The following points from the Code are worth noting at this juncture:

(i) The Code is taken to embody the relevant parts of those Acts of Parliament and Government Regulations which relate to Trade Descriptions and Civil Aviation and also the relevant parts of the regulations of such bodies as the Advertising Standards Authority, the Code of Advertising Practice Committee, the Independent Broadcasting Authority, the Independent Television Companies Authority and the Association of Independent Radio Companies which regulate the standards and practices of tour operators in relation to advertising (regulation 2.2).

(ii) An operator's brochure must give the operator's *legal* identity (in the case of a company this means the full and exact name of the company) (regulation 4.1).

(iii) The operator's brochure must state that, in the event of a dispute between operator and client, ABTA operates an Arbitration Scheme to which the operator must submit if the holiday maker wishes to take advantage of it (regulation 4.11).

The Arbitration Scheme (which is discussed in detail in

Chapter 6) is informal, even more so than the Small Claims Courts (arbitration by the Registrar of the County Court). It has the advantage from a holiday maker's viewpoint of putting upon the operator the onus to ensure that all documents are supplied and that matters proceed as expeditiously as possible to arbitration. It does not apply to claims for an amount greater than £1,500 per person or £7,500 per booking form or to claims which are solely or mainly in respect of physical injury or illness. Further, it does not apply where there is "a commercial dispute" (eg if the tour operator and travel agent dispute who is responsible for the holiday maker's loss). The holiday maker is required to pay a deposit towards the arbitrator's fees and, if unsuccessful, could be ordered to pay all of them. In such an instance, the Scheme would prove more expensive for the holiday maker than if he had issued proceedings in the Small Claims Court.

The procedures for investigating infringements by tour operator members are similar to those for investigating infringements by travel agent members save that the investigations and first hearing are conducted by the Code of Conduct Committee of the Tour Operators' Council. The appeal procedure is the same. An operator member who is found guilty of a breach of the Code of Conduct or the Articles of Association may be reprimanded, fined, suspended or expelled. Alternatively he may be required to give suitable undertakings.

## 3. Tour Operators' Study Group (TOSG)

In 1967 the twenty largest tour operators within ABTA formed the Tour Operators' Study Group ("TOSG"). This association remains separate from ABTA but consists exclusively of ABTA members. One of its aims is to review problems of the trade, taking into account both trade and consumer viewpoints and to report its findings with a view to influencing standards and practices within the trade.

The TOSG is, perhaps, best known for its bonding system, under which its members arrange for banks or insurance companies to enter into bonds in favour of The TOSG Trust Fund Ltd, which bonds can be called upon in the event of a member ceasing to trade. These bonds are accepted by both ABTA and the Civil Aviation Authority as satisfying their respective bonding requirements. In the event of the collapse of a TOSG member, TOSG calls in its bond and applies the bond monies in repatriating stranded holiday makers and thereafter in reimbursing customers whose holidays were due to start after the collapse occurred.

## 4. Civil Aviation Authority (CAA)

The Civil Aviation Authority ("the CAA") is a statutory body, under the ultimate supervision of the Department of Trade, which is responsible for, *inter alia*, the administration of airlines operating within the UK or flying to and from airports within the UK. The principal enactments to be borne in mind for the purposes of this section are the Civil Aviation Act 1982, and the Civil Aviation (Air Travel Organisers Licensing) Regulations 1972.

Section 71 of the 1982 Act reads:

> "Provision may be made by regulations for securing that a person does not in the United Kingdom—
>
> (a) make available, as a principal or an agent, accommodation for the carriage of persons or cargo on flights in any part of the world; or
>
> (b) hold himself out as a person who, either as a principal or an agent or without disclosing his capacity, may make such accommodation available, unless he is the operator of the relevant aircraft or holds and complies with the terms of a licence issued in pursuance of the regulations or is exempted by or under the regulations from the need to hold such a licence".

Regulation 2 of the 1972 Regulations provides that a tour operator who constructs holidays which have air travel as the principal means of transport will be required to obtain an Air Travel Organiser's Licence ("ATOL") from

11

the CAA. Under regulation 3 an application for the grant of a licence must be made in writing to the CAA and the CAA shall either grant a licence to the applicant in the terms requested in the application or in those terms with such modifications as the CAA thinks fit, or refuse to grant a licence. The CAA may refuse to consider an application unless it is accompanied by the appropriate fee and is made not less than six months before the beginning of the period for which the licence is proposed to be in effect.

Under Regulation 3(2) the CAA shall refuse to grant a licence unless it is satisfied that:

(a) the applicant is a fit person to make available accommodation for the carriage of persons on flights (and in determining whether the applicant is a fit person the Authority shall have regard to his and his employees' past activities generally and where the applicant is a body corporate, to the past activities generally of the persons appearing to the Authority to control that body; but shall not be obliged to refuse a licence on the grounds that it considers the applicant has insufficient experience in making available accommodation for the carriage of persons on flights); and

(b) the resources of the applicant and the financial arrangements made by him are adequate for discharge of his actual and potential obligations in respect of the activities in which he is engaged (if any) and in which he may be expected to engage if he is granted the licence.

One of the conditions of the grant of an ATOL is that the ATOL holder should be covered by a bond to protect its customers in the event that it becomes unable to perform its obligations to them. The CAA sets the level of bonds required for licensable activities (ie those activities for which an ATOL is required). The CAA will accept in satisfaction of its bonding requirements bonds granted in favour of TOSG and ABTA. Where an ATOL holder does not belong to either of these bodies, it must procure a bond in favour of the CAA, which will call in and administer the bond monies in the event of the ATOL holder ceasing to trade.

An ATOL may contain such terms as the CAA thinks fit, including terms as to the minimum charges which are to be made and the goods, services and other benefits which are or are not to be furnished by any person whatsoever under or in connection with any contract which includes provision for the making available of the accommodation to which the licence relates. A schedule of standard terms is incorporated in all ATOLs. The current standard terms are reproduced in Appendix B (see page 221).

Some of these terms are discussed in subsequent chapters but at this stage it is worth noting that standard term I requires a licence holder to include its exact company name and ATOL number in all advertising, brochures, and booking and confirmation of booking forms used for package holidays covered by its ATOL. In addition he is required to furnish to the CAA, as soon as it is published, a copy of any brochure in which he, or any agent acting on his behalf, quotes the prices at which he is prepared to make available accommodation for the carriage of persons on flights or to provide an inclusive tour which includes carriage by air, and a copy of any booking form relating to any such brochure.

If the holder of a current ATOL applies for the grant of another one in continuation of or in substitution for the current one and does so not later than three months (or in the case of a licence for a term of three months or less, half the term of the licence) before the expiration of the term of the current licence, then, unless the application is withdrawn, the current licence shall not cease to be in force by reason only of the expiration of that term until the CAA gives its decision on the application. The application must contain any information regarding fitness etc specified by the CAA and be accompanied by the appropriate fee.

An airline is not required to hold an ATOL, nor is an agent of an airline or an agent of an ATOL holder. Consequently a travel agent does not require an ATOL so long as he is selling tickets or holidays on behalf of airlines or tour operators who do hold ATOLs.

In *Jet Travel Limited* v *Slade Travel Agency Limited* (The Times 16 July 1983) it was held that intermediaries who did not sell air tickets directly to the public but only to other tour operators were still required to hold an ATOL. The facts of this case were that the plaintiffs were a subsidiary of a German company, Jet Reisen GmbH, which did not hold an ATOL and which, in the summer of 1981, entered into a number of whole plane charters with Dan Air Services Limited to make flights between Gatwick and cities in Germany. Jet Reisen sold some of their surplus seats to the plaintiffs who, in turn, sold them to the defendants on terms that the defendants should pay for the seats fourteen days in advance. In breach of that agreement, the defendants did not pay for seats sold to them between 30 November and 11 December 1981. The defendants held an ATOL and sold the tickets to the public.

The defendants alleged that the plaintiffs required an ATOL to sell the seats in the first place, the absence of which rendered the contract illegal and unenforceable. Lord Justice May held that the words of regulation 2 of the 1972 Regulations were clear, and that they applied to the plaintiff's obligations under their contract with the defendants. He stated that although the requirement of a bond was no doubt an important and perhaps the most important protection afforded to the travelling public, it was not the only one. The CAA had always to be satisfied that an applicant was a fit and proper person to hold an ATOL and of sufficient financial stability.

The grant of an ATOL does not guarantee that the holder is financially secure but the licence must be renewed each year, the theory being that this will alert the CAA to deteriorating financial positions.

## 5. Air Travel Trust

The Air Travel Reserve Fund Act 1975 established the Air Travel Reserve Fund ("the Fund"). The purpose of the Fund was to provide assistance to the holiday maker if ABTA/TOSG/CAA bonds provide insufficient security. The Fund was dissolved by Order in Council on 27 February 1986 and its assets were passed to the Air Travel Trust ("the Trust") on that date. The Trust had previously been established by the Secretary of State for Transport by means of a Trust deed. It has been given wider discretionary powers than those enjoyed by its predecessor, the Air Travel Reserve Fund Agency. Like its predecessor, the new trust fund extends the protection afforded to those who purchase *package holidays* involving *chartered* air seats offered by ATOL holders. It does *not* protect:

(a) customers who lose money when an airline fails where they have bought tickets from the airline or an agent of the airline; and

(b) customers who purchase holidays from someone who is not an ATOL holder; and

(c) customers who purchase from an ATOL holder a holiday (eg a coach holiday not involving air travel) in respect of which an ATOL is not required.

In 1975 the CAA in exercise of its powers under section 2 of the 1975 Act made the Air Travel Reserve Fund Agency Benefit Rules which contained detailed provisions concerning the application of the former Fund. These included provisions for determining the amount of a customer's loss and the conditions to be satisfied before payments are made out of the Fund. They were considered to be too restrictive and have been replaced by a Statement of Policies on the Administration of Tour Operator's Bonds issued by the Air Travel Trust, the CAA, ABTA and the TOSG.

## 6. Non-licensable holidays

The bonding requirements of the CAA and the back up protection afforded by the Air Travel Trust only apply in respect of holidays for which an ATOL is required. Customers who book holidays, such as coach and cruise holidays, which do not feature air travel are not protected by any statutory scheme against the collapse of the tour operators with whom they book. However, where such holidays are provided by operators who are members of ABTA, a substantial measure of protection is afforded by ABTA's bonding requirements and indemnity insurance schemes. ABTA members must obtain bonds of 10% (20% for members of TOSG) on non licensable turnover and are also covered by an indemnity insurance scheme, whereby each member is covered to £75,000 (there is also a pool of £3 million should this not prove sufficient).

Members of the Passenger Shipping Association are also bonded against financial failure. So holiday makers who book cruise holidays with them enjoy similar protection to those who book non licensable holidays with members of ABTA.

Even if a *coach* holiday operator is not a member of ABTA, a measure of protection will be available if it is a member of the Bonded Coach Holidays Section of the Bus & Coach Council. Members of this Section are required to put up bonds in favour of the Section which can be called up in the event of a member's collapse. The proceeds of the bond are then applied in repatriating stranded holiday makers enabling mid-stream holiday makers to complete their holidays, and in making alternative arrangements for customers whose holidays have been totally aborted by the collapse.

This book is only concerned with the law and practice relating to package holidays. Nevertheless it is worth mentioning in passing that someone who buys an air ticket on its own is vulnerable to the collapse of the airline between the date on which he pays and the date of his flight. The monies which he has paid will almost certainly be the property of the airline, (even if they are still in the hands of a travel agent) and there are no statutory or ABTA bonding or insurance arrangements to provide any protection—as so many Laker customers found to their cost. His only hope of recovering any of "his" money is to claim in the liquidation of the airline.

# Chapter 2

# Tour operators and their responsibilities

## 1. Introduction

When a holiday maker books a package holiday, his contract is with the tour operator who arranges the various component parts of the package, such as travel by air, sea or land, accommodation, guides etc. The travel agent who takes the holiday maker's booking does so in his capacity as booking agent for the tour operator and is not himself a party to the contract for the sale and purchase of the holiday. This chapter considers primarily the nature of the contract between the tour operator and the holiday maker, and the terms normally found in it. The subject of misrepresentation by the tour operator is dealt with separately in Chapter 4.

A feature of the package holiday is that in most cases the tour operator does not himself provide the flights, accommodation, meals etc which go to make up the holidays advertised in his brochure. But it is he who makes the arrangements which enable the holiday to be sold as a package, and it is he who enters into contracts with the airlines, hotels etc, involved in the package. Usually the holiday maker has no contractual link with hotels and so is not in a position to make breach of contract claims against them. He may be able in appropriate circumstances to make non contractual negligence claims against them but that depends on the law of the country concerned, quite apart from which an English holiday maker faces obvious difficulties in conducting court proceedings in a foreign country.

The fact that, in most cases, the tour operator does not

himself provide the flights, accommodation, meals etc which feature in the package which he sells to his customers is a source of interesting contractual problems. What are the tour operator's contractual responsibilities to his customers? Is he responsible in damages for every accident suffered by holiday makers through the negligence of the airlines which he employs or for every bowl of boiling soup which hotel waiters accidentally drop on the laps of his customers? Or is he only liable if he has made what the French describe as a "mauvais choix", namely a failure to choose good airlines, hotels etc?

## 2. Nature of the contract

Many holiday makers consider that any fault in a package holiday, whether on the part of the tour operator or of persons, such as hoteliers, who actually provide the services which make up the package, gives them a claim for breach of contract against the tour operator. This also seems to be the view taken by some county courts. On the other hand tour operators consider that they are not responsible in contract for uncharacteristic lapses by airlines and hotels so long as they (the tour operator) have chosen reputable airlines and hotels of an appropriate standard and given them all necessary information and instructions. The differing viewpoints are best illustrated by a concrete example. If a holiday maker books a package holiday with a tour operator and becomes ill as a result of a meal eaten at his hotel—it being accepted that this had never happened at that hotel before (possibly, it was the fault of the local butcher)—will the tour operator be liable to compensate the disappointed holiday maker for, say, losing the enjoyment of the last few days of his holiday?

Those who seek to impose liability upon a tour operator in such circumstances argue that:

(a) The holiday maker's contract was with the tour operator.

(b) Most brochures detail what the holiday maker

receives in return for the price of his holiday. One of these items is meals. For example one major tour operator's brochure under the heading "What your holiday price includes" states "Meals at your hotels according to the type of holiday you have booked". Thus, the contract is, *inter alia,* for the sale of goods (ie food) the consideration for which was paid to the tour operator.

(c) Section 14 of the Sale of Goods Act 1979 states that where a purchaser, either expressly or by implication, makes known to the vendor the purpose for which the goods are required, and the goods in question are sold in the course of a business, there is an implied term in the contract that the goods shall be reasonably fit for the purpose for which they are supplied. The tour operator contracts in the course of his business and knows, by implication, that the food should be edible. There is, therefore, an implied condition in the contract to this effect.

(d) Section 6(2) of the Unfair Contract Terms Act 1977 provides that—

"As against a person dealing as a consumer, liability for breach of the obligations arising from:

(a) Sections 13, 14, or 15 of the 1893 Act (seller's implied undertakings as to conformity of goods with description or sample, or as to their quality or fitness for a particular purpose);

cannot be excluded or restricted by reference to any contract term".

The holiday maker contracts as a consumer and, by virtue of the above, the tour operator is precluded from excluding the implied condition regarding fitness for purpose.

(e) The tour operator is thus in breach of contract and liable in damages to the holiday maker. The holiday maker would, if the hotel were in

England, also have a valid cause of action in tort against the hotelier if he could show that the hotelier had negligently provided the food in question. It is, however, much simpler for the holiday maker to claim in contract against the tour operator, particularly in relation to overseas holidays.

Tour operators analyse the contract in a very different manner:

(a) The contract was one for the provision of services to be supplied, mainly by independent contractors, one of them being the provision of meals by the hotel.

(b) The tour operator is under an implied obligation to select competent independent contractors, including a competent hotelier.

(c) The tour operator had chosen a reputable hotel and, prior to making a contract with it, had inspected its kitchen and sampled its food, finding them to be satisfactory.

(d) The services contracted for were provided, albeit that one meal was unsatisfactory.

(e) The tour operator has, therefore, acted in accordance with its obligations under the contract and is not in breach.

(f) Any claim which the holiday maker may have is against the hotel or the local butcher in the overseas country's equivalent of negligence.

The mere fact that a party to a contract employs an independent contractor to perform some of his obligations does not by itself exempt him from responsibility if the independent contractor's performance is inadequate. The basic legal principle is concisely set out in *Winfield on Tort* (12th ed) (page 594):

"The true question in every case in which an employer is sued for damage caused by his independent contractor is whether the employer himself was in breach of some duty which he himself owed to the plaintiff"

The relevant passage in *Winfield* continues—

"Such a breach of duty may exist if the employer has not taken care to select a competent contractor or has employed an inadequate number of men. It may also exist if the contractor alone has been at fault, provided that the duty cast upon the employer is of the kind commonly described as "non-delegable". Strictly speaking no duty is delegable but if my duty is merely to take reasonable care, then, if I have taken care to select a competent contractor to do the work, I have done all that is required of me. If, on the other hand, my duty is, eg 'to provide that care is taken' or is to achieve some actual result such as the secure fencing of dangerous parts of machinery, then my duty is not performed unless care is taken or the machinery is fenced. It is no defence that I delegated the task to an independent contractor if he failed to fulfil his duties".

*Winfield* is discussing the situation in tort but the principle which he enunciates is of general application. It indicates that a tour operator will only be liable for the deficiencies of hoteliers etc selected by it where they result in a breach of some duty which the tour operator owes to the holiday maker. The question, then, is whether the tour operator's contractual duties to the holiday maker are such that the tour operator is responsible to the holiday maker for failures on the part of the airlines, hotels etc which feature in a package holiday.

Assuming for the moment that the tour operator's brochure makes it clear that the tour operator does not own or operate the airlines, hotels etc which provide the services comprised in the package holiday, what is the scope of the tour operator's contractual duty to the holiday maker? Obviously and indisputably the tour operator is under a contractual obligation to exercise care in selecting reputable and suitable hotels. This duty, the writers submit, goes far beyond just checking that the hotel is not a place of ill repute. It almost certainly requires the tour operator to conduct a thorough and careful inspection of the hotel and to check all aspects of its operation including safety and sanitary standards, the quality of the hotel's food and service, the adequacy of its air conditioning system, and so on. Furthermore the operator must ensure that all facilities of the hotel which are described, or suggested by pictures, in its brochure are present and genuinely operational.

Do the operator's contractual duties go beyond choosing suitable airlines and hotels and ensuring that what it says and implies in its brochure is accurate? Do they, for instance, require it to guarantee that there will be no failures on the part of the independent contractors which it employs or that there will be no temporary withdrawal of any facility, or even that the holiday maker will enjoy himself? When a developer employs a building contractor to erect a building, the building contractor is normally responsible for all work in connection with that building even though some of it is performed by independent sub-contractors. Are tour operators similarly responsible for every act or omission of the airlines, coach operators, hoteliers etc whom they employ?

## 3. The leading cases

### (a) Wall v Silver Wing

There are few reported cases which deal with the nature of the contract between holiday maker and tour operator. This makes it all the more surprising that the case of *Wall* v *Silver Wing Surface Arrangements Limited (trading as Enterprise Holidays)* (1981) was never reported. In it the plaintiff suffered serious personal injury due to a fire exit at the Marina Aparthol, Puerto de la Cruz being locked (to prevent burglars getting in). Two facts, in particular, should be noted:

(a) In their booking conditions, Enterprise made no reference to liability for injury. They did not try to avoid responsibility for any fault of their own, nor did they say that they were not responsible for the acts or omissions of the airlines, hotels etc featured in the brochures.

(b) The fire escape was defective because the exit

gate had been locked arbitrarily by the hotel management for security reasons. Had the gate not been locked, which it was not when Enterprise's representative inspected the hotel, the fire escape would have proved satisfactory.

The plaintiff's claim was based in contract and/or tort, the former being on the grounds that there was an implied term or condition in the contract that the plaintiffs would be reasonably safe in using the hotel for the purpose for which they were invited to be there. Mr. Justice Hodgson, in deciding in favour of the defendants, specifically rejected this contention. His Lordship made the following comments, *inter alia*:

- "In the normal way it is perfectly well known that the tour operator neither owns, occupies or controls the hotels which are included in his brochure, any more than he has control over the airlines which fly his customers, the airports whence and whither they fly and the land transport which conveys them from airport to hotel".

- "If injury is caused by the default of the hotel owners and occupiers, the airline, the airport controllers or the taxi proprietor, the customer will have whatever remedy (against them) the relevant law allows".

- ". . . I would find it wholly unreasonable to saddle a tour operator with an obligation to ensure the safety of all the components of the package over none of which he had any control at all".

This case supports the view that the contract between tour operator and holiday maker is a contract whereby the tour operator undertakes to exercise skill and care in making suitable arrangements with airlines, hotels etc and that it will not be liable for their negligence so long as it exercises sufficient care in selecting and instructing them. The tour operator's position in this respect is likely to be even stronger if he makes it clear to the holiday maker that he (the tour operator) is only engaged in arranging for the provision of services and that the flights, accommodation and meals are being provided by independent contractors. But any normal holiday maker should know that anyway.

## (b) Jarvis v Swan Tours

Another interesting case is that of *Jarvis* v *Swan Tours Limited* [1973] 1 All ER 71, the facts of which were that the defendant's 1969/70 winter sports brochure described one of its holidays as a "house-party in Morlialp", Switzerland with "special resident host". The brochure stated that the price of the holiday included the following house-party arrangements: "Welcome party on arrival. Afternoon tea and cake . . . Swiss dinner by candlelight. Fondue party. Yodler evening . . . farewell party". It also stated that there was a wide variety of ski runs at Morlialp, ski packs could be hired there, the hotel was chosen because of its comfort, the hotel owner spoke English and the hotel bar would be open several evenings a week. The brochure added . . . "You will be in for a great time when you book this house-party holiday". The plaintiff booked a fifteen day holiday between 20.12.1969 and 3.1.1970 for a cost of £63.45. In the first week of the holiday, the house-party consisted only of 13 people, and for the second week he was the only person there. There was no welcome party, the ski runs were some distance away and no full length skis were available except on two days in the second week. The hotel owner did not speak English. The cake for tea was only potato crisps and dry nutcake. There was not much entertainment at night— the yodler was a local man in his working clothes singing a few songs quickly and the hotel bar was an annexe open only on one evening. During the second week there was no representative at the hotel.

It would seem that in this case the tour operator had committed offences under the Trade Descriptions Act 1968 and had engaged in serious misrepresentations. However, this chapter is concerned only with the position in contract. The tour operator was, not surprisingly, found to have been in breach of contract:

> *Per* Edmund Davies LJ: "Those travel agents made

it clear by their lavishly illustrated brochure with its ecstatic text that what they were contracting to provide was not merely air travel, hotel accommodation and meals of a certain standard. To quote the assurance which they gave regarding the Morlialp House-Party Centre 'no doubt you will be in for a great time when you book this house party holiday'. The result was that they did not limit themselves to the obligations to ensure that an air passage was booked, that hotel accommodation was reserved, that food was provided and these items would measure up to the standards they themselves set up. They went further than that. They assured and undertook to provide a holiday of a certain quality, with 'Gemutlichkeit' (that is to say, geniality, comfort and cosiness) as its overall characteristics, and 'a great time', the enjoyable outcome which would surely result to all but the most determined misanthrope".

What Edmund Davies LJ was saying was that in this case the tone and wording of the brochure constituted an undertaking that any normally sociable person would have 'a great time'. It was not merely representing that the hotel was a good hotel in a pleasant ski-ing setting but that the ambience of the hotel was such that enjoyment and pleasure were guaranteed. In such a case it does not matter that the tour operator does not own the hotel and that the holiday maker knows that he does not because the tour operator has taken upon himself the burden of ensuring a "great time".

### (c) *Rogers v Night Riders*

The question of what a party to a contract represents itself as doing arose in the case of *Rogers* v *Night Riders (a firm) and Others* [1983] RTR 324. The plaintiff's mother telephoned the first and third defendants, who were two firms under the same management and control operating a mini-cab service, to request a mini-cab to take her husband and daughter to Euston railway station. The defendants contacted one of their drivers by car radio to take the fare. Their drivers owned, maintained and controlled their own vehicles but the defendants ensured that they had held a driving licence for at least two years and had their own private hire insurance. In the course of the journey there was an accident caused by the defective nature of the mini-cab and negligent driving as a result of which the plaintiff suffered personal injury.

The Court of Appeal held that on the facts the defendants had held themselves out to the general public as a car hire firm undertaking to provide a vehicle to convey the plaintiff to her destination; that the defendants could foresee that the plaintiff might be injured if the vehicle provided for her was defective and, accordingly, they owed the plaintiff a duty to take reasonable steps to ensure that the vehicle was properly maintained. Furthermore this duty could not be delegated by the defendants to a third party, such as the driver, so as to avoid responsibility for breach of it.

The crucial point was the way in which the defendants held themselves out to the general public. Unlike tour operators, who make it clear that they themselves do not provide the services and facilities featured in their brochures, the defendants gave the impression that they did actually provide the service. The following comments by Dunn LJ should be noted:

> "The firm Night Riders or A1 Cars hold themselves out to the general public as a car hire firm and they undertook to provide a hire car to take the plaintiff to Euston Station. In those circumstances, they owed the plaintiff a duty to take reasonable steps to ensure that the car was reasonably fit for that purpose. It matters not whether the duty is put in contract or in tort, either way it is a duty they could not delegate to a third person so as to evade responsibility if the car was not fit for that purpose. There was no suggestion in the evidence in the Court below, and it was never put to the plaintiff, that she was told of the true position of the firm, that is to say, the car did not belong to them and that the firm was no more than a booking agent for owner drivers'

cars over which they had no control. If there had been such evidence and if the true nature of the defendant's business had been known to the plaintiff, then the situation would have been different. But, so far as the plaintiff was concerned, she was dealing with a car hire firm not a mere booking agency and, accordingly, the defendants were under a primary duty to her".

A tour operator is not a mere booking agent but nor is it a provider of travel and accommodation services in its own right. The writers consider that the Court of Appeal and House of Lords will, when put to the test, imply into package holiday contracts warranties that the tour operator has exercised reasonable care and skill to select hotels by visiting and inspecting them carefully before its brochure was compiled and by checking their sanitary and safety arrangements, and that the hotel in normal circumstances matches its description in the brochure but would expect them, as in the *Wall* v *Silver Wing* case, to stop short of imposing any absolute liability to guarantee safety, sanitariness etc. However good the hotel, the possibility of legionnaires disease being contracted at it cannot be ruled out. Nor can one be sure that once in a blue moon some member of the hotel's staff will not cause injury or loss by some act of personal negligence. Tour operators owe their customers a high standard of care but not, in the writers' submission, an absolute one unless they go overboard in their brochures and promise a great, carefree, time of your life, everything possible for your comfort and enjoyment etc, holiday.

## (d) Craven v Strand Holidays

The writers' opinion concerning the responsibilities of tour operators is reinforced by the views expressed by the Ontario Court of Appeal in the case of *Craven* v *Strand Holidays (Canada) Limited* (1982) 40 OR (2d) 186. In this case the plaintiffs claimed damages for injuries received when the bus in which they were travelling overturned. They had booked a holiday in Columbia through the defendant tour operator which in turn had booked the bus transport with an independent bus company. The judge who heard the case found for the plaintiffs but the Court of Appeal reversed his decision and held that Strand was not liable since it had exercised due care in the selection of the bus company. The following quotations indicate the reasons for the Court of Appeal's decision:

"If a person agrees to perform some work or services he cannot escape contractual liability by delegating the performance to another. It is his contract. But if the contract is only to . . . arrange for the performance of services, then he has fulfilled his contract if he has exercised due care in the selection of a competent contractor. He is not responsible if that contractor is negligent in the performance of the actual work or service, for the performance is not part of his contract".

"A person is not liable for the negligence of an independent contractor unless he has a primary obligation to carry out a non-delegable duty imposed upon him by law or by contract. It is clear on the evidence that Strand never undertook to perform the bus transfers but merely to arrange for this to be done by a third party".

"The relationship of the bus company to the appellant (Strand) being that of independent contractor precludes any liability, either in tort or contract, unless the appellant itself was guilty of negligence. By the brochure containing the essential terms of the contract, Strand agreed to supply the respondents with a Columbia tour including transportation, hotels and certain meals, but did not ensure the safety of the travellers. The disclaimer in the brochure quoted is inconsistent with an agreement or an intent to assume any implied obligations for the safety of the transportation".

"To support the implied term (that Strand was responsible for ensuring the safety of its holiday makers) the respondents rely on the dicta contained in the line of cases illustrated by *Jarvis* v *Swan*

*Tours Limited* and *Jackson* v *Horizon Holidays Limited.* As I understand them, these cases, the first of which was relied upon by the trial judge awarded damages as compensation for loss of entertainment and enjoyment where the facilities glowingly described in the travel agent's brochure were found to be lacking. Where a misrepresentation is made with promissory intent and is a term of the contract, the common law gives a remedy in damages for breach of contract. *Jarvis* v *Swan Tours Limited* founded liability on this basis. Damages were awarded because the tour operators 'broke their contract and provided . . . a holiday lacking in some of the things which they contracted to include in it'."

The Ontario Court of Appeal also overruled the trial judge's finding that the limitation of liability wording contained in Strand's brochure was ineffective to relieve Strand of liability, Lacourciere JA stating:

"I am of the opinion that under the circumstances of this case, it was open to the appellant, Strand, to rely on the exclusionary provisions of the contract. This is not a case where the respondents accepted a standard form contract containing onerous provisions in small type in circumstances where no-one could be reasonably expected to read it. This was not a transaction carried out in a hurried manner where speed could be said to be one of the attractive features of the services provided".

## (e) Recent county court cases

The authors' assessment of current English law regarding the responsibilities of tour operators is supported by some recent county court cases, most notably *Kaye* v *Intasun* [1987] CLY 1150, *Gibbons* v *Intasun* [1987] 1 CL 16A and *Usher* v *Intasun* [1987] CLY 418. In the *Kaye* case, the plaintiff's room was invaded by cockroaches during the first three nights of his holiday. He lost sleep and his daughter was badly upset. The evidence indicated that the hotel had not been afflicted by cockroaches before or after the plaintiff's stay, and that the defendants had not failed in their monitoring or other responsibilities. The plaintiff contended that the mere existence of the cockroach problem while he was there represented a breach of contract. The court rejected this contention and dismissed the plaintiff's claim.

In the *Gibbons* case, the plaintiff's luggage was lost during transfer from airport to hotel. She lost all her, and her children's, clothes. They flew home without taking their holiday. She sued Intasun for breach of contract and negligence, but during the trial these allegations were withdrawn. She also sued them for breach of an alleged duty as bailees. It was held that it is well known that tour operators employ local independent coach companies to effect transfers. The fact that the tour operator's representative works with the coach driver during the transfer process did not establish Intasun as bailees of the plaintiff's luggage. The claim failed.

In the *Usher* case, industrial action and technical problems resulted in the plaintiffs, a honeymoon couple, arriving a day late in Tenerife. But the court held that a tour operator is not responsible for problems experienced in connection with a properly selected airline. However, the court did accept the plaintiffs' claim that Intasun should have done more to reassure the plaintiffs. This was held to constitute a breach of an implied contractual term and the plaintiffs were awarded £50.

## 4. Strict liability and the proposed EEC directive

Consumer organisations and many genuinely disaffected holiday makers reject out of hand the suggestion that "strict liability" should not be imposed upon tour operators. Much of the reasoning behind this is on the basis of the balance of convenience. If strict liability is not imposed, holiday makers will have, as their only avenue of recourse, to sue abroad (eg a Spanish hotelier) for negligence. This will be something beyond the means of many and, in any event, the sums of money involved would usually be far outweighed by the cost of taking such a step. The answer in many cases could be for tour operators to accept, or be required to accept, more responsibility for obtaining recompense for holiday makers where a hotel has slipped up. An operator should ensure that its contracts with hotels will enable it to recover in circumstances where the customer himself would be able to recover if he were in a contractual relationship with the hotel. The operator has a representative on the spot and a continuing relationship with his hotels and so should be able to obtain a reasonable settlement of any genuine grievance.

The justification for strict liability is analogous to the commonly accepted justification of vicarious liability, enunciated by Lord Pearce in *Imperial Chemical Industries Limited* v *Shatwell* [1965] AC 565:

> "The doctrine of vicarious liability has not grown from any very clear, logical or legal principle but from social convenience and rough justice".

But in relation to package holidays it is important that "rough justice" should be applied with discrimination. One of the commonly accepted benefits of package holidays is their cheapness, which has made foreign holidays available to a far wider market. If "strict liability" is imposed upon operators, it is bound to increase their financial liabilities which will be reflected in the cost of package holidays. This is particularly so because there are some holiday makers who will press excessive claims if it is made easy to do so. It is a relatively simple matter to pick on something that has gone a bit wrong and blow it up out of all proportion. Unfortunately there are in life a few people who will exploit any opportunity of financing their next year's holiday; others who, possibly with the help of lawyers, claim to have fads or allergies of exceptional intensity which, if not accommodated, apparently justify massive distress claims; and others whose equilibrium is so delicate as to be upset by what most people would take in their stride. It is in the interests of the average holiday maker as well as of the tour operator that these people should not be given too much scope.

Be that as it may, it looks as if the EEC is likely to

impose at least a measure of strict liability on UK tour operators. The European Commission has published a draft directive on package travel, including package holidays and package tours. This draft directive deals with all aspects of the package holiday contract. As regards strict liability, the relevant passage is Article 5. It requires member states of the EEC to ensure that:

(i) all services provided in the course of a package holiday, whether by the organiser (i.e. "tour operator") or by a third person, shall be rendered punctually and efficiently;

(ii) *vis-à-vis* the consumer, liability for any deficiency in the provision of those services lies either with the organiser or (in those member states which so prefer) with the travel agent.

The wording of Article 5 is not totally clear, but it is believed that the intention is to make the tour operator liable for all negligence or other default by the airlines, coach companies, hotels etc whose services feature in a package holiday. It is not within the scope of this book to discuss the pros and cons of the draft directive. Readers who are interested in such a discussion are referred to the report on the draft directive of the Select Committee on the European Communities of the House of Lords (HL Paper 107) which is available from HMSO. The final version of the directive may be modified so that strict liability is imposed on tour operators in relation to hotels but not to airlines, shipping lines and other international carriers. But it is almost certain that by 1992 the EEC will have made a radical intervention in favour of the holiday maker, albeit one which will have to be paid for by some increase in package holiday prices.

## 5. Standard booking conditions

### (a) Unfair Contract Terms Act 1977

Having discussed the general contractual position, the terms and conditions which normally appear in package holiday brochures fall to be considered. But first, some relevant sections from the Unfair Contract Terms Act 1977 should be noted:

"2. (1) A person cannot by reference to any contract term or to a notice given to persons generally or to particular persons exclude or restrict his liability for death or personal injury resulting from negligence".

"3. (1) This section applies as between contracting parties where one of them deals as consumer or on the other's written standard terms of business.

(2) As against that party, the other cannot by reference to any contract term—

(a) when himself in breach of contract, exclude or restrict any liability of his in respect of his breach; or

(b) claim to be entitled—

(i) to render a contractual performance substantially different from that which was reasonably expected of him; or

(ii) in respect of the whole or any part of his contractual obligation, to render no performance at all;

except in so far as (in any of the cases mentioned above in this sub-section) the contract term satisfied the requirement of reasonableness".

"11. (1) In relation to a contract term the requirement of reasonableness is that the term shall have been a fair and reasonable one to be included having regard to the circumstances which were, or ought reasonably to have been, known to or in the contemplation of the parties when the contract was made".

Schedule 2 of the 1977 Act lays down the following guidelines regarding reasonableness which are relevant to a contract between a holiday maker and a tour operator—

(a) the relative strength of bargaining position of the parties;

(b) whether the customer could have entered into a similar contract with other persons but without having to accept a similar term;

(c) whether the customer knew or ought to have known of the existence and extent of the terms;

(d) whether or not the customer received an inducement to enter into the contract.

A holiday maker contracts as consumer with a tour operator and this imposes a greater responsibility on the operator than if the contract was between equal parties. Most operators recognise this and ABTA, after consultation with the Office of Fair Trading over a code of conduct which is mandatory for all ABTA members, forbids its members to include in their brochures clauses which purport to—

(a) exclude or limit liability for misleading statements made by the operator, his employees or agents;

(b) exclude or limit liability for the operator's contractual duty to exercise diligence in making arrangements for a package holiday;

(c) exclude liability for any alleged cause of dissatisfaction if complaint is not made within a fixed period unless that period is at least 28 days.

In addition, ss. 2 and 3 of the Unfair Contract Terms Act 1977 (see above) mean that a tour operator's brochures cannot contain clauses purporting—

(a) to exclude liability for death or injury caused by the operator's own negligence; and

(b) to exclude liability for breach of contract, or loss or damage caused by negligence or the rendering of a service different from that expected, unless reasonable within the Act to do so.

The provisions of the Unfair Contract Terms Act which are set out in the preceding paragraphs are particularly relevant in the case of holidays, such as most cruise and many coach holidays, where the tour operator itself provides transport or accommodation. In such cases any attempt by the tour operator to exclude liability for its own negligence or failure to perform will have to meet the requirements of the 1977 Act, except insofar as they are overridden by the Athens and Geneva Conventions (see Chapter 7). But the requirements of the 1977 Act are also relevant in the more normal case where the tour operator does not provide any transport or accommodation because its obligation to make suitable arrangements is one which frequently gives rise to liabilities which some tour operators might wish to exclude; and also because of the provisions in most brochures which seek to enable tour operators to withdraw from or vary their obligations in certain specified circumstances.

## (b) Brochures and booking conditions

The terms and conditions of the contract between holiday maker and tour operator are contained in the operator's brochure. It must give the exact name of the tour operator (ie the name under which it is registered at the Companies Registration Office) and where applicable specify its ATOL number. It also specifies the price of the holiday and when it is payable, flight departure times, the accommodation, the location of the resort, and all the items which are comprised in the holiday price. Descriptions and pictures of the facilities available are representations (and will be considered as such in Chapter 4) but they are also, following a booking, incorporated in the holiday contract as either terms or warranties.

Brochures issued by tour operators must have regard to the relevant provisions of the Misrepresentation Act 1967, the Trade Descriptions Act 1968, the Civil Aviation Act 1982, the Unfair Contract Terms Act 1977 and Part III of the Consumer Protection Act 1987. In addition the brochures of ABTA members must satisfy the requirements of Rule 4 of the Tour Operators' Code of Conduct and ABTA's Guidelines for Booking Conditions, both of which are reproduced in the Appendix to this book.

Most tour operators' brochures contain booking conditions,

sometimes described as guarantees of fair trading which provide:

(i) That the contract becomes effective from the date on which the operator confirms the booking, from which date any monies paid by the holiday maker to a travel agent in connection with the holiday will belong to the operator.

(ii) That the operator provides a service of arranging for other people (hotels, airlines etc) to provide services, but does not himself own the airlines, hotels etc or provide the services which contribute to the holiday package.

(iii) That the operator accepts responsibility for the negligence of its own employees but that it neither has nor accepts liability for the negligent acts or omissions of independent contractors over whom the tour operator has no direct control. The first part of such a clause enables the operator to meet ABTA's requirements and those of the 1977 Act. If the views expressed in the *Wall* v *Silver Wing* case are correct, such a clause is not an exclusion clause since it does not seek to exclude a liability which in its absence would otherwise be imposed.

(iv) That the facilities and amenities offered by the various hotels etc, as described in the brochure, have been checked by the operator's representatives and found to be normally available but are liable to be affected by, for example, climatic changes, off peak seasons or local regulations. What the operator is stating is that proper care has been taken to select competent independent contractors but that the operator is not in a position to guarantee that normal circumstances will prevail each day of the year.

(v) What the holiday price is, or a clear statement of how it is to be calculated.

(vi) That the operator reserves the right to cancel the holiday as a result of *force majeure* events such as wars, in which case the customer will be notified as soon as possible and offered a total refund or an alternative holiday of similar standard. Again, this follows the OFT's code of conduct.

(vii) What the holiday maker must do if he wishes to alter or cancel his holiday. Most brochures set out a schedule of cancellation charges. It is rare for such charges to be queried—perhaps because holiday makers usually insure against cancellation.

(viii) That the operator reserves the right at any time before the balance of the holiday price becomes payable to cancel the holiday if the operator has not taken a sufficient number of bookings to make the holiday an economically viable proposition. In such a case the customer will be notified as soon as possible and offered a total refund or an alternative holiday of similar standard.

## (c) Surcharges

In contract law there is no objection to a supplier or arranger of future services reserving the right to increase the price of the services to reflect supervening increases in costs. Historically this is something which tour operators have usually done, though from time to time there are spells when no surcharge guarantees are fashionable.

The need for some regulation of surcharging arrangements to protect the consumer was recognised many years ago. Paragraphs 4.14–4.17 of the ABTA Tour Operator's Code of Conduct (see page 213) and paragraph 3 of ABTA's accompanying Guidelines for Booking Conditions (see page 216) contain important provisions regarding surcharging which ABTA tour operators must observe.

Rule 4.15 requires tour operators to comply with ABTA's Standards on Surcharges. The current Standards (November 1988) oblige tour operators to absorb the first 2% of any cost increases and to give holiday makers the right to cancel and obtain a full refund if surcharges increase the holiday price by more than 10%.

Amongst other things the Standards contain important rules for notifying surcharge conditions. They give tour operators a choice of policies which they may adopt, and specify a mandatory clause to be used in connection with each policy. These rules and clauses are reproduced in Appendix C.

## (d) Cancellation and material alteration

The Tour Operator's Code of Conduct draws an important distinction between cancellation and material alteration (see paragraphs 4.5 and 4.6 reproduced on pages 209–210). The distinction is amplified in paragraphs 4.3 and 4.4 of the Guidelines which accompany the Code (see pages 217–218).

A tour operator's booking conditions must not reserve the right for the operator to cancel a holiday after the date when the balance of the holiday price has to be paid unless it is necessary to do so as a result of *force majeure* circumstances. If an operator does cancel, whether before or after the balance becomes payable, in circumstances permitted by the Code he must offer the holiday maker the choice of an alternative holiday of at least comparable standard (if available) or of a prompt and full refund of all money paid by the holiday maker.

Booking conditions may reserve the right for the operator to make material alterations at any time so long as he is able to notify the alteration not less than fourteen days before the commencement of the holiday. But if, other than for *force majeure* reasons, the operator makes a material alteration after the date when the balance of the holiday price should be paid, he shall ensure that the holiday maker receives *compensation* which may be in accordance with a scale of payments. The right to receive compensation and any scale of payments must be clearly stated in the operator's booking conditions.

## (e) Overbooked hotels

The Tour Operator's Code provisions regarding over-booking are clearly stated in paragraph 4.7 (see page 210). The requirements regarding offers to holiday makers specified in sub-paragraphs (iii) and (iv) of paragraph 4.7 should be mentioned in the operator's booking conditions.

Broadly speaking, if a holiday maker arrives to find a hotel overbooked, he is to be offered alternative accommodation and, where the hotel and/or facilities of the alternative accommodation can reasonably be regarded as inferior to those originally booked, reasonable compensation for "disturbance" must be paid.

## (f) ATOL requirements

When granting ATOLs, the CAA imposes various requirements regarding the contents of brochures/booking conditions. These are contained in Standard Terms 1(i)(b), 8 and 9. In addition, Standard Term 11 imposes important requirements regarding the contents of the operator's confirmation of booking. This confirmation must be supplied to the holiday maker within fourteen days of the operator receiving notification of the booking and not later than the date of departure.

The tour operator and the holiday maker who actually signs the booking form and makes the contract are able to enforce it. It is, though, common for one person to book a holiday on behalf of others who will not in the strict sense be contracting parties. *Jackson* v *Horizon Holidays* [1975] 3 All ER 92, which is considered in detail in Chapter 5, established the important principle that the person who actually makes the booking can sue on behalf not only of himself but also of any other person for whom he makes a booking. The court can award damages in favour of all on whose behalf the holiday was booked and apportion the total damages as it thinks fit.

The conclusions reached by the Court of Appeal, and in particular by Denning LJ, in *Jackson* v *Horizon Holidays* were disapproved of by the House of Lords in *Woodar* v *Wimpey* [1980] 1 WLR 277. Lord Wilberforce said, *inter alia*:

"I am not prepared to dissent from the actual decision in that case (i.e. *Jackson* v *Horizon Holidays*). It may be supported either as a broad decision on the measure of damages or possibly as an example of a type of contract — examples of which are persons contracting for family holidays, ordering meals in restaurants for a party, hiring a taxi for a group — calling for special treatment ... There are many situations of daily life which do not fit neatly into conceptual analyses, but which require some flexibility in the law of contract. Jackson's case may well be one. I cannot however, agree with the basis on which Denning LJ put his position in that case ..."

Lord Wilberforce's comments were supported by the other Lord Justices in the Woodar case. The present position, therefore, appears to be that the result of the Jackson case is approved, although its *ratio decidendi* is not.

Holiday contracts entered into by minors (children under the age of eighteen) are governed by both the common law and the Minors' Contracts Act 1987. The effect of the 1987 Act is to repeal previous legislation which invalidated most contracts entered into by minors and to allow the courts, if it is just and equitable, to require a defendant, who was a minor at the time when the contract was made, to transfer back to the plaintiffs any property acquired under that contract.

The general common law rules still prevail, though. The effect of these is that holiday contracts entered into by minors are voidable on the part of the minor.


# 6. Implied duties

## (a) Nature of tour operator's duties

Many of the obligations which the courts regard tour operators as owing to their customers are ones which are not spelt out in the holiday contract. The extent of these obligations is, as yet, not clearly defined, and the various reported and unreported decisions known to the writers suggest that there is no total judicial consensus regarding the nature of the holiday contract.

If, contrary to the writers' understanding of the law, the contract imposes strict liability on the operator, it will be the operator's duty to ensure that the holiday is satisfactory in all respects and conforms fully with the descriptions set out in the brochure. Taking things a stage further it might even be argued by analogy with the position in law regarding the contract which exists between a hotel and its restaurant customers that that part of the holiday contract which relates to the provision of meals is one for the sale of goods, and that liability for any inadequacy in the hotel's meals, no matter by whom caused, cannot be excluded. This is because section 6(2) of the Unfair Contract Terms Act 1977 does not allow exclusion of liability for breaches of section 14(3) of the Sale of Goods Act 1979 which implies into a contract for the sale of goods a condition that the goods will be fit for their normal purpose.

If the holiday contract is a contract to make suitable arrangements and does not involve strict liability for the outcome of those arrangements, the operator's duty will be to do his best to ensure that all facilities described or implied in the brochure will be available on any given holiday, that the airlines, hotels etc will be reasonable value for money and that their normal standards are high. The writers' opinion as to the view which the Court of Appeal and the House of Lords would adopt has already been set out and the following merely amplifies it.

The operator's primary duty is to select suitable airlines, hotels etc. So far as airlines are concerned, the operator is, in the writers' view, entitled to choose any state or reputable private airline and rely on the CAA to monitor its safety standards. Few operators are equipped to check aircraft safety standards themselves and it seems superfluous to expect them to hire outside experts to duplicate the function of the CAA.

Operators should avoid using airlines which are in severe financial difficulties. Depending on the wording in its booking conditions, an operator which uses an airline that ceases trading will either have to arrange alternative flights (usually at extra cost) or will be able to cancel the booking and provide a full refund. If the collapse occurs while the holidaymaker is on holiday, the operator will have to make alternative arrangements to repatriate him.

## (b) Vetting of facilities

It is not sufficient for an operator merely to choose hotels which have a reasonable reputation and which appear to provide good value for money. It should carry out a careful check of a hotel's safety and sanitary arrangements, its kitchens, the standard of its meals, and of all the hotel's facilities which are mentioned in the operator's brochure. It will not do to rely on a visit to a hotel during a cool season as evidence that the hotel's air conditioning works well in hot weather, nor merely to accept assurances from the hotel manager that the hotel's sanitary arrangements are excellent.

Moreover, it will not suffice to make an initial investigation and rely upon it for the next ten years. Admittedly, Mr. Justice Hodgson in the *Wall* v *Silver Wing* case (see page 22) did state that following one inspection he did not think "that there was any duty upon the operators to make routine inspections thereafter". However, the writers doubt whether operators should rely on this as a statement of general application. Circumstances can change rapidly at a hotel and recent county court decisions suggest that operators should check a hotel carefully each time that they include it in one of their brochures. In addition they should arrange for their local representatives to report any significant changes following the printing of the brochure so that the operator can either get things put right or give his customers the opportunity to change their bookings.

Examples of matters which should be notified to a customer as soon as it becomes at all likely that they will affect his holiday are a breakdown in a hotel's air conditioning system, the closure of its only swimming pool, or the commencement of noisy building works on an adjoining site. The inference to be drawn from decisions of the county courts is that anything which might reasonably be expected to have caused a significant number of customers not to have booked a holiday had they known about it before booking should be notified to them if it happens before their departure date. It is then for them to decide whether to go ahead, or to ask for an alternative holiday of a similar standard in the same resort or a total refund.

Where possible, the operator will first seek to have anything which goes wrong at a hotel put right. The hotel proprietor will naturally be inclined to give optimistic estimates of how long it will take to put something right. Often it will be difficult (even with help from its on the spot representative) for the operator to make a definite assessment. Sometimes this may result in it relying on assurances from the hotel proprietor and then being proved wrong. In practice this may not matter too much so long as it is able to re-locate holiday makers quickly at a hotel of similar or better standard without any extra cost to them.

### (c) Industrial action

Industrial action and threats of industrial action can create difficult problems. Where the industrial action affects flights, the position will usually be catered for in the operator's booking conditions. For instance Intasun's brochure provides that:

> "We would like to guarantee that our flights will never be delayed and, in fact the vast majority of flights do depart on time. Unfortunately though delays do occasionally occur. These are completely beyond our control and we have a Duty Office working closely with airlines and our overseas offices to make sure any delay is as short as possible and your overseas transfer and accommodation arrangements are changed if necessary. Our aim is to minimise the inconvenience of delay so far as possible. All Intasun holidaymakers are entitled to

our special Flight Delay Benefit insurance as follows; if there is a long delay to your outward flight:

- £15 compensation per person after the first 12 hours delay;
- £10 compensation per person after each further full 12 hours delay.

These benefits are available to all our passengers whether or not our holiday insurance has been taken.

**Important Notes**

Periods of delay are calculated by reference to the departure time on your ticket and the time you leave. Exclusions: Claims arising from (a) industrial action existing at the time of booking; (b) war (declared or otherwise); (c) late arrival of the insured person at the airport unless due to industrial action; (d) Claims in respect of infants under two years. Claims should be made to our Customer Services Department at our Bradford office within 28 days of your return flight.

**EXTRA CANCELLATION BENEFIT**

If you take our special recommended holiday insurance you may cancel your holiday after a 24 hour delay and obtain a full refund of your holiday cost (less £20 and the insurance premium paid)''.

Industrial action, or the threat of industrial action, at a hotel is more difficult to cater for. If there is a likelihood that when a holiday maker arrives at his hotel all or most of the hotel staff will be on strike or working to rule, he should be told in advance and given the choice of a suitable alternative holiday or a refund. Indeed, he should be given this choice in any case where there is a likelihood that industrial action at the hotel will spoil his holiday. This is so even though the operator is in no way responsible for or able to control the industrial action. Through neither party's fault a situation has arisen in which the holiday contract cannot be properly performed. In such circumstances it is submitted that the holiday maker has a legal entitlement to rescind the contract if a suitable alternative cannot be provided.

## (d) Exceptional occurrences and health risks

Similar considerations apply where a pending holiday is threatened by civil commotion, natural disaster (eg a volcano or hurricane) or some substantial health risk (eg typhoid). In the authors' opinion there is an implied condition in all holiday contracts—with the possible exception of certain adventure holidays—that the operator will not knowingly expose the holiday maker to significant risk to life, limb or health. In any event the operator is almost certainly under a duty of care in tort not to do so—see *Anns* v *London Borough of Merton* [1978] AC 728.

An interesting instance occurred when it became widely reported and well known within the travel industry that a few holiday makers had died while on self catering holidays in the Algarve as a result of defective gas installations. In such a situation the authors consider that a tour operator is under an obligation to notify customers whose holidays have not commenced and give them the opportunity of deciding whether to go ahead, despite the risks involved, or to take a suitable alternative holiday or a refund. Many holiday makers might be inclined to take precautions and go ahead but where there is a special—albeit relatively slight—chance of a fatal accident occurring, tour operators would be wise to give holiday makers the opportunity not to proceed with the holiday. If something does go wrong the court's sympathy would be with the holiday maker (or his dependants) and damages of many hundreds of thousands of pounds might be awarded to the dependants of a deceased holiday maker.

A recent interesting county court case on the same subject is *Davey* v *Cosmos Air Holidays* (1989) CLY 327. Mr. Davey booked a holiday for himself and his family for two weeks in October 1984, including accommodation at the Hotel Do Cerro, Albufeira at a cost of £726. On the third day of the holiday his daughter was taken ill and subsequently the remaining members of the family became ill. The symptoms included severe stomach pains and diarrhoea. Other holidaymakers at the hotel suffered similarly. The outbreaks of illness were reported, and had been reported, not only in the local press but also in the British press. The cause of the illness appears to have been that raw sewage was pumped into the sea fifty yards from the beach. The family sued for damages for breach of contract and/or negligence.

Cosmos were held to be negligent in that they were or should have been aware of the situation before Mr. Davey and his family arrived, and had taken no precautions to reduce or eliminate the risk of injury to them. Cosmos were also held to be in breach of an implied term of the contract "to take such steps as are reasonable taking all the circumstances into account to avoid exposing their clients to any significant risk of damage or injury to their health". The Davey family were awarded £1,000 "for breach of contract and for the ruin of their holiday"; Mrs. Davey, who contracted dysentery, was awarded £500 for pain and suffering; Mr. Davey and his daughter were each awarded £200 for pain and suffering; the young son was awarded £250. Special damages of £217.30 (for the cost of replacement of soiled clothing) were also awarded.

## (e) Notification of changes

The extent of the operator's obligation to notify customers in advance of matters which might spoil their holidays was indicated in an unreported county court case. It concerned a hotel whose guests during one fortnight included a large uncontrolled party of secondary school children. More as a result of boisterousness than malevolence they made life unpleasant for the other guests in the hotel. The county court judge held that in these circumstances the holiday maker who brought the proceedings was entitled to damages from the operator even though the operator was not responsible (in the normal sense of the word) for what had gone wrong.

In the writers' view this decision might well have been reversed had the operator appealed. But, although the county court's decision was not based on a failure by the operator to notify the holiday maker in advance, comments made in the course of the hearing indicate that a tour operator should notify its customers of potential trouble of any significant nature and give them an opportunity to withdraw from the holiday and take a refund. The deputy recorder's comments also suggest that operators are under an obligation to make use of their local representatives to obtain early warning of trouble at a hotel—whether it takes the form of unruly guests, a breakdown of the air conditioning, or anything else calculated to diminish materially a holiday maker's enjoyment.

What if the unruly guests arrive or the air conditioning breaks down during the course of the holiday? The authors consider that there is an implied condition in the holiday contract that the tour operator will use all reasonable endeavours to remedy matters. But in many cases all that it can do is, through its local representative, to make urgent representations to the hotel manager and check carefully that the manager does whatever he promises to do.

Usually a breakdown of the air conditioning system can be rectified within two or three days. In the authors' opinion, the holiday makers so affected would not normally have a claim in law against the operator. Indeed, if the breakdown is an isolated event and the operator is doing its best to encourage the hotel to have it rectified, it is arguable (depending on the wording of the operator's booking conditions) that the operator is not liable, even if the air conditioning is out of action for, say, the last ten days of the holiday.

Once a large party of unruly guests is installed at a hotel it may be difficult for the hotel manager—let alone the tour operator—to do much about it. Representations and pleas for better behaviour and control can be made but may not be of much avail. The local police may be called but may neither attempt nor achieve anything much. If the hotel is owned by the tour operator or, possibly, a member of the same group of companies, there is a reasonable case for saying that it should never have accepted a booking for a large party of secondary school children without ensuring that adequate control would be kept at all times. But if, as is more usual, the operator has no proprietary connection with the hotel, it is a big step to hold that it is in breach of contract as a result of the antics of unexpected "intruders".

### (f) Local representatives

Despite their reservations about the above mentioned county court decision, the writers consider that the legal duties of a tour operator during the course of a holiday are greater than is often realised. One of the services which a tour operator normally agrees to provide is that of its local representative. The representative is usually an employee or agent of the operator over whom there is direct control and so the operator will be responsible for any default on the representative's part. The main duties of the representative are to meet holiday makers on arrival at the resort, to assist in transportation to and from the hotel or other accommodation, to help holiday makers in settling in, and to be readily available to deal with any queries or complaints. In addition, he assists holiday makers to book excursions and helps with the final day departure arrangements.

It is natural for local representatives to become friendly with many of the hotel managers with whom they are in contact. It is also natural for them to shrug their shoulders about what they may regard as relatively minor (or totally insuperable) problems and to seek to avoid the more difficult type of holiday maker. But it is important for operators to train their representatives to overcome these temptations. In law tour operators are responsible for the acts and omissions of their local representatives. It is the local representative who has to perform the operator's obligation to use all reasonable efforts to provide guidance and assistance to holiday makers and to help have any deficiencies at the hotel put right. Numerous county court cases bear witness to the heavy price which tour operators can pay for negative or unimaginative handling of complaints by their local representatives.

In *Glover* v *Kuoni* (1987) CLY 1151 Mr. and Mrs. Glover booked a package holiday with Kuoni, to include sixteen days accommodation in the Maldives. The flight on which they travelled lost their luggage which contained valuable photographic equipment. One of their purposes in visiting the Maldives was for underwater photography. They had no clothes or items whatsoever of their own for the duration of the holiday, there were no available places to purchase replacements and they had to borrow from other holiday makers. For the first week Kuoni's on the spot representative did nothing to help, and was abrasively dismissive. The court held that Kuoni were not responsible for the loss of the luggage. Nevertheless it ordered them to pay damages (see page 141) because of the ineptitude and lack of interest of their representative. The court considered that if she had done her job properly the luggage would have been recovered sooner and the holiday salvaged.

Readers are referred also to the case of *Usher* v *Intasun* (see page 30) where the holiday maker was awarded £50 because of a failure on the part of Intasun to provide reassurance. This case did not involve a local representative but it indicates clearly the hand-holding empathetic approach expected of local representatives.

### (g) Duty after holiday over

Does the tour operator have any duties after a holiday is over? In particular is it under any obligation to assist a holiday maker in obtaining redress from a hotel for some accident or failing for which the operator clearly has no responsibility itself? The writers are not aware of any cases (even unreported ones) on this point. But, in their opinion, it is more likely than not that such a duty would nowadays be implied into the holiday contract. It is unlikely that this duty would require the operator to incur legal expenses on the holiday maker's behalf but it would require it in a clearcut case to press the aggrieved holiday maker's claim actively and diligently.

### (h) Insurance

Another duty which the courts might be tempted to

imply in a suitable case is for operators at least to draw their customers' attention to the desirability of insuring certain holiday risks. Most operators do include an insurance package and proposal form in their brochures. But even this may not be enough in cases where the cover is set relatively low. The safest course for an operator is to suggest in the insurance package section of its brochure that the customer should consult his travel agent or insurance broker if he has any doubt whether the operator's insurance package is sufficient for his needs.

## 7. Conclusion

In the preceding paragraphs the writers have expressed views regarding the implied duties of tour operators based upon *obiter dicta* in the leading cases on holiday contracts discussed in pages 22-30, on various county court cases and on general trends in the common law relating to consumer contracts. As yet, there is no conclusive case law authority for many of the views expressed. Sooner or later some of these matters may be litigated up to the Court of Appeal, and possibly even the House of Lords. Alternatively, and more likely, new principles will be introduced into English law by the EEC.

In conclusion a brief word about The Supply of Goods and Services Act 1982. In the writers' opinion, the holiday contract is clearly a contract for the supply of services by the tour operator. The services which the tour operator contracts to supply are, in most cases, not the transport and accommodation services described in its brochure but rather the service of arranging for transport, accommodation and other holiday services to be provided in a manner which, barring uncharacteristic lapses or exceptional circumstances, will provide a holiday which conforms with what is said and implied in the brochure.

The only section of the 1982 Act which appears to be of any practical significance to the holiday contract is section 13 which implies into contracts for the supply of a service an implied term that the supplier will carry out the service with reasonable care and skill. However it is doubtful whether this codification of the relevant common law principles adds anything of substance to the views regarding the responsibilities of tour operators expressed in this chapter.

# Chapter 3

# The travel agent

## 1. Introduction

The contract for a package holiday is between the holiday maker and the tour operator. *Prima facie,* the travel agent is the selling agent for the tour operator. It is the travel agent who provides the holiday maker with the tour operator's brochure, who takes from the holiday maker details of the holiday desired, who communicates these details to the tour operator and confirms with him the availability of a particular holiday, who collects payments from the holiday maker for despatch to the tour operator and who despatches the tickets to the holiday maker. This role imposes upon a travel agent liabilities and duties in law to the tour operator. These will normally be encapsulated in a written agency agreement between them—at least where ABTA members are involved.

Although a travel agent who sells package holidays for the tour operating companies who assemble them is clearly acting as their agent in certain respects and receives his commission from them, he is not a sales agent in the normally accepted sense of the term. He will usually be acting as agent for a large number of operators rather than just promoting the products of one. He will not often sally forth and call on potential customers. Although there are signs that this is beginning to change, he will not normally perform a positive selling role—at any rate not in the hard sell sense—on behalf of any particular operator. In general, his role as agent for the operators whose brochures he stocks is a less active one than that of the sales agent appointed by a manufacturer of goods. Historically, it has in many respects, been more akin to that of a mere booking agent, such as Keith Prowse and other agencies through whom theatre tickets can be booked. However, there is now a tendency for some agents, mainly the larger ones, to concentrate in their brochures, window displays and staff recommendations, on promoting a few preferred tour operators.

Although travel agents owe duties in contract to the tour operators they represent, it is submitted that they also have duties and liabilities in law to the holiday maker— the other principal to the package holiday contract. This chapter examines the relationships between travel agent and tour operator and between travel agent and holiday maker, and considers whether the travel agent is agent of both tour operator and holiday maker, something which, on the face of things, would be contrary to the general principle in agency law that an agent should not put himself in a position where he is purporting to act for both the buyer and the seller.

This chapter does not consider a travel agent's liabilities and duties in law when he is merely selling, for example, a train ticket. Nor is the position of "direct sell travel companies" specifically considered. Their duties and liabilities will be owed direct to the holiday maker, since there is no intermediary to take into account, and will encompass the duties and liabilities to the holiday maker of both tour operator and travel agent.

Before considering the contractual relationship between tour operators and travel agents, it is appropriate to indicate briefly some of the basic legal principles which govern relations between principals and agents generally.

## 2. Common law principles of agency

### (a) Contractual relationships

The basic notion behind the present day English common law rules of agency can be expressed in the maxim "He who does an act through another is deemed in law to do it himself". In contractual terms this is traditionally expressed to mean:

> "The contract is the contract of the principal, not that of the agent, and *prima facie* at common law the only person who can sue is the principal and the only person who can be sued is the principal". (*Montgomerie* v *UK Steamship Association* [1891] 1 QB 370 per Wright J).

Accordingly, when a travel agent effects a sale on behalf of his tour operator principal, he is putting the holiday maker into a direct contractual relationship with the operator. If anything goes wrong with the holiday, the holiday maker must sue the operator and not the travel agent through whom the holiday was booked. This principle is affirmed in the International Convention on Travel Agents which was signed in 1970 but which to date only Belgium and Italy have incorporated into their national law. It states that a travel agent who merely arranges the provision of holidays by others will not be liable to the holiday maker provided that he has not been negligent in making the arrangements.

In modern times, most agency relationships involve an actual contract of agency between the principal and agent. In English law, there is no necessity for the contract to be in writing except where the authority given to the agent is to execute a deed (ie a document under seal which may subject a party to obligations for which he receives no consideration), in which case the agency must be created by a deed. However the use of written agency contracts in the travel industry and elsewhere is increasing. The usual contractual stumbling blocks of fraud, duress, mistake or misrepresentation must be absent from any express agency appointment but it is not proposed to discuss these basic aspects of contract law in this book.

### (b) Authority of agent

In the case of contractual agents, such as travel agents, the scope of the agent's authority will mainly be dealt with by the contract itself. In addition, authority may be implied from the nature of the business in which the agent is employed or by the custom in a particular trade. Generally speaking an agent has implied authority to do everything necessary for and ordinarily incidental to carrying out his express authority according to the usual way in which such authority is executed.

Where an agent is acting for his principal in a specific business, the agent is impliedly authorised to act according to the usages and customs of that business. The custom must be known to the principal or be so commonly known that he is taken to have knowledge of it. For example in the case of *Limako BV* v *Hentz & Co Inc* [1979] 2 Lloyds Rep 23, brokers in the cocoa trade were held to be agents even though in accordance with custom they had acted in their own name and made themselves personally liable to a third party. However, if the agent acts in accordance with an unreasonable custom, by which is meant one inconsistent with the nature of the transaction, the agent will not be taken to have authority so to act, unless the principal had notice, in which case he will be presumed to have consented.

An agent's implied authority supplements the authority which is expressly given to him and is another type of actual authority. Actual authority contrasts with apparent authority which arises where X by words or conduct represents to Y that Z has authority to act on X's behalf. In such circumstances X may be bound to Y by acts of Z even though Z did not have actual authority to bind X. This apparent, or ostensible, authority arises because a principal allows his agent to appear to have more authority than he actually has, as where unknown to others a principal makes reservations in his agent's authority that limit the authority which the agent would normally have. For instance, in the case of *Watteau* v *Fenwick* [1893] 1 QB 346, Willis J stated that "the principal is liable for all the acts of the agent which are within the authority usually confided to an agent of that character (despite) ... limitations as between the principal and the agent put upon that authority".

*Watteau* v *Fenwick* involved an agent employed to manage a beer house by a firm of brewers. The agent was forbidden by the principal to buy certain articles for the business. Nevertheless, he ordered some from a third party who did not know of the limitation on the agent's authority. The principal was held liable to the third party on the basis that it was in the usual course of business for a manager to purchase this type of item and therefore he had ostensible authority to do so.

## (c) Duties of agent

Where the agency is a contractual agency, it is the agent's duty to do what he has undertaken to do and to obey the lawful instructions given to him by his principal. These instructions may be contained in his express authority or may be implied from established trade customs. In circumstances which are covered neither by express instructions nor trade customs or usages the overriding considerations are that the acts of the agent must be lawful and for the principal's benefit.

An agent is bound to his principal to use reasonable care in the exercise of his powers. This is a comprehensive obligation which includes the duty to use customary diligence, care and skill. The agent will be responsible to his principal for any loss caused by a failure to observe these standards. The liability of an agent does not depend upon the success of his efforts but upon whether he has acted in as reasonable a manner as could be expected from an agent employed in such a capacity. Should the principal require a *higher* standard of care and skill to be exercised, he should provide for it by express terms in the contract.

It is a general rule of law that an agent must perform his undertaking personally and may not delegate the task unless specifically authorised to do so. The reasoning behind this rule is that the principal may well consider the personality of the agent to be essential to the relationship.

Under common law an agent is obliged to keep proper accounts of money and property received for and on behalf of the principal and to make them available for inspection by the principal. Further the agent must pay over to his principal all monies received on the latter's behalf. However in normal circumstances an agent is not obliged to bank his principal's monies in a separate bank account and if he does not, the principal has no preferential claim to "his money" if the agent goes into liquidation (*Henry* v *Hammond* [1913] 2 KB 515). In normal circumstances if a principal allows his agent to retain monies for more than six years from the date on which they should have been accounted for, the principal's claim to such monies becomes statute-barred.

### (d) Duties of principal

The main duties of a principal are to pay his agent's commission and to indemnify him against liabilities properly incurred by him on behalf of his principal when acting within his express, implied or customary authority. In the absence of any express provision regarding when commission is earned an agent's entitlement in respect of a particular sale will normally vest at the time when the principal accepts the customer's order. Accordingly, if the principal subsequently repudiates his contract with his customer, he will still have to pay commission to the agent. However, if the principal's customer fails to complete the purchase, the agent will normally lose his entitlement to commission in respect of the "sale". This is because the agent's obligation is to introduce a purchaser ready and willing to purchase and able to purchase and to complete his purchase. Matters of this nature are normally dealt with in express terms in contracts between principals and agents and it is highly desirable that they should be.

## 3. Travel agency agreements

### (a) Standard terms

Article 13(6) of ABTA's Articles of Association, which article is commonly known as "Stabiliser", provides that, in the absence of special permission, no ABTA Travel Agent should sell foreign package tours organised or promoted by a non-ABTA tour operator, and that no ABTA tour operator should sell foreign package tours through a non-ABTA travel agent. An ABTA tour operator can only sell such tours directly to the public or through an ABTA retail agent. Further, ABTA requires that all ABTA tour operators dealing through agents establish formal agency agreements.

Consequently, each ABTA travel agent will have a formal agency appointment agreement with every tour operator with whom he deals.

Normal terms to be found in these agreements are—

   (a) the travel agent must stock and display the tour operator's brochures;

   (b) he must use the operator's booking form when selling one of the operator's holidays;

   (c) the agent must forward bookings to the operator and not purport to accept any booking without the express authority of the operator;

   (d) the agent's responsibility for collecting cancellation charges;

   (e) the rate of commission to be received by the agent and how and when it is to be paid;

   (f) the time at which monies received from holiday makers are to be transmitted to the tour operator;

   (g) a prohibition against the agent making representations or warranties on behalf of the operator;

   (h) the agent's right to be indemnified by the tour operator and *vice versa*;

   (i) the time from which any deposit or other monies paid by a holiday maker to the travel agent in respect of a booking are held by the travel agent as agent for the tour operator.

## (b) ATOL requirements

As regards (i), standard term 9(1) of the Civil Aviation Authority's standard ATOL terms, requires all holders of

Air Travel Organisers' Licences (ATOLs), which includes all operators offering holidays abroad which involve significant air travel, to make it clear to the travel agent and the customer in writing, that any money paid by the customer to the agent in respect of a holiday the provision of which requires an ATOL are held by the agent as agent for the operator from the date on which the customer receives confirmation of his booking from the operator. This only refers to ATOL holders. There are other tour operators who appoint travel agents whose holidays do not need an ATOL.

Standard term 9(2) also requires ATOL tour operators to make it clear in writing to travel agents whether monies collected by them from a customer in connection with a holiday booking are held by them as agent for the operator until the date on which the operator confirms the booking. The authors' research suggests that most ATOL tour operators notify their agents that monies held by them pending confirmation of a holiday are held by them for the customer. In addition, the authors believe that most ATOL tour operators include a statement to this effect in their booking conditions so that their customers are aware of the position.

## (c) Discounting

On 1 August 1984 the Director General of Fair Trading asked the Monopolies and Mergers Commission to investigate the alleged practice whereby tour operators prevented travel agents from discounting the price of tour operators' holidays and bearing the cost of the discount themselves. The conclusions of the Commission can be summarised as follows:

> (i) Tour operators did prohibit travel agents from supplying tour operators' package holidays at a discount from the price prescribed by the tour operator.

> (ii) Tour operators had sought to prevent Ilkeston Co-operative Society from introducing a voucher system, and this prevented competition between travel agents.

(iii) Public interest was not best served by such restrictions of competition among travel agents.

As a result of the Commission's findings (readers who are interested in the details should refer to the Report, reference Cmnd 9879) the Restriction on Agreements and Conduct (Tour Operators) Order 1987 was introduced. It provides that:

(i) it is unlawful for a tour operator to make an agreement which prohibits a travel agent from offering "inducements" to the public; and

(ii) an inducement is defined as "a benefit, whether pecuniary or not, offered to a class or classes of persons or to the public at large by a travel agent expressly on his own behalf as an incentive to that class or those classes of persons or the public at large to acquire foreign package holidays through him rather than through another"; and

(iii) it is unlawful for a tour operator to withhold or to threaten to withhold the sale of package holidays through travel agents who offer inducements; and

(iv) it is unlawful for a tour operator to give any preference to a travel agent who does not offer inducements.

Tour operators are not prevented from specifying the prices at which their holidays are to be sold. What they cannot do is to forbid travel agents to offer cash discounts or other inducements at the agent's own expense.

## 4. Travel agent and tour operator

As previously stated, a principal is responsible to his customer for those acts of his agent which are within the agent's actual or ostensible authority. These normally include all steps necessary to process a holiday maker's booking. This is what the preface describes as the travel agent's "booking agent role".

If a travel agent, for whatever reason, incorrectly notes the dates on which a holiday maker wishes to travel and arranges the holiday contract on the basis of this error, will the tour operator be liable to the holiday maker, since this is clearly an act within the travel agent's authority? (Any liability of the travel agent to the holiday maker is considered later in this chapter).

It is established law that an agent for reward (which a travel agent is) must exhibit such a degree of skill and diligence as is appropriate to the performance of the duties that he has accepted (*Lage* v *Siemens Bros & Co Ltd* (1932) 42 Ll.L Rep 252). A professional agent must show the degree of care to be expected of those in his profession. He is not responsible to his principal for a mere mistake or error of judgment not amounting to a failure to exercise proper care or skill (*Nitrate Producers' Co* v *Wills* (1905) 21 TLR 699). However, a failure to exercise proper care or skill will lose the agent his normal right of indemnity against his principal.

A form of agency agreement which is widely used provides for the operator to "keep the agent indemnified against all claims and liabilities relating thereto save to the extent that they are attributable to the acts and omissions of the agent" and that the agent should "keep the operator indemnified against all claims and liabilities attributable to acts or omissions committed by him in breach, or outside the scope, of this agreement".

A principal will be liable to a customer for mistakes by the principal's agents provided that the agent is acting within his actual or ostensible authority. In such circumstances the principal will normally be entitled to be indemnified by the agent. As a general rule a customer cannot sue an agent for a known principal for breach of contract. If incorrect departure dates have been noted by the travel agent and the error is not spotted by the holiday maker, the fault is that of the travel agent and not the tour operator. However, at the time of making the mistake the agent is acting within the scope of his authority. *Prima facie*, therefore, the tour operator will be liable to the holiday maker and entitled to a full indemnity from the agent.

As explained in the preceding chapter, the travel agent does not assume any contractual responsibility for faults in the package holiday provided by the tour operator. This is something for which only the principal to the contract can be liable. This is also the case where a holiday maker suffers personal injury and loss while on holiday, unless the circumstances were within the agent's control and attributable to his acts or omissions. It is normal for agency agreements to state that the agent will accept liability for any loss or injury suffered by a customer as a result of the negligent acts or omissions of the agent. This could happen where the agent gives a negligent answer to a customer's question or fails to deliver the customer's tickets or pass on information provided by the operator for onward transmission to the customer.

It is also necessary to consider the agent's position vis à vis the operator when the holiday maker fails to honour his contract with the operator, by, for example, failing to make payment in full or to take the holiday reserved. Normally this is catered for in agency appointment agreements by wording such as:

> "If the Agent has used his best endeavours to collect such balances, cancellation charges or other monies, but has failed to do so, the operator will release the Agent from his obligation hereunder, whereupon the operator will take steps to exercise his right at law to collect monies due . . ."

## 5. Whose agent?

Generally speaking, there is no contract or other written terms delineating a travel agent's responsibility to the holiday maker. Case law is not of much assistance and the travel agent's liabilities and duties must be derived from general principles of law and accepted practice in the holiday industry. Valuable guidance regarding the latter is given in ABTA's *Code of Conduct for Travel Agents*.

At the time of Clarkson's collapse in 1974 there was

considerable controversy concerning for whom travel agents act. This was a matter of vital importance because if travel agents were acting as agents for customers, they would be able to refund deposits paid by customers rather than accounting for them to the liquidator. In the normal course of events this question would have been decided by the courts in the fullness of time. But it never was because the Government decided to put all Clarkson's customers out of their misery by compensating them out of the proceeds of a special levy imposed on people who booked holidays with ATOL holders in subsequent seasons.

Some lawyers who in 1974 advised that travel agents were the agents of the holiday maker and not of the tour operator regarded the position of travel agents as analogous to that of insurance brokers. It has been established in cases such as *Rozanes* v *Bowen* (1928) 32 Ll.L.R, 98 and *Anglo-African Merchants Ltd* v *Bayley* [1970] 1 QB 311, that insurance brokers, as distinct from insurance agents appointed to sell policies exclusively on behalf of a single insurer, are the agents of the insured and not of the insurer. And this is so notwithstanding that the broker is remunerated by commission paid by the insurer.

In certain respects travel agents engaged in selling package holidays are comparable with insurance brokers. They stock the brochures of numerous tour operators and do not normally seek to promote the holidays of any one operator in preference to those of others. They answer questions regarding holidays featured in a brochure and on occasions make comparative judgements regarding the suitability for a customer's purposes of different holidays. They assist customers in completing the operator's booking form and then forward it to the operator for acceptance.

On the other hand there are differences in the respective roles of insurance brokers and travel agents. Many more members of the public choose their holidays without asking questions than do people who take out insurance. The contents of a holiday brochure are much more intelligible to the average member of the public than those of an insurance policy. And the choice of a holiday is a much more subjective matter than the choice of an insurance policy. But these differences do not conclusively establish the agent as acting for the operator rather than the holiday maker.

At the time of Clarkson's collapse in 1974 the legal documentation employed in the holiday industry was rudimentary. Many tour operators did not even enter into formal agency agreements with the agents who stocked their brochures. And their brochures, instead of making it clear whose agent they were, used language which afforded great scope for litigation.

Since then there has been a considerable improvement. Nowadays all ABTA operators enter into formal agreements appointing travel agents as their agents. By itself this is not necessarily conclusive because it is arguable that holiday makers have no knowledge of these agreements and so should not be prejudicially affected by their existence. However the formal agreement does create an initial presumption which may be difficult to displace. Furthermore the position regarding the main bone of contention, namely who owns deposits etc held by a travel agent, has to be made clear in brochures which feature ATOL holidays.

Although the matter is not entirely free from doubt, and in any particular case will be affected by the wording of the documentation employed, the authors consider that in most cases a travel agent is not acting as the agent of customers who book package holidays through him—not even where the operator's brochure refers to him as "your" travel agent. This is particularly so in the case of ABTA agents because of the wording of the agency agreements entered into between them and the ABTA tour operators whom they represent. Admittedly, the customer may be able to contest a position purportedly established by an agreement to which he is not a party and of which he is probably not aware. But the absence of any written or express oral agency agreement between a travel agent and its customers makes it difficult to override the written agreements entered into between ABTA operators and agents which, in the authors' opinion, establish ABTA agents as being booking agents for the tour operators whom they represent. In this respect there is an interesting contrast with freight forwarding agents who, like travel agents, do not receive any remuneration from their customers but who enter into written agreements with their customers which clearly establish them as agents for their customers.

In *Kemp* v *Intasun Holidays Ltd*, full details of which are set out on page 135, the issue of whose agent is a travel agent arose peripherally. This case concerned a casual conversation between Mrs. Kemp and the travel agent, before the booking for the package holiday had been made, in which Mrs. Kemp referred to her husband's asthmatic condition and whether that casual conversation was sufficient to put the defendant, through the travel agent, on notice of Mr. Kemp's particular state of health. The Court of Appeal did not find it necessary to hold whose agent the travel agent was, Parker LJ stating:

> "I for my part would not be prepared without further consideration to make any pronouncement upon when, or in what circumstances, the travel agent is or is not the agent of the tour operator or is or is not under a duty to communicate information which he receives to the tour operator."

Kerr LJ did, however, state in the course of his judgment:

> "At the time of that conversation, *Thomas Cook* (the travel agent) *were not the agents of the defendants* . . . Whether they became their agents at a later stage and, if so, for what purpose, it is unnecessary to decide."

## 6. Monies held by agent

To some extent the question of whose agent a travel agent is is an academic one because of the protection afforded to holiday makers by the law of tort and misrepresentation discussed later in this chapter. However, it can assume great practical significance when a tour operator goes into liquidation and its liquidator claims that monies held by travel agents in respect of holidays which as a result of the liquidation will never take place belong to the tour operator. Because of the standard term 9 included in all ATOLs the position regarding monies held by travel agents on behalf of a collapsed ATOL holder will normally be clear. However, in other cases the ownership of monies held by an agent in respect of bookings taken for a tour operator who goes into liquidation may well depend on whose agent the travel agent is in law.

It was stated by Scrutton LJ in *Fullwood* v *Hurley* [1928] 1 KB 498 that:

> "No agent who has accepted an employment from one principal can in law accept an engagement inconsistent with his duty to the first principal . . . unless he makes the fullest disclosure to each principal of his interest, and obtains the consent of each principal to the double employment".

The writers consider that the problem of conflicts of interest does not arise in relation to the normal activities of travel agents engaged in selling package holidays. They doubt whether travel agents can be regarded as agents of customers as well as booking agents for tour operators. In any event the agent's role in helping members of the public to choose and book their holidays is, it is submitted, not inconsistent with his role as a mere booking agent (as distinct from promotional sales agent) for the tour operators for whom he acts. What would give rise to a conflict would be for an agent who is a party to an express written agreement to hold money received in respect of a confirmed holiday as agent for the operator to allow himself to get into a position in which he is under an obligation to hold the same money as agent for the customer. In the authors' opinion, most travel agents do not allow that to happen.

Although, in the writers' opinion, travel agents, when engaged in connection with package holidays, do not act as agents for "their" customers, this does not mean that they do not act for the customer in certain other matters. For instance, if a customer asks a travel agent to make bookings for a hotel in Paris, the agent may well be acting as agent for the customer even though he receives his remuneration by way of commission from the hotel. It is necessary in relation to any category of work undertaken by travel agents to consider a range of questions (eg is there a formal agency agreement? what role does the travel agent play? what is said in any relevant advertisements? how is the agent paid?) before arriving at a decision. But to do that for anything other than the sale of package holidays is outside the scope of this book.

## 7. The booking agent role

Brief mention has been made already in this chapter of the travel agent's role as booking agent for the tour operator. This involves the displaying of brochures, the taking of bookings, the subsequent servicing of bookings, and dealing with cancellations. In those cases, and there are some, where the holiday maker selects a holiday from a brochure and asks the agent to book it, the agent's role as the operator's booking agent may be his only role— albeit that in performing it he may owe duties to the holiday maker as well as to the tour operator.

The agent owes a contractual duty to the operator to transmit accurately all details given to him by the holiday maker, such as location, length of stay, departure dates etc. Although it is possible to imply a contract between a booking agent and a customer whereby in consideration of the customer agreeing to book through the agent the agent agrees to exercise all due care in processing the customer's booking, there must be doubts about whether an operator's booking agent, whose sole remuneration consists of a commission from the principal whose tickets, holidays etc he sells, has any *contractual* obligations to "his" customers. In particular it is difficult to formulate a contract which imposes duties in respect of answers to pre-booking queries. The only obvious consideration for obligations which it may be desired to impose on the agent at that stage is that the prospective holiday maker accepts a commitment to book his holiday through the agent. But nobody would seriously contend that an agent who gives advice to a prospective holiday maker is entitled to sue him if he decides to book his holiday through another agent. However, under the general principles of the tort of negligence, as laid down in cases such as *Anns* v *London Borough of Merton* [1978] AC 728 and *Junior Books Ltd* v *Veitchi Co Ltd* [1982] 3 WLR 477, the holiday maker is entitled to assume that the travel agent will give accurate answers to questions and process his booking with due care.

In certain circumstances the courts may be prepared to treat a statement intended to have contractual effect as a separate contract or warranty collateral to the main transaction (eg *Esso Petroleum Co Ltd* v *Mardon* [1976] QB 801). Lord Denning MR in *J Evans & Sons (Portsmouth) Ltd* v *Andrea Merzario Ltd* [1976] 1 WLR 1078 stated—

> "When a person gives a promise or an assurance to another, intending that he should act on it by entering into a contract, and he does act on it by entering into the contract, we hold that it is binding".

*Shanklin Pier Ltd* v *Detel Products Ltd* [1951] 2 KB 854 established that a collateral contract could exist where the main contract was not between the plaintiff and the defendant but the plaintiff and a third party. The plaintiffs, owners of Shanklin Pier, wished to have their pier painted with suitable paint and the defendants, paint manufacturers, assured them that their paint would be suitable. In the plaintiff's contract with the contractors the plaintiffs inserted a term that the defendant's paint would be used. The paint was used, proved to be unsuitable and the plaintiffs sued. It was held that the assurance constituted a contract, collateral to the main contract, the consideration for which was the plaintiff's entry into the main contract on the condition that the defendant's paint was to be used.

A holiday maker's contract for a package holiday is with the tour operator but sometimes a travel agent, in response to pre-booking enquiries will give certain assurances about the standard of the holiday. If these assurances are not based solely upon information supplied by the tour operator, it is possible to contend that a collateral contract exists between the holiday maker and the travel agent. However, it is doubtful whether such a contract, if it exists, would impose liabilities upon a travel agent in excess of those imposed by common law and the Misrepresentation Act 1967.

Even in cases where a customer selects a holiday without asking any questions and then asks the travel agent to effect the booking, it is by no means certain that the agent is merely a booking agent for the operator. As a result of the promotional material employed by travel agents customers can be forgiven for believing that, at least up to the time the operator confirms a booking, the travel agent is acting as agent for them. Looked at in this way the holiday maker uses "his" agent to relay certain information and sums of money to the operator to secure a contract between him and the operator. Operators naturally regard the travel agent as their agent because he has entered into a written agency agreement with them but this does not preclude holiday makers from regarding the travel agents as their agent. That some do so can be seen from the fact that many dissatisfied holiday makers ask the travel agent to take their complaints up with the operator on their behalf, much as they would ask their insurance broker to pursue an insurance policy claim.

Paragraph 2 of ABTA's Code of Conduct for travel agents specifies numerous obligations which in any court case would provide persuasive evidence regarding the standards which a travel agent can reasonably be expected to achieve. Amongst them are:

> (i) Travel agents shall maintain a high standard in serving the public and shall comply with all relevant statutory requirements.

> (ii) Travel agents shall make every effort to ensure that accurate and impartial information is provided to enable their clients to exercise an informed judgement in making their choice of facilities.

> (iii) Travel agents shall make every effort to

ensure that their clients are not sold tours holidays or travel arrangements incompatible with their individual requirements.

(iv) When alterations are made to travel arrangements for which bookings have already been accepted, travel agents shall inform their clients immediately they are advised of the situation and act as intermediaries between their principals and clients in any subsequent negotiations.

(v) Travel agents shall ensure that their counter staff carefully study all tour, holiday and travel programmes and brochures so that they are able to impart accurate information to their clients and to sell more efficiently.

(vi) Travel agents shall ensure that booking forms are completed correctly in every detail.

(vii) Travel agents shall draw the attention of their clients to any insurance facilities and cover available, including insurance relating to cancellation, and shall indicate any exclusions and limitations so that their clients may seek additional cover if deemed desirable or necessary.

(viii) Travel agents shall ensure that all travel and other documents received from principals are checked before delivery to their clients and that any points requiring clarification are explained to their clients.

(ix) Travel agents shall advise clients of the necessary passport, visa and health requirements for the journeys to be undertaken and shall assist them with any other ancillary services which they may request and which are not covered by the booking (eg currency).

A travel agent will usually be liable to a holiday maker in tort if he negligently records, for example, the holiday maker's desired departure dates and effects a booking with the tour operator on the basis of such an error. What must be considered now is whether this means that liability for all resultant damages will attach to the travel agent. *Prima facie,* the answer to this must be in the affirmative. The holiday maker may regard the tour operator as being partly to blame but if the error arose solely through the travel agent's negligent recording of details which were passed on to the operator, the operator will be able to seek a full indemnity from the travel agent. This is because he acted in reliance upon the agent, as he was entitled to do, but the agent failed to exercise the proper care and skill reasonably expected of him. If the holiday maker issues proceedings solely against the tour operator, on the basis that the operator issued the actual tickets and it was presumed that the information given to the agent had been correctly relayed, the operator should join the agent as third party to those proceedings. If proceedings are issued against both operator and agent, the operator should serve a contribution notice upon the agent.

## 8. Contributory negligence

Would it be possible for the travel agent to allege that the holiday maker had been contributorily negligent through a failure to check the details on the tickets? Although it is perhaps cavalier for a holiday maker not to check his tickets upon receipt, it does not follow that it is incumbent upon him to do so. *Prima facie* he should be entitled to rely upon the travel agent and the tour operator who issues the tickets. This is particularly so if the booking is a late booking and the tickets are collected on the day of departure. Then the holiday maker's primary concern is to ensure a smooth departure and a certain disregard for things such as return dates must be expected.

When, though, the holiday maker has had the tickets in his possession for some weeks, he has had more than sufficient time to check their accuracy. To most people a holiday is still an annual event not to be treated lightly. This point is advanced most strenuously when complaints are made about a holiday but there is no reason to suppose that it should not apply in reverse. Thus, a holiday maker who has failed to check the accuracy of his tickets should, if he claims against the travel agent in tort, be regarded as contributorily negligent and have to bear at least a small percentage of any resultant financial loss. A nominal percentage, such as 10-15% will sometimes be appropriate, but where there is clear evidence that the customer was specifically asked to check his tickets, a significantly higher contribution would seem to be called for.

Obviously any holiday maker who could be shown to have been aware of an error and who relied upon it to obtain financial advantage from the travel agent should not be allowed to do so and should bear any financial loss himself. This would not be an example of contributory negligence. Rather it would be a case where the holiday maker acted in full knowledge of the mistake and any loss does not flow from the mistake but the holiday maker's deliberate actions.

On occasions a travel agent will make a mistake when helping to fill in a customer's booking form for him. The customer should spot it when he reads through the form before signing it. In those rare cases where he does not, there are further opportunities for doing so. Many travel agents provide receipts for deposits which summarise the essential details of the booking. In many cases the customer will at the same time also receive a computerised summary of his booking. About ten days after signing and handing over his booking form he should receive a confirmation of booking which he can check. Subsequently he receives a final invoice and the tickets themselves at which time he is normally specifically asked to check them.

Rushed late bookings, sometimes involving collecting tickets at the airport, are a different matter and do occasionally give rise to mistakes which are not discovered in time. And, even with normal bookings, strange misunderstandings occasionally arise and persist. In such circumstances a minute dissection of what happened may be required to apportion responsibility.

On occasions flight times are changed after the initial booking of a holiday. It is then the duty of the tour operator to notify the agent, and of the agent to notify the customer. If the agent fails to pass on such information, or any other material post-booking information which he receives from the operator, he will be liable to make good any resulting loss suffered by the operator or the customer. If he notifies the customer, but in a manner which gives rise to misunderstanding, the apportionment of responsibility will depend on the facts of the particular case.

The subject of mistakes by travel agents in taking bookings is complicated by their role as booking agent for the tour operator. In legal theory the mistake of an agent made when he is acting within the scope of his agency duties is the mistake of his principal. Accordingly, in the circumstances outlined in the preceding paragraphs the customer should have a good claim against the tour operator—who in turn will have a good claim to be indemnified by the travel agent. The customer's claim against the operator could be presented as a claim in contract in which event the doctrine of contributory negligence could not be invoked to reduce it.

## 9. The agent's role as consultant

### (a) The duty of care

*Derry* v *Peek* (1889) 14 App Cas 337, established that a duty of care in the making of statements did not exist unless the duty arose out of a contractual relationship. However, *Nocton* v *Ashburton* [1914] AC 932, decided that such a duty to take care could arise out of a fiduciary relationship, and that decision was greatly extended by *Hedley Byrne Co Ltd* v *Heller and Partners Ltd* [1964] AC 465.

The relevant facts of *Hedley Byrne* are that the appellants were advertising agents who had placed substantial forward advertising orders for a company on terms by which they were personally liable for the cost of the orders. They asked their bankers to inquire into the company's financial stability and their bankers made inquiries of the respondents, who were the company's bankers. The respondents gave favourable references but stipulated that these were "without responsibility". In reliance on these references the appellants placed orders which resulted in a loss of £17,000. They brought an action against the respondents for damages for negligence.

It was held that a negligent, though honest, misrepresentation, spoken or written, may give rise to an action for damages for financial loss caused thereby, apart from any contract or fiduciary relationship, since the law will imply a duty of care when someone seeking information from a party possessed of a special skill trusts him to exercise due care, and that party knew or ought to have known that reliance was being placed on his skill and judgement. In the *Hedley Byrne* case there was an express disclaimer of responsibility, so no duty of care was implied but travel agents do not normally publish or utter disclaimers of responsibility.

Lord Morris of Borth-y-Gest, in giving judgment, stated:

> "It should now be regarded as settled that if someone possessed of a special skill undertakes, quite irrespective of contract, to apply that skill for the assistance of another person who relies upon such a skill, a duty of care will arise. The fact that the services are to be given by means of or by the instrumentality of words can make no difference. Furthermore if, in a sphere in which a person is so placed that others could reasonably rely upon his judgement or his skill or upon his ability to make careful enquiry, a person takes it upon himself to give information or advice to, or allows this information or advice to be passed on to, another person, who, as he knows or should know, will place reliance upon it, then a duty of care will arise".

It is considered, applying the above and for the following reasons, that a travel agent does owe a holiday maker a duty of care when answering questions, despite the absence of a contractual or fiduciary relationship:

(a) Travel agents hold themselves out as experts in their particular field, and depth of experience is an aspect which large or specialised travel companies are anxious to impart to the public.

(b) Travel agents "take it upon themselves to give information or advice" to the general public.

(c) The public rely—and this is something of which travel agents are aware—upon the agent's skill and expertise, and trust that it will be properly exercised.

## (b) Extent of duty of care

How extensive is the travel agent's duty of care? Clearly it applies where he answers questions which are put to him, or volunteers information or advice of his own accord. But is it his duty to advise, even if advice is not sought? To what extent is he entitled to rely upon warnings and advice given to the holiday maker by the tour operator (usually in his brochure)? Is he under a duty to disclose information known to him which could materially affect a particular holiday? If he is, it is also necessary to consider his position as regards the tour operator since disclosure by the agent of adverse information about a particular holiday may be tantamount to advising the holiday maker either not to contract with an operator or to break a contract already made.

The writers consider that travel agents are seldom under a duty to volunteer advice to a holiday maker who chooses a holiday without asking for guidance. If a holiday maker bungles his choice of holiday, he cannot blame the travel agent unless the agent gives a wrong answer to a clear and material question. If the faulty choice is the result of misrepresentations in the operator's brochure, the holiday maker will have a claim against the operator—but not against the agent.

It is instructive to compare the agent's responsibilities when selling holidays with his responsibilities when selling air flight tickets. On the face of it they should be the same but, in the writers' opinion, there is a vital difference. Nowadays there are a wide range of special offers, Apexes, Super Apexes etc which provide opportunities for vast savings. The travel agent in his role as expert adviser to "his" customers should have some responsibility to advise them concerning the more obvious possibilities. For instance, if he lets his customer pay the full fare in circumstances where the normal agent would have known of a large (legitimate) discount, he must be vulnerable to a claim under the *Hedley Byrne* principle. But booking a holiday is different. It is a much more personal decision—not just a matter of getting from A to B quickly and cheaply. It is dominated by considerations of taste and personal preference. The agent has a responsibility to answer questions carefully—and to say that he does not know the answer where he does not. But it is doubtful whether more can reasonably be expected of him.

In the writers' submission there is a class of information which a travel agent is legally bound to communicate to holiday makers as a result of his supposed knowledge and expertise. The class is limited, and excludes information which is either highly specialised or commonplace. It is not, for example the travel agent's responsibility to point out to travellers that Beirut is not at present to be recommended for family holidays or that the Costa Brava in August will not afford quiet empty beaches. Nor is it his job to advise upon the circumstances in which an elephant will charge a Landrover. However, it is his duty to counsel the holiday maker about matters known to him but probably not known to the holiday maker which could prevent the holiday maker from reaching his destination or put him at risk once he has arrived.

In January 1983 the Sunday Times revealed that some holiday makers had died in self-catering apartments in the Algarve as a result of carbon monoxide poisoning. It was further revealed that the poisoning was a result of faulty gas heating appliances within the apartments. This was information which very quickly circulated within the holiday industry and caused great concern. The duty of tour operators to notify holiday makers who have booked with them about such a problem seems clear cut. What, though, is the position of a travel agent?

There are two basic types of travel agent whose positions must be considered—those which do not have a tour operations division, and those which do and whose tour operations division ceased to supply package holidays pending rectification of the problem.

There is also a third intermediate category, namely travel agents whose company does not have a tour operations division but which is a member of a group of companies one of which is a tour operator. In legal theory the knowledge of its tour operating affiliate company should not be imputed to such a travel agent but a court might be tempted to depart from that doctrine in the circumstances discussed below.

The same basic duty of care applies to both categories of agent. Customers who have booked through a travel agent rely upon his skill and knowledge of the industry. This reliance, and the agent's attendant duty, cannot be taken to end once the travel agent has effected the holiday maker's booking with the tour operator. It would be illogical and, in the writers' opinion, incorrect to state that a travel agent has a duty to advise a holiday maker of matters known to the agent which could endanger the life of the holiday maker before the operator confirms the booking but that thereafter no such duty exists. Such a duty must, it is submitted, exist up to the date of departure of the holiday maker—either under an extension of the *Hedley Byrne* principle or, more likely, as a result of the neighbourliness principle enunciated in *Anns* v *London Borough of Merton.*

Accordingly, it is submitted that in the circumstances pertaining to the Algarve the travel agent, irrespective of whether or not he had a tour operations division, owed a duty to holiday makers to do the following:

(a) seek immediate assurances from those tour operators whose brochures included self catering holidays in the Algarve that their holidays were free from risk and confirmation that such assurances were as a result of inspection by suitably qualified experts (preferably British);

(b) inform the tour operators that their holidays

77

would not be sold pending receipt of the assurances and confirmation sought;

(c) advise those holiday makers who had already booked of the problem and suggest that they contact the relevant tour operator;

(d) advise the tour operators what steps were being taken.

A travel agent with a tour operations division which had withdrawn its own package holidays which utilised apartments thought to be dangerous but continued through its retail division to sell similar holidays provided by other operators would be placed in a particularly anomalous situation which would be difficult to justify either legally or morally.

Some travel agents have available for distribution booklets outlining various requirements for travelling abroad and details of conditions known to be prevalent in some countries. These do not purport to be extensive and usually refer holiday makers to embassies etc at which further detailed enquiries can and should be made. What they do is to put the holiday maker on notice of basic prerequisites for travelling abroad and gaining entry to the country being visited. It is submitted that this adequately fulfils the travel agent's duty of care. Most travel agents do not have at their fingertips full details of the visa requirements for Outer Mongolia, nor would holiday makers expect them to have such knowledge. What holiday makers do expect is that travel agents will give general advice and put them on notice of, say, medical and visa requirements so that each holiday maker can make his own arrangements.

The position of travel agents who offer specific services regarding such requirements is different. A detailed consideration of the duties of travel agents offering such services is outside the scope of this book but, in general terms, it is submitted that those agents who take it upon themselves to offer services over and above the norm must assume duties and responsibilities over and above the norm.

A travel agent does not hold himself out as being

responsible for the overall well-being of his customers while abroad nor is he so regarded. In particular, a travel agent cannot be presumed to know whether or not a particular individual has special health requirements. It is for the holiday maker to advise the travel agent of these and any failure to do so will absolve the travel agent from liability for any ill-health consequently suffered by the holiday maker.

It can be seen that the travel agent's duty to the holiday maker goes beyond merely conveying statements made by a particular tour operator. There is a wider duty, albeit in limited circumstances, to provide advice and information. There must, however, be circumstances in which the travel agent is entitled to rely solely upon a tour operator's description in a brochure about facilities available on a particular holiday. Can these circumstances be readily defined?

Consider the example of the holiday maker who tells a travel agent that he requires a holiday in a hotel in Athens. He is interested in the packages offered by three tour operators and seeks the travel agent's recommendation concerning which to choose. *Prima facie* the travel agent must be able to rely upon a comparison of the descriptions given in each of the operator's brochures and any oral comments which can be elicited over the phone. If the holiday maker is subsequently dissatisfied, any recourse should be against the particular operator.

A travel agent would be placed in an impossible situation if a duty was imposed upon him to warn a holiday maker about all possible problems associated with a particular holiday—including, for example, the risk of food poisoning, sun stroke and dehydration. Such a duty would be tantamount to a duty to dissuade a holiday maker from making his contract with the tour operator.

## 10. Conclusion

The obvious conclusion is that a travel agent has different duties to different people, and indeed different duties to the same people. For this reason, although described as an "agent", he does not easily fit in with the general principles of agency law which apply to a "selling agent" and he is, in fact, something of a hybrid. Primarily the travel agent is the agent of the tour operator but there are several important points which distinguish him from a normal selling agent:

(a) Selling agents, when answering questions about their principal's products, can properly be regarded as answering them on behalf of their principals. This is particularly the case where the agent is precluded from selling competitive products—something which practically never occurs in the travel industry. Travel agents often answer questions in their own right, and incur the attendant liabilities for a false or misleading answer.

(b) Many holiday makers regard, and are encouraged to regard, the travel agent as their agent and certain of his duties are consistent with this.

(c) The travel agent has duties of care in tort which to some extent make him a consultant to the customer.

## 11. Sunday trading

The Shops Act 1950 provides that "shops" are to be closed for the serving of customers on Sundays. The case of *Erewash Borough Council* v *Ilkeston Consumer Co-operative Society Ltd* (1988) The Times 30 June, considered whether or not a travel agent's premises constituted a shop for the purposes of this Act.

The Queens Bench Divisional Court held that a travel agent's premises did not constitute a shop for the offence of Sunday trading within the meaning of sections 47 and 74 of The Shops Act 1950. The following extracts from the judgment of Bingham LJ should be noted:

(i) "The travel agency was not a shop for no thing was in any ordinary sense offered or sold."

(ii) "... A travel agency business was not one where customers resorted to the premises in circumstances comparable with those in which the business of selling goods by retail to similar customers was carried on".

(iii) "The travel agent's business of booking hotel accommodation and issuing travel tickets was not at all closely comparable with or analogous to the typical retail shopkeeper's activity of selling goods across the counter or off the supermarket shelf."

The upshot of this case is that travel agents are at present free to trade on Sundays. The distinction drawn by the Divisional Court does seem somewhat semantic. Its implication is that services can be provided for reward but goods cannot be exchanged for reward on a Sunday.

# Chapter 4

# False and misleading statements

## 1. Introduction

Tour operators and, to a lesser extent, travel agents are frequently accused by customers of making false or misleading statements regarding the facilities available on a package holiday. In most cases the complaints relate to statements made in the tour operator's brochure, such as that a lift or a tennis court is available at a hotel when it is not, or that all rooms have a view of the sea when some do not, or that there is a good bus service to the nearest town whereas buses are practically non-existent. They can also be about oral statements made by either the tour operator or the travel agent. All such statements (whether oral or written) are usually referred to as representations.

Under common law a representation must be a statement of *fact,* past or present, as distinct from a statement of opinion (*Sanders* v *Gall* (1952) CPL 343), or of intention (*Angus* v *Clifford* [1891] 2 Ch 449), or of law (*Beesly* v *Hallwood Estates Ltd* [1960] 1 WLR 549). Further, it must be a statement of fact made before the contract is entered into or be incorporated as a term of the contract. Civil liability in respect of erroneous statements will be on the grounds of misrepresentation, which is the subject of the Misrepresentation Act 1967 and also of various common law principles. Criminal liability, insofar as the travel industry is concerned, will stem from breaches of s.14 of the Trade Descriptions Act 1968 and of Part III of the Consumer Protection Act 1987.

## 2. Criminal liability – Trade Descriptions Act 1968

*(a) Section 14, Trade Descriptions Act 1968*

Section 14(1) reads as follows:

"It shall be an offence for any person in the course of any trade or business:

(a) to make a statement which he knows to be false; or

(b) recklessly to make a statement which is false;

as to any of the following matters that is to say—

(i) the provision in the course of any trade or business of any services, accommodation or facilities;

(ii) the nature of any services, accommodation or facilities provided in the course of any trade or business;

(iii) the time at which, manner in which or persons by whom any services, accommodation or facilities are so provided;

(iv) the examination, approval or evaluation by any person of any services, accommodation or facilities so provided; or

(v) the location or amenities of any accommodation so provided".

It should be noted that sub--subsections (i) to (v) qualify both sub-sections (a) and (b).

Various other passages from s.14 should also be noted:

"For the purposes of this section—

(a) anything (whether or not a statement as to any of the matters specified in the preceding subsection) likely to be taken for such a statement as to any of those matters as would be false shall be deemed to be a false statement as to that matter;

(b) a statement made regardless of whether it is

true or false shall be deemed to be made recklessly, whether or not the person making it had reasons for believing that it might be false". (s.14(2))

"In this section 'false' means false to a material degree . . . " (s.14(4)).

## (b) Enforcement of section 14

Section 14 is enforced by Trading Standards Departments of local authorities. Local Trading Standards Officers work in liaison with the Department of Prices and Consumer Protection and the Office of Fair Trading and must report to the OFT any prosecutions brought under the Act. Although prosecutions are normally brought by Trading Standards Departments, it is open to an individual to bring a private prosecution.

For a successful prosecution to take place under s.14 the prosecution must show that a relevant statement of fact has been made; that at the time of making it was false; and that at that time the maker knew it to be false or was reckless as to its falsity. A relevant statement of fact may be one about services, accommodation or facilities to be provided by someone other than the persons making the statement. This proposition was categorically laid down in *Bambury* v *Hounslow Borough Council* [1971] RTR 1 (DC). Statements of fact made by tour operators about their package holidays and the services provided by, say, hoteliers do therefore come within the ambit of the Act.

Reported cases on prosecutions of travel companies under s.14 appear to involve only tour operators. If a travel agent makes a false statement about a package holiday, he will probably merely be repeating something which appears in the operator's brochure in which event it may be difficult for the prosecution to satisfy the court that the statement was made either knowingly or recklessly. It is possible for a travel agent to make a false statement of fact about services which he himself offers to assist customers in making their holiday arrangements but in practice it is not very likely.

## (c) Meaning of "false statement"

It was established by *Breed* v *Cluett* [1970] 2 QB 459, that for the purposes of s.14 the false statement of fact need not induce the contract and that it can be made during the existence of the contract.

There have been no cases to date which have specifically reviewed the meaning of "false to a material degree". However, two cases in 1972/73 did indicate that the 1968 Act was not meant to cover what were in effect mere breaches of warranties. To create a criminal offence something more serious must have occurred. In *R* v *Clarksons Holidays Limited* (1972) 57 Cr App Rep 38, it was declared that "the count as framed converted what was at worst a breach of contract into a crime". The facts of this case involve a description of a hotel in Spain which was depicted in Clarkson's brochure by a drawing qualified by the words "Artist's impression of Hotel Calypso". The holiday maker requested a room with a balcony and Clarksons confirmed that this facility would be available. When the holiday maker arrived at the hotel, he complained that the balcony did not match its description in the brochure. Clarksons were convicted in the first instance but the Court of Appeal quashed the conviction making the comment mentioned above. It should be noted in passing that Clarksons were prosecuted on 10 counts in all and that the Court of Appeal upheld their conviction on the remaining counts. The 1973 case which reiterated this ruling was *Beckett* v *Cohen* [1973] 1 All ER 120.

## (d) Mens rea

Section 14(1)(a) requires knowledge of the false statement of fact. Following the decision of the Divisional Court in *Wings Limited* v *Ellis* [1984] 1 All ER 1046 (the facts of which are set out later in this chapter) it had been thought that some element of dishonesty was required to impose liability. However, the view taken by the Divisional Court was the subject of an appeal to the House of Lords ((1984) 3 All ER 576).

The certified question for the opinion of the House of

Lords was "whether a defendant may properly be convicted of an offence under section 14(1)(a) of the Trade Descriptions Act 1968 where he has no knowledge of the falsity of the statement at the time of its original publication but knew of it at the time when the statement was read by the complainant". Their Lordships answered this question in the affirmative, holding that where a holiday company innocently issues brochures giving false information and takes steps to correct them immediately it discovers its mistake, it nevertheless commits a breach of section 14(1)(a) if a customer is subsequently issued with an uncorrected brochure, unless it can avoid strict liability by invoking one of the statutory defences specified in ss. 23 and 24.

The effect of the House of Lords decision is that unless a tour operator can successfully invoke one of the statutory defences, it will be liable under s.14(1)(a) for a false statement made in a brochure if, at the time the brochure comes into the hands of a customer it knows that a statement in it is false even though it believes that all copies held by its agents have been corrected.

*(e) Recklessness*

The question of what is or is not reckless as defined by the Act was specifically dealt with in *MFI Warehouses Ltd* v *Nattrass* [1973] 1 All ER 762. In this case the appellants issued an advertisement containing the words "folding doors gear (carriage free)" and offered folding door sets on 14 days approval. Two purchasers thought that the folding door gear sets could be bought separately without the doors. One of them found that he was expected to pay carriage on the gear set and the other discovered that he could not obtain it on approval without paying for it before despatch. The appellant's chairman had examined the advertisement for some 10 minutes before approving it but had not appreciated that it offered the gear set as an item which could be bought separately. The Divisional Court (Lord Widgery CJ, Ashworth and Willis JJ), in upholding conviction under s.14(1)(b), held—

(i) while the word "recklessly" in the context of section 14 did not involve dishonesty, it was not necessary to prove that the statement was made with the degree of irresponsibility which was implied in the phrase "careless whether it be true or false";

(ii) it was sufficient in this case for the prosecution to show that the advertiser did not have regard to the truth or falsity of his advertisement even though it could not be shown that he was deliberately closing his eyes to the truth, or that he had any kind of dishonest intention.

The criteria for deciding whether a statement of fact is misleading to such an extent as to come within the ambit of the 1968 Act were one of the matters considered in *British Airways Board* v *Taylor* [1976] 1 All ER 65. The following comment of Viscount Dilhorne should particularly be noted—

"indeed, it is an essential feature of the Act that, when it has to be considered whether descriptions or statements are misleading, it is the meaning which they are likely to bear to the person or persons to whom they are addressed that matters, and not the meaning which they might, on analysis, bear to a trained legal mind".

Section 24(1) of the Act, which, *inter alia,* applies to possible offences under both paras. (a) and (b) of s.14(1), provides that:

"In any proceedings for an offence under this Act it shall, subject to sub-section 2 of this section, be a defence for the person charged to prove—

(a) that the commission of the offence was due to a mistake or to reliance on information supplied to him or to the act or default of another person, an accident or some other cause beyond his control; and

(b) that he took all reasonable precautions and exercised all diligence to avoid the commission of such an offence by himself or any person under his control".

(Sub-section 2 merely refers to the need to give notice to the prosecution that this defence will be relied upon).

The difficulty with this defence is that if the court decides that the defendant has acted recklessly, it is difficult to see how he can successfully contend that he has taken all reasonable precautions and exercised all due diligence. A tour operator who is prosecuted under s.14(1)(b) for, say, failing to notify a holiday maker of a change of itinerary on a coach tour can plead not guilty, relying upon the provision of details about the operator's normal *modus operandi* in such circumstances and the fact (if it is true) that only one person out of, say, 50 had not been notified. If the court still considers that the operator has been reckless, he has ready-made grounds for a plea of mitigation. If only one person out of, say, 2,000 had not been notified, it is submitted that there are good grounds not only for proving the absence of recklessness but also for showing that all reasonable precautions and diligence had been exercised in an effort to avoid commission of the offence.

The standard of proof required to establish recklessness was refined and raised by the *Wings Limited* v *Ellis* case. The pertinent facts of this case are that on 13 January 1982 a Mr Wade booked, through travel agents, a holiday with Wings Limited for himself and his wife at the Seashells Hotel, Nogombo, Sri Lanka commencing on 3 March 1982. Mr Wade booked his holiday in reliance upon Wing's Brochure entitled *Wings Faraway Holidays Winter Oct 1981/Apr 1982,* which stated that the bedrooms at the hotel were air conditioned, and contained a photograph which purported to be of the hotel but was not. The photograph had originally been approved by the contracts manager and it was only someone with personal knowledge of the hotel, such as the contracts manager, who could have detected the error. Wings discovered the error in May 1981 and by a memorandum dated 1 June 1981 instructed their staff to amend their brochures, to inform travel agents of the error and to inform customers of the error when bookings were being made. Further, a letter was despatched to customers who had already booked holidays. When Mr Wade booked his holiday some seven months after discovery of the error, neither Wings nor the travel agents advised him of it. Wings were prosecuted, and convicted by a magistrates' court, of knowingly making a false statement contrary to s.14(1)(a) (this related to the statement in the brochure that the hotel bedrooms were air conditioned) and of recklessly making a false statement contrary to s.14(1)(b) (this related to the inclusion in the brochure of the incorrect photograph).

Wings appealed against both convictions. Various questions were referred to the Divisional Court in the case stated and some of those which it answered are set out below with the answers:

> "Whether the two facts (a) that the appellant's customer Mr Wade read the brochure containing the statement 'AC' (this refers to air conditioning) on 13 January 1982 and (b) that employees of the appellant discovered that the said statement was false before that date in about May 1981, by themselves suffice to support a conviction of the appellant under s.14(1)(a) of knowingly making a false statement, regardless of any other evidence, or of evidence that Mr Wade's travel agent in common with all other persons inquiring about bookings at the Seashells Hotel was told that it was not air conditioned?"
>
> *Answer: No (Reversed by the House of Lords)*
>
> "Whether to secure a conviction under s.14(1)(b) it was necessary for the prosecution to prove recklessness on the part of an employee of the appellant responsible for the publication of the said brochure?"
>
> *Answer: No*
>
> "Whether there was evidence on which the court could make the finding of fact made by it that the appellant was reckless?"
>
> *Answer: No*
>
> "Whether to secure a conviction under s.14(1)(b) it was necessary for the prosecution to prove recklessness on the part of a director or a controlling manager of the appellant who represents the

directing mind and will of the company and controls what it does?"

*Answer: Yes*

As regards liability for recklessness under s.14(1)(b), Mr Justice Mann, who read the judgment of the court, made the following particularly noteworthy comments:

"A company cannot be guilty of an offence unless the specified state of mind was a state of mind of a person who is or forms part of the directing mind and will of the company . . . We can find nothing in the evidence which suggests that a person ruling the company was privy to the selection of the photograph. In particular, we reject the respondent's suggestion that Michael Stephenson who approved the photograph and who variously called himself a "long haul development manager" and the "contracts manager" could be inferred to be a member of the relevant class. The most that could be said for the respondent (ie against Wings) is that the members of this class, although establishing a system, failed to establish a system which would have prevented the mistake which occurred. That failure cannot, in our judgment, constitute "recklessness". There may be cases where the system is such that he who establishes it could not be said to be having regard to the truth or falsity of what emerged from it but that is not this case".

The Wings case indicates that tour operators who discover mistakes and take proper steps in accordance with an established system to notify customers of them cannot be successfully prosecuted under s.14(1)(b) merely because of an isolated failure in the system. But it will be paramount for there to be a well established and *provable* system. The absence of such a system, and of proof of steps taken to correct false statements, will render likely a successful prosecution under s14(1)(b).

In *Yugotours Ltd.* v *Wadsley* (1988) The Guardian 3 June, the Divisional Court heard an appeal by Yugotours against a conviction under section 14(1)(b). The relevant facts were that Yugotours' 1986 summer brochure advertised a holiday headed Adriatic Island Adventure with a photograph of a three-masted schooner and a description of the holiday offered, including the words "the excitement of being under sail on board this majestic schooner" and "lie back and enjoy the wind-filled sails". A letter dated 13 March 1986 to customers stated, *inter alia*, "your cruise will be a combination of sailing and motor sailing" and went on to state that the schooner had a minimum of two showers.

Two customers, who booked the holiday with Yugotours, complained that the schooner provided for them was not the one in the brochure, was not three-masted, had no sails and only had one shower. Trading Standards officers instituted proceedings against Yugotours on the grounds, *inter alia*, that the schooner provided was not the one depicted in the brochure, that it had one shower, not two, and that the cruise was not a combination of sailing and motor sailing.

Yugotours claimed, and this emerged from the evidence, that in September 1985 they had contracted with another company to provide a schooner with sails but, at some undetermined point, bookings became too great and Yugotours, in obtaining another vessel, arranged for a two-masted schooner to be provided. This was, though, before the letter of 13 March.

The Divisional Court upheld the conviction of Yugotours by the magistrates under section 14(1)(b). In the course of his judgment, Parker LJ stated that if a statement is false and is known to be false, and nothing whatever is done to correct it, the company making the statement can properly be found guilty of recklessness notwithstanding the absence of specific evidence. The state of mind envisaged by section 14(1)(b) is one which can only be a matter of inference and there was sufficient evidence from which such an inference could be drawn.

*(f) Compensation*

Prosecutions under the Act do not preclude civil proceedings. Although not widely invoked, it should be borne in mind that under the Criminal Justice Act 1972 the court can (if an application is made to it) make an award against the defendant in favour of the individual who first brought the matter to the notice of the Trading Standards Department if he has suffered any loss. In *R* v *Thomson Holidays Limited* [1974] 1 All ER 823, for example, Thomson Holidays were ordered to pay compensation to the original complainants. This order was upheld by the Court of Appeal which stated that the court had to consider under s.1(1) of the 1972 Act whether the loss or damage could fairly be said to have resulted from the offence for which the accused had been convicted. Compensation under the 1972 Act is limited to £2,000 per complainant. The maximum fine under the Trade Descriptions Act is also £2,000 but a prosecution can be brought on more than one count in respect of the same booking and it is each count which has a limit of £2,000.

The pertinent facts of the Thomson Holidays case mentioned above were that, following the distribution in August and September 1970 of two million copies of Thomson's brochure for the 1971 season, two complaints were made by unrelated individuals about the amenities described at a particular hotel in Greece. Separate prosecutions were instituted. At the hearing of the first, Thomsons pleaded guilty but at the second entered a plea of *autrefois convict*—ie that they could not be convicted twice for the same offence. The Court of Appeal held that this was not a valid plea. A false statement is made within the meaning of s.14(1)(b) when it is communicated to someone and each time a false statement in a brochure is communicated to a reader a fresh offence is committed. Thus, a tour operator whose brochure contains a false statement within the meaning of the Act could, in theory, have separate prosecutions brought against him by every person who reads his brochure.

### (g) Time at which statement is made

The Court of Appeal in *R* v *Thomson Holidays Limited* held that a new statement was made on every occasion that an interested member of the public read it in a brochure published by a company engaged in attracting custom. It considered that communication was of the essence of making a statement. The House of Lords, in reaching their decision regarding the question referred to it in the *Wings* case, also considered the question of when a statement is made for the purposes of s.14(1)(a). Their decision is best summarised by the following extracts from the judgment of Lord Hailsham:

> "The Divisional Court used the authority of *R* v *Thomson Holidays* [1974] QB 592, 597 to establish the general proposition, taken out of context, that 'a statement is made when it is communicated to someone'.
>
> When, in the course of trade or business, a brochure containing a false statement was issued in large numbers through a chain of distribution involving several stages, and was intended to be read and used at all or some of the stages, it did not follow that it was only 'made at its ultimate destination'.
>
> It might be 'made' when posted in bulk, when the information was passed on by telephone or in smaller batches in the post, and when it was read by the ultimate recipient — provided that at each stage what happened was in accordance with the original intention of the issuing house.
>
> The statement in the present case was made when Mr. Wade read the brochure on January 13th 1982. It might also have been made at various other stages in the chain of distribution, and was certainly made to other recipients. On January 13th 1982 Wings knew that the hotel was not air conditioned, and therefore knew that the statement, if made in its uncorrected form (as it was), was false."

Lord Scarman stated in *Wings* v *Ellis* that it was unnecessary for the Court of Appeal in *Thomson* to hold that communication was of the essence of a statement. In his view, which is now the law, a statement in a brochure is originally made when the brochure is first published. But further statements to the same effect are made whenever persons do business with the operator on the strength of the uncorrected brochure.

## (h) Statements of intention

The 1968 Act does not cover a statement of intention or future promise which is unfulfilled. This is because the statement is neither true nor false at the time it is made. The Court of Appeal, in *R* v *Sunair Holidays Limited* [1973] 2 All ER 1233, specifically held that s.14(1) of the Act had no application to statements which amounted to promises regarding the future and so which, when they were made, could not have the character of being either true or false. However it did state, *per curiam,* that a promise about the future may be within s.14 if it can be construed as an implied statement of present intention, means or belief which is false at the time of making and is made knowingly or recklessly. The case involved Sunair's 1970 brochure and *inter alia,* a statement that a hotel in Spain would have a swimming pool. The hotel's season began on 7 March 1970 and ended on 6 October. Its owners planned to improve it during the winter of 1969-70 and builders were instructed to construct a swimming pool on the roof immediately the hotel closed for the 1969-70 winter season. Building work progressed slowly and, when the brochure was read by the complainants—7 January 1970—the hotel was closed and the pool incomplete. Further, when the complainants arrived at the hotel on 27 May 1970, they discovered that the pool could not be filled with water because it had not been properly completed. The Court of Appeal quashed Sunair's conviction under s.14(1)(b) on the basis that the comments in their brochure about the swimming pool related to the future but stated that, had the charges in the indictment been framed to the effect that the brochure impliedly represented that satisfactory arrangements had already been made for the provision of the facilities for services in the future and that such arrangements had not, in fact, been made at the time of the brochure, Sunair would have been convicted.

## (i) Overbooking

This case should be contrasted with that of *British Airways Board* v *Taylor* [1976] 1 All ER 65. The facts were as follows. BOAC wrote on 14 August 1973 to a passenger, who had paid in advance, confirming his reservation for a specified flight on a particular date and at a particular time. Unknown to the passenger, BOAC operated a deliberate policy of overbooking whereby passengers were booked in excess of space on each flight. When BOAC wrote on 14 August 1973 the flight was not overbooked but it was at the time of the flight and the passenger was not allowed on board. The House of Lords held that the letter and ticket would be understood as a statement of fact that the booking was certain, which statement, in view of the overbooking policy, was false within s.14(1) of the 1968 Act since the passenger was exposed to the risk that he might not get a seat. It should be noted, in passing, that British Airways Board escaped liability on the grounds that the statement had been made by BOAC and not by British Airways Board which had replaced BOAC following BOAC's dissolution in 1974.

The question of overbooking will now be considered with specific reference to overbooking by foreign hoteliers. If a tour operator issues a confirmation invoice to a holiday maker that accommodation will be available at a particular hotel in, say, Greece but upon the holiday maker's arrival accommodation is not available at the hotel, will the tour operator be liable under s.14(1)(b)? It will be assumed for the purposes of this question that the tour operator had a contract for accommodation with the hotelier and that it was the hotelier who operated the policy of overbooking. The following are the material considerations:

    (a) By analogy with the *British Airways Board* v *Taylor* case, the confirmatory invoice is a statement of fact. Subject to the wording of the particular invoice, it would not normally be a statement of fact that accommodation had been booked in a specific room at a specific hotel for a specific period but that accommodation had been arranged at a specific hotel for a specific period.

    (b) At the time of the confirmatory invoice was the statement of fact false?

    (c) Was the statement made recklessly?

(d) The facts which affect (b) and (c) above must be considered together since the same facts are material to each point. Whether or not a prosecution will be successful must depend upon the contractual arrangements between the tour operator and the hotelier. If, before the issue of the confirmatory invoice, the operator had concluded a contract with the hotelier to the effect that, say, twenty rooms would be available per day for the period June to September for occupation by clients of the operator, and if, at the time of the issue of the confirmatory invoice, the operator had not already confirmed bookings for twenty other rooms for the period during which the client in question was to stay, it is difficult to see how the operator can be said to be making a statement which is false—let alone be making a false statement recklessly. An arbitrary act of the hotelier, over which act the operator had no control, has created the overbooking.

(e) Most tour operators do have a system of making block bookings at apartments. So long as the operator's confirmatory invoice cannot be interpreted as stating that a specific room has been booked, and so long as the operator is not exceeding his allocation, it appears to follow that no false statement of fact has been made by the operator.

(f) The operator should be entitled to rely upon his contract with the hotelier. In normal circumstances it is unreasonable to suggest that at the time of making a booking with a holiday maker the operator should check with the hotelier that the accommodation contracted for is still available.

## 3. Criminal liability – Consumer Protection Act 1987

Part III of The Consumer Protection Act 1987 (hereinafter referred to as "the 1987 Act") makes it a criminal

offence for a business to give a misleading price indication to consumers about goods, services, accommodation or facilities. It came into force on 1 March 1989
together with regulations – the Price Indications Regulations 1988 – and a Code of Practice regarding its
interpretation.

It is beyond the scope of this book to provide a detailed
analysis of the 1987 Act. What follows is a brief summary
of the relevant provisions.

The 1987 Act creates two offences. The first is contained
in s20(1) which provides that:

> "A person shall be guilty of an offence if, in the
> course of any business of his, he gives (by any means
> whatever) to any consumers an indication which is
> misleading as to the price at which any goods,
> services, accommodation or facilities are available
> (whether generally or from particular persons)."

This section will apply however the price indication is
given – whether in a TV or press advertisement, in a
catalogue or leaflet, or notices in windows or even orally
(say over the telephone).

Section 20(6) defines price. It makes it clear that the total
sum to be paid is to be regarded as the price. The Code
of Practice advises traders to "make clear in your price
indications the full price customers will have to pay for
the product". For example, the price should include VAT.
There is also a section in the Code of Practice which deals
with "holidays and travel prices". The following points
should be noted:

(a) If a variety of prices is offered, the brochure
should make clear the basic price and what are
optional additional charges.

(b) Any non-optional extra charges which are for
fixed amounts should be included in the basic
price.

(c) Details of non-optional extra charges which may
vary, such as holiday insurance, should be made
clear to customers in the brochure near to the
information on the basic price.

(d) If there are any circumstances in which prices could be increased after customers have made their booking (for example a surcharge), this must be clearly stated with all indications of prices together with details of where in the brochure customers will find full information on the circumstances in which an increase could be made.

A price indication includes not only a statement as to price but also a comparison with another price. The Code of Practice deals at some length with price comparisons. The principal points to note are:

(a) Price comparisons should always state the higher price and the intended price. "Reduced to £50.00" is wrong: the price from which the reduction has been made should also be given.

(b) It should be made clear what sort of price the higher price is. For example, comparisons with something described in terms such as "regular price", "usual price" or "normal price" should say whose regular, usual or normal price it is (ie "our normal price").

The 1988 Regulations further qualify the position on price comparison. They make it clear that a comparison with an earlier price is only authorised where it has been charged for a continuous period of not less than twenty-eight days within a period of six months before the new price. It is also necessary that the earlier price related to the supply of the relevant item at the same premises.

The second offence under the 1987 Act is contained in s20(2). It makes it an offence for a person in the course of his business to give a price indication which, after it was given, has become misleading unless he takes all reasonable steps to prevent consumers from relying on it. It is a pre-requisite for this offence to have been committed that some or all of those consumers to whom the price indication was given might reasonably be expected to rely on it at a time after it became misleading.

The Code of Practice comments upon this offence with

particular reference to the holiday industry. It recommends as follows:

(a) Tour Operators who sell direct to holidaymakers must make the correct price clear when a package holiday is being booked, indicating where the original price is misleading. This must be done before the holidaymaker has entered into a contract for the package holiday.

(b) If a price indication becomes misleading while a brochure is current, all travel agents to whom the tour operator has distributed the brochure must be advised. Further, tour operators should be prepared to cancel any bookings made on the basis of a misleading price indication.

(c) Travel agents who are advised of a misleading price indication must ensure that the correct price is made clear to holidaymakers before a booking is made.

The Code of Practice is most important. It provides guidance as to the interpretation of the 1987 Act. Breach of the Code will not in itself give rise to any criminal or civil liability (s25(2) of the 1987 Act); but failure to follow it will be used as evidence of an offence.

The 1987 Act applies not only to tour operators but also to travel agents. For an offence to be committed it is not necessary for the person making the price indication to be the person providing the holiday.

There are various defences to prosecutions brought under s20(1) and s20(2). The five possible defences to a prosecution under s20(1) are contained in s24(1) − (4) and s39. The three possible defences to a prosecution under s20(2) are contained in s24(1) − (3).

Section 25(2)(b) states that:

"Compliance by that person (ie the defendant) with such a code (ie the Code) may be relied on in relation to any matter for the purpose of showing that the commission of the offence by that person has not been established or that that person has a defence."

This makes it clear that the Code of Practice will be of immense importance in defending any prosecutions.

Section 24(1) provides that it is a defence for a defendant to show that the acts or omissions allegedly creating the offence were authorised by regulations made under s26. Section 26 gives the Secretary of State the power to introduce regulations which, for example, govern the way in which price indications may be given. The Price Indications Regulations 1988 were introduced pursuant to s26.

Section 24(2) provides that if the price indication complained of is published in any book, newspaper, magazine, film or radio or television broadcasts or in a programme included in a cable programme service, it will be a defence to show that the indication was not contained in an advertisement.

Section 24(3) is what could be described as the "publishers" defence. It applies if the defendant can show that, in the course of his business, he publishes advertisements, that he received the advertisement in question for publication in the ordinary course of his business, and at the time of publication did not know and had no grounds for suspecting that the publication would involve commission of the offence. The third limb of the defence is important. If the "publisher" becomes aware that there are persistent complaints about a particular advertisement, it may be difficult for him to show that he did not suspect the publication would involve the commission of the offence. The burden of proof will rest with the defendant.

Travel agents who give misleading price indications based on documentation, promotional literature etc from tour operators may well be able to take advantage of the defence in s24(4). It provides that it is a defence if:

"(a) The indication did not relate to the availability from him of any goods, services, accommodation or facilities;

(b) A price had been recommended to every person from whom the goods, services, accommodation or facilities were indicated as being available;

    (c) The indication related to that price, and was misleading as to that price only by reason of a failure by any person to follow the recommendation;

    (d) It was reasonable for the person who gave the indication to assume that the recommendation was for the most part being followed."

Section 39 provides that it is a defence to show that "all reasonable steps" were taken and "all due diligence" exercised to avoid committing the offence. The burden of proving this lies with the defendant.

Where this defence involves an allegation that the commission of the offence was due to the act or default of another or to reliance on information given by another, it is necessary to serve on the prosecution a notice identifying the person who committed the act or default or who gave the information. If the defence involves an allegation of reliance on information from another, it will be necessary to satisfy the court that it was reasonable in all the circumstances to rely on the information having regard in particular:

    (a) "to the steps which he (the defendant) took and those which might reasonably have been taken for the purpose of verifying information; and

    (b) to whether he had any reason to disbelieve the information."

This sub-section also makes it clear that those who on the face of it may be unconnected with an offence but who have been put on notice of, for example, complaints or previous offences may not be able to escape a successful prosecution.

Until the 1987 Act was implemented the travel industry had not faced any legislation which dealt with statements as to price, other than the Price Marking (Bargain Offers) Regulations 1979 which have been repealed by the 1987 Act. The 1987 Act will be enforced by Trading Standards Officers. They are likely to pay great attention to the travel industry following the public controversy over surcharges during 1988.

## 4. Civil liability

Civil liability in respect of false or misleading statements can arise from written or oral representations by either tour operator or travel agent. The reader should keep in mind the two basic principles outlined at the start of this chapter, namely that a representation must be a statement of fact and that it must be made before the contract is entered into or form one of its terms. It should also be borne in mind that misrepresentation can give rise to actions based in contract or in tort. The contractual action will normally be between the tour operator and the holiday maker—they are the principals to the contract and it is generally only the principals who can sue or be sued upon the contract. Actions for tortious misrepresentation will normally be brought by the holiday maker against the travel agent, with whom alone the holiday maker is in personal contact.

This chapter merely considers the circumstances in which liability may attach to a tour operator and/or travel agent as a result of a misrepresentation made to a holiday maker. The remedies available to a holiday maker are discussed in Chapter 5. Contractual misrepresentation is considered first by relating specific legal points to a tour operator's *modus operandi* and then by an overall assessment of the operator's position.

### (a) Contractual misrepresentation

To mount an action for contractual misrepresentation, the misrepresentation must have been made either by the other party to the contract (ie the tour operator) or by that party's agent acting within the scope of his authority (ie the travel agent relaying to the holiday maker information obtained from the tour operator). In either case, the holiday maker should sue the tour operator alone and, if proceedings are instituted against the travel agent, the agent will be entitled to claim an indemnity against the operator on the basis that he acted at all times within his authority and upon information supplied by the operator. If a travel agent has misrepresented the situation outside the scope of his authority he may be liable to the holiday maker in tort for fraudulent or negligent misrepresentation.

## (b) Representee

The person commencing an action on the grounds of misrepresentation (ie the holiday maker) must be able to show that he is a representee. There are three classes of representee—

(a) Persons to whom the representation is directly made. Holiday makers to whom a direct oral representation is made by a tour operator are in this category.

(b) Persons to whom the representor intended or expected the representation to be passed. Holiday makers to whom a travel agent acting within the scope of his authority communicates representations made by a tour operator are in this class.

(c) Members of a class at which a representation was directed, which includes the public at large. This covers anyone who reads a tour operator's brochure.

## (c) Representation

As has already been emphasised, to constitute a representation a statement must be one of fact, past or present. A statement of opinion does not in general constitute a representation. However, this is not always so. If it can be shown that the person expressing the opinion did not honestly hold it, or that a reasonable man in possession of the same facts as the person expressing the opinion would not have held it, the statement may be regarded as a statement of fact which is actionable (*Smith* v *Land and House Property Corporation* (1884) 28 Ch D 7). Further, a statement of opinion published as if it was a fact may be regarded as a statement of fact (*Reese River Silver Mining Co Ltd* v *Smith* (1869) LR 4 HL 64). Statements in a tour operator's brochure regarding facilities available at a particular resort or hotel are usually made as if they were statements of fact and must, therefore, be regarded as such.

A statement of intention can be regarded as a misrepresentation of existing fact if, when made, it is not possible to give effect to it (*Edgington* v *Fitzmaurice* (1885) 29 Ch D 459). Accordingly, an argument by a tour operator that a statement made in his brochure was only one of intent will not enable him to escape liability if at the time of confirming a particular holiday maker's booking it was clear that the original intention was unlikely to be fulfilled. In this context it should be remembered that an invoice confirming the holiday arrangements to the holiday maker is regarded by the courts as containing an implied statement that the relevant statements included in the brochure are correct.

*Chitty on Contracts* (25th edition page 214) states, as regards statements of intention or opinion:

> "It is suggested that the fundamental principle which underlies the cases is not so much that statements as to the future, or statements of opinion, cannot be misrepresentations, but rather that statements are not to be treated as representations where, having regard to all the circumstances, it is unreasonable of the representee to rely on the representor's statements rather than his own judgment".

### (d) Non-disclosure

Mere non-disclosure does not constitute misrepresentation (*Percival* v *Wright* [1902] 2 Ch 421), unless the contract is one *uberrimae fidei* (ie of the utmost good faith), in which case there is a fiduciary relationship between the parties and non-disclosure of a material fact creates a misrepresentation out of a representation. A contract between a tour operator and a holiday maker is not one of the utmost good faith, nor is there a fiduciary relationship between the parties. Nevertheless, there are circumstances in which non-disclosure may amount to misrepresentation. Suppose a picture in a brochure shows a hotel set against a luscious, verdant landscape and the accompanying literature elaborates the idyllic landscape. This would distort reality considerably if, in fact, a mere fifty yards to the west of the hotel is a power station continually belching out noxious fumes. Because most holiday makers have only the tour operator's representations to guide them in their choice of resort the circumstances hypothesised should, in the writers' opinion, impose a liability on the operator for non-disclosure of a material fact. But the duty to disclose can only be a duty to disclose facts which are contrary to what is implied by the brochure and which substantially and materially affect the package holiday.

A failure by the representor to inform the representee of a change in circumstances which has rendered an originally true representation false can be a misrepresentation (*With* v *O'Flanagan* [1936] Ch 575). This can apply to either tour operator or travel agent in circumstances such as a failure to notify a holiday maker that, for example, a particular hotel which used to have all-night discotheques every night of the week has stopped them and does not intend to recommence the facility.

In certain circumstances, a representation is treated as continuing until the contract is concluded, particularly when it was innocently made in the first instance but the representor, upon being made aware of the true position, does not inform the representee of the change in circumstances (*Davies* v *London Provincial Marine Insurance Co* (1878) 8 Ch D 469). ABTA tour operators are required to notify the holiday maker as soon as possible of a material change in circumstances and offer a similar alternative holiday or a total refund, provided that the change materially alters the nature of the holiday. This reflects the legal position, although the law goes further by allowing the holiday maker damages if the change does not so materially affect the holiday as to justify cancellation and a total refund.

The representation need not be material nor need it have been the sole inducement to enter into the contract. But, for the representation to be actionable, the representee must be able to show that it affected his assessment of the situation. So long as the holiday maker relied upon it, as the tour operator or travel agent should expect him to do, the misrepresentation will be actionable. However, its materiality will affect the relief available to a holiday maker (see Chapter 6).

At common law damages have always been recoverable for a *fraudulent* misrepresentation. The 1889 case of *Derry* v *Peek* decided that, in order for fraud to be established, it is necessary to prove the absence of an honest belief in the truth of what has been stated. In that case Lord Herschell stated—

> "fraud is proved when it is shown that a false representation has been made (i) knowingly, or (ii) without belief in its truth, or (iii) recklessly, careless whether it be true or false".

The onus of proof in this cause of action rests upon the representee.

### (e) Negligent misrepresentation

The position of people who suffer as a result of misrepresentations which are not fraudulent was revolutionised by s.2(1) of the Misrepresentation Act 1967 which reads as follows:

> "Where a person has entered into a contract after a misrepresentation has been made to him by another party thereto and as a result thereof he has suffered loss, then if the person making the representation would be liable to damages in respect thereof had the misrepresentation been made fraudulently, that person shall be so liable notwithstanding that the misrepresentation was not made fraudulently, unless he proves that he had reasonable grounds to believe and did believe up to the time the contract was made that the facts represented were true".

The effect of this is that a tour operator will be liable in damages for a negligent misrepresentation (ie one made carelessly or without reasonable grounds for believing it to be true) unless he can show that he had reasonable grounds for believing the truth of the representation made by him. It must be stressed that the onus of proof rests with the tour operator.

## (f) Reasonable grounds for belief

The case of *Howard Marine and Dredging Company Limited* v *A Ogden & Sons (Excavations) Limited* [1978] QB 574 is instructive concerning what constitutes reasonable grounds for belief. In this case, the plaintiffs misrepresented to the defendants the carrying capacity of two barges which the defendants wished to hire for carrying large quantities of clay out to sea and then dumping. The defendants entered into the contract in reliance on this misrepresentation and used the barges for some time before they discovered the true facts and returned the barges. The plaintiffs' misrepresentation was based upon their recollection of an entry in Lloyd's Register about the capacity of the barges but the entry was incorrect. The correct capacity could have been ascertained from the ship's documents in the plaintiffs' possession. A majority of the Court of Appeal held that the defendants were entitled to damages for breach of s.2(1) of the 1967 Act. It was held that to avoid liability the plaintiffs had to prove that they had reasonable grounds to believe and did believe up to the time the contract was made, that the facts represented were true and that on an analysis of the evidence that burden had not been discharged since the person making the representation had not shown any objectively reasonable ground for disregarding the capacity stated in the ship's documents and for preferring the Lloyd's Register incorrect figure. The following *dicta* in particular should be noted:

> "If the representee proves a misrepresentation which, if fraudulent, would have sounded in damages, the onus passes immediately to the representor to prove that he had reasonable grounds to believe the facts represented. In other words the liability of the representor does not depend upon his being under a duty of care the extent of which may vary according to the circumstances in which the representation is

made. In the course of negotiations leading to a contract the statute imposes an absolute obligation not to state facts which the representor cannot prove he had reasonable ground to believe ... But the question remains whether his evidence, however benevolently viewed, is sufficient to show that he had an *objectively reasonable* ground to disregard the figure in the ship's documents and to prefer the Lloyd's Register figure". (*per* Bridge LJ).

A point also arose regarding an exclusion clause upon which the plaintiffs sought to rely to exempt responsibility for negligent misrepresentation. Bridge LJ stated:

"What the judge said in this matter was: If the wording of the clause is apt to exempt from responsibility for negligent misrepresentation as to carrying capacity, I hold that such exemption is not fair and reasonable. The judge having asked himself the right question and answered it as he did in the exercise of the discretion vested in him by the Act (section 3 of Misrepresentation Act 1967), I can see no ground on which we would say that he was wrong".

Two other cases which, although not directly relating to s.2(1) of the Misrepresentation Act, set out analogous principles are:

*Greenwood* v *Leather Shod Wheel Company* [1900] 1 Ch D 421. This case involved a misrepresentation by a company in its prospectus. Section 38 of the Companies Act 1867 stated that no person is liable for a misrepresentation in a prospectus provided that he can prove that he had reasonable cause to believe and did believe that the statement was true; in other words that there was not notice of matters which would cast doubt on the veracity of any statement of fact in the prospectus. (These are the same criteria as in s.2(1) of the Misrepresentation Act). Lindlay MR stated:

"Notice in the section (ie s.38, Companies Act 1867) means not what is called 'constructive notice' but actual notice, that is notice which brings home to the mind of a

reasonable, intelligent and careful reader such knowledge as fairly and in a business sense, amounts to notice
of a contract. In other words, liability under s.38 could be
avoided provided that the person who had included the
representation in the prospectus could show that he did
so upon information which to a reasonable intelligent
and careful person in a business sense would justify the
inclusion of the representation."

*Brown* v *Raphael* [1958] 2 All ER 79. This was a case
which arose from a negligent misrepresentation at
common law as to certain matters affecting the sale of a
house. The vendor relied upon information provided by
his solicitors but it was held that he could not rely upon
this information. Lord Evershed, MR, stated—

> "The question then arises: was that information
> such as to justify a reasonable person who had any
> awareness of the significance of the matter, assert-
> ing as an inducement to a reasonable purchaser that
> the annuitant was believed to have no aggregate
> estate? . . . it is quite plain that that very meagre
> information formed no basis whatever on which a
> responsible person could put forward that view as an
> inducement for somebody to buy the reversion".

To obtain the protection of the proviso under s.2(1) of the
Misrepresentation Act 1967 tour operators have two
burdens of proof, one of which is subjective and one of
which is both objective and subjective. The subjective
burden of proof is to show to the court that it was believed
that the statements in the brochure were true. The
objective burden of proof is to show that there were
reasonable grounds for this belief. Reasonable grounds
will of course be subjective in that different people will
come to different decisions based upon the same information. The starting point must, therefore, be objective.
Adapting Lindlay MR's words—would a reasonably intelligent and careful person with knowledge of the travel
industry be entitled to form the belief that was formed?

It is accepted practice in the travel industry that tour
operators rely for their information upon inspections by
their products departments, reports which they receive

from their representatives, trade publications and information provided by hotels themselves. The *Brown* v *Raphael* and *Greenwood* v *Leather Shod Wheel Co* cases indicate that information from hotels alone would not provide a basis to justify the inclusion of representations in brochures. However, reports from products managers and representatives constitute actual notice and, in the writers' opinion, should be accepted as providing reasonable grounds for making representations.

*Chitty on Contracts* (25th edition page 231) states as follows (when commenting on the *Howard Marine & Dredging Co* case):

> "It was also stressed that the question was, strictly speaking, not one of negligence but that the Act imposed an absolute obligation not to state facts which the representor cannot prove he had reasonable grounds to believe. No doubt it is correct to say that it is not a question of negligence, as at common law, where a duty of care is in issue; and it is possible that circumstances may exist in which a person may make a statement without having reasonable grounds to believe it, in which case it would be held that he was not (having regard to all the circumstances) negligent. Nevertheless, for most practical purposes it will usually be correct to equate liability under section 2(1) of the Act with liability for negligence".

This statement reinforces the following *dicta* by Mr Justice Hodgson in the *Wall* v *Silver Wing* case (the *dicta* arose in connection with negligence)—"Before it (the representation) was included in the brochure the Martina was inspected and found not only to have adequate but admirable fire escape facilities. I think that that fulfilled any duty of care owed to the customers and I think it robbed of any suggestion of misrepresentation anything contained in the brochure. I do not think that there was any duty upon the tour operators to make routine inspections thereafter".

## (g) Remedies

Section 2(2) of the Misrepresentation Act 1967 reads as follows:

> "Where a person has entered into a contract after a misrepresentation had been made to him otherwise than fraudulently, and he would be entitled, by reason of the misrepresentation, to rescind the contract, then, if it is claimed, in any proceedings arising out of the contract, that the contract ought to be or has been rescinded, the court or arbitrator may declare the contract subsisting and award damages in lieu of rescission, if of the opinion that it would be equitable to do so, having regard to the nature of the representation and the loss that would be caused by it if the contract were upheld, as well as to the loss that rescission would cause to the other party".

In the event of an innocent misrepresentation (ie an inaccurate representation which is not fraudulent within the meaning of fraudulent specified in *Derry* v *Peek*) the common law normally only entitled the representee to claim rescission of the contract. As discussed above, s.2(1) entitles the representee to claim damages in the event of a negligent misrepresentation and the effect of s.2(2) is to enable the court to award damages in lieu of rescission in the event of a misrepresentation which is neither fraudulent nor negligent. This remedy is only available at the discretion of the court in lieu of rescission and does not provide a right to claim damages.

## (h) Exclusion clauses

At common law a representor could not exclude liability for fraudulent misrepresentation but could for innocent (including negligent) misrepresentation. Section 3 of the Misrepresentation Act 1967, as amended by s.8 of the Unfair Contract Terms Act 1977, states—

> "If a contract contains a term which would exclude or restrict:
>
> (a) any liability to which a party to a contract may

be subject by reason of any misrepresentation made by him before the contract was made; or

(b) any remedy available to another party to the contract by reason of such a misrepresentation;

that term shall be of no effect except in so far as it satisfies the requirement of reasonableness as stated in s.11(2) of the Unfair Contract Terms Act 1977; and it is for those claiming that the term satisfies that requirement to show that it does".

The requirement of reasonableness is discussed in Chapter 2 but it should be noted that the onus will be on the tour operator to show that the exclusion clause is reasonable.

It is the tour operator's brochure which contains the main body of representations about the facilities on a particular holiday and, if inaccurate, it will provide the holiday maker with a valid cause of action unless the operator can prove that he had reasonable grounds to believe and did believe up to the time the contract was made that the representation was true. This burden is in broad terms the same as a tour operator faces in disposing of a claim for breach of contract by providing satisfactory details of checks made concerning the facilities offered by hotels and other independent contractors. This onus of proof, and the viability of exclusion clauses in view of the "reasonableness" test imposed by the Unfair Contract Terms Act 1977, are both discussed in Chapter 2.

Misrepresentations by a tour operator are not necessarily confined to statements made in its package holiday brochure. Sometimes a holiday maker will ask his travel agent a question which will lead to the latter ringing the tour operator for an answer, which is then passed on to the holiday maker. For instance, the holiday maker may want to know whether there is a golf course in his resort or a casino. Some travel agents will know the answer but others will need to check with the operator. If the operator gives an answer which is false without having reasonable grounds for believing it to be true, the holiday maker should normally be in a position successfully to claim against the operator under the Misrepresentation Act.

### (i) Tortious misrepresentation

As previously stated, claims of tortious misrepresentation will normally be brought by the holiday maker against the travel agent. It is not necessary to consider in any detail the legal basis of tortious misrepresentation since—

    (a) the general principles regarding what constitute a representation are applicable; and

    (b) the effect of the 1964 case of *Hedley Byrne & Co Ltd* v *Heller & Partners Limited*, which is discussed in Chapter 3, will mean that any proceedings brought will generally be for negligent advice rather than misrepresentation.

Some travel agents adopt the practice of specially recommending holidays offered by a particular tour operator by the endorsement of recommendation stickers on the front of the tour operator's brochures displayed in the agent's premises. It is suggested for the following reasons that such travel agents can be liable to a holiday maker who is justifiably dissatisfied, even if only with one aspect of the facilities offered:

    (a) The effect of such a recommendation sticker must be that the travel agent, in his own capacity as a travel expert, is endorsing the holidays in the operator's brochure. In the absence of wording to the contrary this must mean every holiday detailed in the brochure. Obviously the wording of the sticker is most important but the writers have in mind those which merely say "Specially recommended by . . ."

    (b) The agent must intend that holiday makers will rely upon his recommendation that the operator's holidays will be more than satisfactory—a classic example of an inducement to enter into a contract.

(c) Normally the travel agent has not actually inspected the operator's hotels etc and, therefore, will not be able to prove that he has taken reasonable care in the way that the operator may be able to.

Travel agents who use such stickers argue that it is not each and every holiday which is being recommended but rather that the sticker is a pointer towards a generally reputable tour operator. This is not likely to be the interpretation put upon it by members of the public and, in the writers' opinion, would not be how a court of law would see it. However reputable a tour operator may be, his reputation will not justify a travel agent in recommending a holiday of which he had no personal knowledge.

Whether or not the travel agent is entitled to obtain an indemnity from the tour operator will depend upon the background to the use of the recommendation stickers. If they are used pursuant to an agreement between operator and agent, it is likely that it will provide that the agent be indemnified in the event of complaints/court proceedings. If there has been no agreement, the operator may well consider that the agent has acted outside his normal scope and should bear the consequences himself.

## 5. Advertising standards

There is one further aspect of misrepresentation which must be examined and which is not associated with any of the foregoing. A brochure as well as being a source of representations and a contractual document in its own right is a promotional document which is required to observe the standards laid down by the Advertising Standards Authority.

The Advertising Standards Authority prepares the British Code of Advertising Practice. It establishes criteria for professional conduct by advertisers and indicates to the public the limitations accepted by those in advertising. The following aspects of the code should be noted in particular:

(a) All advertisements should be legal, decent, honest and truthful.

(b) All descriptions, claims and comparisons which relate to matters of objectively ascertainable fact should be capable of substantiation.

(c) Advertisements should not contain any statement or visual presentation likely to mislead the consumer either directly or by implication, omission, ambiguity or exaggeration.

(d) All comparative advertisements should respect the principles of fair competition and should be so designed that there is no likelihood of the consumer being misled.

It is open to members of the public or other travel companies to complain to the ASA about a breach of its code in a tour operator's brochure. The ASA's sanctions are, basically, the withholding of advertising space or time and adverse publicity due to the reports which they publish about complaints. They do, though, require a certain length of time to investigate the situation.

It is worth noting that comparative advertising is not much practised by ABTA members who are generally keen to avoid internecine strife. Where it does occur, an aggrieved operator may consider that the ASA are not the most effective body to deal with it and may prefer to complain to ABTA.

Other options which are available to an operator who is aggrieved by the contents of a competitor's brochure are to report the matter to the Trading Standards Department or to seek immediate relief from the courts by means of an injunction. In blatant cases there is considerable merit in involving the Trading Standards Department since they have the authority to enter upon an operator's premises, seize its records for examination and seriously disrupt trading. Relief by means of injunction can be difficult to obtain since, if it is a case of a minor operator at fault, there is a risk that the courts will decide that the threat to business is not sufficient to justify the grant of an injunction. Any situation of this nature will require that the operator and his legal advisers consider the circumstances peculiar to the case—it is not possible to set down hard and fast guidelines, and it is outside the scope of this book to review possible causes of action in any detail.

# Chapter 5

# Damages

Chapters 2, 3 and 4 have considered the various ways in which a tour operator and/or a travel agent can be liable in law to a holiday maker who is dissatisfied with his package holiday arrangements—for example, breach of contract, misrepresentation, negligent misstatement, breach of duty of care. This chapter presumes liability and examines the remedies available in law to the holiday maker. The relevant general principles in law will be covered first followed by an examination of the principal cases to date.

## 1. Meaning of damages

Lord Blackburn, in *Livingstone* & *Rawyards Coal Co* (1880) 5 App Cas 25, defined damages as—

> "that sum of money which will put the party who has been injured, or who has suffered, in the same position as he would have been in if he had not sustained the wrong for which he is now getting compensation".

This definition is equally applicable to damages in contract or in tort but it must be stressed that there is a basic distinction between damages in contract and in tort. In contract, the "wrong" to which Lord Blackburn refers is breach of the contract and, as stated by Parke B in *Robinson* v *Harman* (1848) 1 Ex 855, a plaintiff is entitled to be put into the position he would have been in if the contract had been fully performed. The claim, in essence, is for loss of bargain. In tort, on the other hand, the "wrong" is the doing of that which gives rise to the complaint and a plaintiff is entitled to have the position restored, so far as is possible, to the *status quo ante*.

## 2. Damages for breach of contract

*(a) Causation*

For damages to be recoverable for breach of contract there must be a causal connection between the defendant's breach of contract and the plaintiff's loss, *and* the particular loss must be within the contemplation of the parties. The first question to be considered is whether or not the defendant's breach caused the plaintiff's loss, in respect of which two alternative situations must be borne in mind—

(a) the defendant's breach *directly* causes the plaintiff's loss; or

(b) the defendant's breach *indirectly* causes the plaintiff's loss, ie a "new intervening event" occurs pursuant to the defendant's breach and causes the plaintiff's loss.

In either of these situations what must be determined is the extent of the plaintiff's loss for which the defendant, by reason of his breach, should be held liable. The question of causation can be somewhat complicated, and a detailed analysis is beyond the scope of this book. The writers do not propose to dwell on this subject, save to bring it to the reader's attention and comment briefly on "indirect" causation.

Indirect causation can stem either from the intervening act of a third party, or from an intervening act of the plaintiff. Regarding the latter, the effect of s.1(1) of the Law Reform (Contributory Negligence) Act 1945 is that damages *in tort*, will be reduced if the plaintiff "suffers damage as the result partly of his own fault and partly of the fault of any other person". There has been doubt whether or not damages in *contract* may be reduced by the application of this Act. In *Forsikringsaktieselskapet Vesta* v *Butcher* [1986] 2 All ER 488, Hobhouse J identified three categories of case to which the Act could possibly apply, namely:

"(i) Where the defendant's liability arises from some contractual provision which does not depend on negligence on the part of the defendant.

(ii) Where the defendant's liability arises from a contractual obligation which is expressed in terms of taking care (or its equivalent) but does not correspond to a common law duty to take care which would exist in the case independently of contract.

(iii) Where the defendant's liability in contract is the same as his liability in the tort of negligence independently of the existence of any contract."

*McGregor on Damages* concludes that the Act does not apply to damages in contract for category (i) cases, but does for category (ii) and (iii) cases.

## (b) Foreseeability

Assuming that the plaintiff's loss is attributable to the defendant's breach, what has to be considered is whether the loss was within the contemplation of the parties and was not too remote from the breach to merit compensation. The first definitive outline of what damages are or are not too remote is contained in the following words of Alderson, B in *Hadley* v *Baxendale* (1854) 9 Exch 341—

"Where two parties have made a contract which one of them has broken, the damages which the other party ought to receive in respect of such a breach of contract should be such as may fairly and reasonably be considered either arising naturally, ie according to the usual course of things, from such breach of contract itself, or such as may reasonably be supposed to have been in the contemplation of both parties, at the time they made the contract, as the probable result of the breach of it. Now, if the special circumstances under which the contract was actually made were communicated by the plaintiffs to the defendants, and thus known to both parties, the damages resulting from the breach of such a contract, which they would reasonably contemplate, would be the amount of injury which would ordinarily follow from a breach of contract under these special circumstances so known and communicated. But, on the other hand, if these special circumstances were wholly unknown to the party breaking the contract, he, at the most, could only be supposed to have had in his contemplation the amount of injury which would arise generally, and in the great multitude of cases not affected by any special circumstances, from such a breach of contract. For, had the special circumstances been known, the parties might have specifically provided for the breach of contract by special terms as to the damages in that case; and of this advantage it would be very unjust to deprive them".

The above principle was restated by Asquith LJ in *Victoria Laundry* v *Newman* [1949] 2 KB 528 as follows:

" (1) It is well settled that the governing purpose of damages is to put the party whose rights have been violated in the same position, so far as money can do so, as if his rights had been observed. This purpose, if relentlessly pursued would provide him with a complete indemnity from all loss *de facto* resulting from a particular breach, however improbable, however unpredictable. This, in contract at least, is recognised as too harsh a rule.

(2) Hence, in cases of breach of contract the aggrieved party is only entitled to recover such part of the loss actually resulting as was at the time of the contract reasonably foreseeable as liable to result from the breach.

(3) What was at the time reasonably so foreseeable depends on the knowledge then possessed by the parties, or, at all events, by the party who later commits the breach.

(4) For this purpose, knowledge 'possessed' is of two kinds; one imputed, the other actual. Everyone, as a reasonable person, is taken to know the 'ordinary course of things' and consequently what loss is liable to result from a breach of contract in that ordinary course. This is the subject matter of the 'first rule' in *Hadley* v *Baxendale*. But to this knowledge, which a contract breaker is assumed to possess whether he actually possesses it or not, there may have to be added in a particular case knowledge which he actually possesses, of special circumstances outside the 'ordinary course of things', of such a kind that a

breach in those special circumstances would be liable to cause more loss. Such a case attracts the operation of the 'second rule' so as to make additional loss also recoverable.

(5) In order to make the contract breaker liable under either rule it is not necessary that he should actually have asked himself what loss is liable to result from a breach. As has often been pointed out, parties at the time of contracting contemplate not the breach of contract but its performance. It suffices that, if he had considered the question, he would as a reasonable man have concluded that the loss in question was liable to result.

(6) Nor, finally, to make a particular loss recoverable, need it be proved that upon a given state of knowledge the defendant could, as a reasonable man, foresee that a breach must necessarily result in that loss. It is enough if he could foresee it was likely so to result. It is indeed enough ... if the loss (or some factor without which it would not have occurred) is a 'serious possibility' or a 'real danger'. For short, we have used the word 'liable' to result. Possibly the colloquialism 'on the cards' indicates the shade of meaning with some approach to accuracy".

Asquith LJ's use of the test of reasonable foreseeability was, however, qualified by the House of Lords in *Czarnikow* v *Koufos* [1969] 1 AC 350. To use Lord Reid's words in that case the test should now be regarded as whether the loss is "of a kind which the defendant, when he made the contract, ought to have realised was not unlikely to result from the breach ... the words 'not unlikely' denoting a degree of possibility considerably less than even chance but nevertheless not very unusual and easily foreseeable".

Asquith LJ's proposition that "foreseeability" depends upon both imputed and actual knowledge is still, however, regarded as correct in law. The question of "knowledge" is important since it establishes a holiday maker's duty to disclose material facts if he subsequently wishes to claim damages in contract for an unusual result occurring from the tour operator's breach of contract due to such material facts. If, for example, there is a particular health reason whereby air conditioning is a necessity for a particular holiday maker, the operator, in the event of a hotel not providing air conditioning in breach of the operator's contract with the holiday maker, will only be liable for damages which would ordinarily result, if the special circumstances have not been communicated to him by the holiday maker. He will not be liable for those damages which result due to the plaintiff's particular state of health. This principle is set out in the 1987 Court of Appeal case of *Kemp* v *Intasun Holidays Limited* (see page 135).

*(c) Indirect damage*

Reference was made earlier to a breach of contract which directly causes a loss and one which only does so indirectly (through a new intervening event). The writers submit that this distinction can be misleading in relation to damages and that it causes confusion in the drafting of exclusion clauses. For instance, does an exclusion clause which excludes liability for indirect or consequential loss exclude liability for every sort of loss which would not have occurred but for a new intervening event? This depends on what is meant by a new intervening event.

In the case of *Saint Line* v *Richardsons Westgarth & Co* [1940] 2 KB 99 Atkinson J said direct damage is that which flows naturally from the breach without other intervening cause and independently of special circumstances while indirect damage does not so flow. Consequential has come to mean "not direct" and refers to something which is not the direct or natural result of the breach. It would seem to follow from this that:

(a) "indirect" and "consequential" are synonymous;

(b) damage is not direct if it is attributable to a new intervening cause; and

(c) damage is direct if it is the natural result of a breach.

It is submitted that there is an inconsistency between (b) and (c) above. Something may well be a natural result even though it involves the intervention of a new third party event. In *London Joint Stock Bank* v *MacMillan*

[1918] AC 777 a customer of the plaintiff bank, in breach of his duty of care not to draw cheques so as to facilitate fraud, signed a cheque drawn by a clerk of his in such a way as to enable the clerk to alter the amount from £2 to £120. The clerk cashed the cheque and absconded. The House of Lords held that the customer was liable to the bank for the forged increase, Lord Finley LC saying that the fact that an *intervening* crime was necessary to bring about the loss did not prevent the loss being the natural consequences of the carelessness. Does this mean that the loss resulting from the intervening third party crime should be regarded as loss flowing directly from the customer's duty of care so as not to be rendered irre- coverable by a (hypothetical) clause excluding liability for indirect loss? The writers believe so but there appears to be no conclusive authority on this subject.

### (d) Mitigation of loss

It is an established principle in contract law that a plaintiff must mitigate his loss—ie he must take reasonable steps to avoid loss. If he does not and could have avoided loss by so doing, he will not recover damages. But a plaintiff is not obliged to take every conceivable step to minimise his loss. The onus of proof rests with the defendant to show that the plaintiff, as a reasonable man, ought to have taken a particular step. What is, or is not, reasonable will depend upon the particular circumstances of each case but it is easy to conceive circumstances in which a holiday maker clearly has a duty to mitigate his loss. If, for example, an operator incorrectly details a flight time as a result of which the holiday maker misses his flight but the operator is able to arrange a flight to the same desti- nation from the same airport some two hours later, the holiday maker must be under a duty to mitigate his loss and take that flight. If he does not but instead returns home, the only compensation to which he should be entitled is a nominal sum for the inconvenience of a two hour wait to catch the alternative flight. It is patently unreasonable not to accept the alternative flight and so is clearly a breach of the holiday maker's duty to mitigate his loss.

There are certain other points regarding mitigation which should be borne in mind:

(a) If a plaintiff succeeds in mitigating his loss wholly, he cannot recover for such avoided loss.

(b) If the plaintiff incurs loss or expense in taking reasonable steps to mitigate, the defendant will be liable to compensate him in damages for such loss or expense. Thus, in the example above, if the alternative flight is from another airport, the tour operator is liable to compensate the holiday maker in damages for the cost of travelling to the other airport.

(c) A plaintiff's inability to mitigate his loss due to his impecuniosity should not reduce the damages to which he is entitled. This was specifically stated in *Clippens Oil Co* v *Edinburgh and District Water Trustees* [1907] AC 291, and appears to have been accepted in *Leisbosch Dredger* v *SS Edison* [1933] AC 449. Although the principle was not applied in *Dodd Properties* v *Canterbury City Council* [1979] 2 All ER 118, the authors consider that it will be applied in holiday cases. If, for example a holiday maker is accommodated in a hotel abroad which is totally unsatisfactory and the tour operator refuses to relocate him or return him to the UK straightaway, the holiday maker's damages will not be reduced merely because he did not have the funds to relocate himself or arrange his own immediate flight to the UK.

*(e) Special and general damages*

Damages are usually divided into special and general damages. The former are those "out of pocket" expenses which have arisen as a result of the breach of contract. The remaining items of general damage—for example loss of enjoyment of a holiday—are not amenable to precise monetary quantification by the holiday maker. Their assessment is left to the courts and it is submitted that there are three main questions which a court will bear in mind when assessing a claim for general damages:

(i) What is the value of that part of the holiday package which the holiday maker has not received? This is the head of general damages known as diminution of contract value. If a package holiday to Greece at a cost of £600 per person was supposed to include the services of the operator's courier to take the holiday makers to various sites of antiquity and explain the history, architecture, etc but the courier was not available, the court would assess the extent to which such services were reflected in the price of the holiday and make an appropriate award. If, in a two week period, there would only have been two excursions to sites of antiquity, the reduction in the value of the contract would be minimal—say £50— but, if daily excursions had been contracted for, a judge might assess it at £250.

(ii) Did the holiday maker suffer any physical inconvenience and discomfort as a result of the operator's breach? If so, damages will be awarded. Cases such as *Hobbs* v *LSW Ry* (1875) LR 10 QB 111, *Stedman* v *Swan's Tours* (1951) 95 SJ 727, and *Feldman* v *Allways Travel Service* (1957) CLY 934, have established that damages are recoverable for physical inconvenience and discomfort. If, in the example in (i), the non-availability of a courier had resulted in holiday makers becoming stranded, and having to spend one night by the ancient temple of Corinth without any accommodation, food etc, damages would be awarded for that physical inconvenience and discomfort.

(iii) Did the holiday maker suffer mental distress, annoyance and disappointment because of the breach? If so, damages will be awarded to compensate him. This head of damages has only been available since the historic decision of the

Court of Appeal in *Jarvis* v *Swan Tours* [1973] 1 All ER 71, the facts of which are set out on page 24. It is a rule in contract law that damages will not be awarded for mental distress, annoyance and disappointment unless the contract is of a type to make such damages appropriate. In *Jarvis* v *Swan Tours* the court held that holiday contracts were of such a type. It is occasionally submitted that the decision in *Jarvis* creates an exception to the rule that damages for mental distress etc will normally not be awarded. The writers disagree. The rule is that such damages will not be awarded unless the mental distress is of a kind which the defendant, when he made the contract, ought to have realised was not unlikely to result from a breach such as that which occurred. Tour operators, in effect, peddle dreams, and broken dreams are bound to produce mental distress, annoyance and disappointment.

The court can at its discretion add interest to any damages awarded. The amount of interest will reflect current commercial rates. In the High Court interest is awarded under the Supreme Court Act 1981 and in the County Court under s.69, County Courts Act 1984.

## 3. Damages in tort

At the start of this chapter, mention was made of the basic distinction between the measures of damages in contract and in tort. The purpose of damages in tort is to restore the plaintiff, so far as money can, to the position that he would have been in had the tort never been committed. The succeeding paragraphs give a broad statement of the relevant principles, but lawyers advising about a particular case should also consult textbooks such as *McGregor on Damages*.

A plaintiff will recover damages for a particular loss if he can show that the defendant's tort caused it—whether directly or indirectly—and that the loss was reasonably foreseeable. As in contract, this incorporates elements of causation and remoteness. The Judicial Committee of the Privy Council in *Overseas Tankship (UK)* v *Morts Dock and Engineering Co, The Wagon Mound* [1961] AC 388 (PC) purported to make foreseeability the sole test of the extent of liability in an action for negligence, since when the subject has been much litigated. However *McGregor on Damages* (20th edition) suggests that elements of causation cannot be easily excluded and will, at least in some cases, be a valid consideration.

There are two points of difference with contract law which must be mentioned:

(a) The provisions of the Law Reform (Contributory Negligence) Act 1945 apply to an assessment of damages in tort.

(b) In contract, if there are circumstances peculiar to a plaintiff which would result in him suffering abnormal damage in the event of a breach, the plaintiff must disclose those circumstances if he seeks to recover compensation for the abnormal damage. This is not so in tort. A defendant must take a plaintiff as he finds him.

Under contract law, a holiday maker can recover damages, for physical inconvenience, mental anguish, distress and disappointment. It is submitted that in cases where they are "reasonably foreseeable" these are also material considerations in tort.

Whether damages for misrepresentation under common law or the Misrepresentation Act 1967 should be assessed under tortious or contractual principles is a difficult question which can only be dealt with properly by reference to the various types of misrepresentation. A detailed examination is beyond the scope of this book and what follows is no more than a brief synopsis:

(a) The Court of Appeal in *Doyle* v *Olby (Ironmongers)* [1969] 2 QB 158 unreservedly held that tortious principles should apply in the event of fraudulent misrepresentation.

(b) *McGregor on Damages* suggests that, at common law, damages for negligent misrepresentation, where no contract results, should be assessed on tortious principles but that, where a contract results, both contractual and tortious principles may be applicable.

(c) Despite the decision of Graham J in *Watts* v *Spence* [1976] Ch 165 that by virtue of s.2(1) of the Misrepresentation Act 1967 the plaintiff was entitled to damages for loss of bargain where he had suffered loss as a result of the defendant's negligent misrepresentation, it is suggested that tortious principles should apply in the event of negligent misrepresentation under s.2(1) of the 1967 Act.

(d) The assessment of damages for an innocent misrepresentation under s.2(2) of the Misrepresentation Act 1967 creates a more difficult problem. Section 2(3) of the 1967 Act states:

"Damages may be awarded against a person under subsection (2) of this section whether or not he is liable to damages under subsection (1) thereof, but where he is so liable any award under the said subsection (2) shall be taken into account in assessing his liability under the said subsection (1)"

This provides a clear indication that damages under s.2(2) can be less than under s.2(1). *McGregor* suggests that the purpose of damages under s.2(2) should be to put the plaintiff into the same position as he would have been if a decree of rescission had been granted.

## 4. The leading cases

In recent years there have been five major cases regarding the damages to be awarded to justifiably aggrieved holiday makers. These will now be considered in detail.

### (a) Jarvis v Swan Tours Ltd

The material facts of this case are detailed on pages 24 and 25.

In the first instance, the trial judge held that the plaintiff was entitled to damages for breach of contract. He assessed these as being worth £31.72 (half the holiday price), on the basis that the contractual measure of damages was the difference between what the plaintiff had paid for the holiday and what he had got. The plaintiff appealed.

**Held:** In a proper case damages for mental distress could be recovered in an action for breach of contract. The plaintiff was not necessarily restricted to damages for physical inconvenience suffered by the breach. Breach of a contract to provide a holiday or entertainment and enjoyment was a proper case in which to award damages for mental distress, or inconvenience, because in such a contract it was foreseeable that a material breach might well cause frustration, annoyance and disappointment, and damages could be awarded for such inconvenience. The measure of the damages to which the plaintiff was entitled was not restricted to compensation for the loss of entertainment and enjoyment which he had been promised and did not get. He was also entitled to be compensated for the vexation and disappointment which he had suffered. On a broad view of the case, the plaintiff was awarded £125 and, accordingly, his appeal was allowed.

The following *dicta* in particular should be noted. *Per* Lord Denning MR:

> "If the contracting party breaks his contract, damages can be given for the disappointment, the distress, the upset and frustration caused by the breach ... A good example was given by Edmund Davies LJ in the course of the argument. He put the case of a man who has taken a ticket for Glyndbourne. It is the only night on which he can get there. He hires a car to take him. The car does not turn up. His damages are not limited to the mere cost of the ticket. He is entitled to general damages for the disappointment he has suffered and the loss of the entertainment which he should have had ... He (Mr Jarvis) is entitled to damages for the loss of those facilities and/or his loss of enjoyment ... The

right measure of damages is to compensate him for the loss of entertainment and enjoyment which he was promised, and which he did not get."

*Per* Edmund Davies LJ:

"The court is entitled, and indeed bound, to contrast the overall quality of the holiday so enticingly promised with that which the defendants in fact provided ... I am of the opinion that ... vexation and being disappointed in a particular thing which you have set your mind upon are relevant considerations which afford the court a guide in arriving at a proper figure".

## (b) *Jackson v Horizon Holidays* [1975] 3 All ER 92

**The facts:** The plaintiff booked a package holiday with the defendants for four weeks for himself, his wife and two children at a hotel in Ceylon at a total cost of £1,200. The plaintiff told the defendants that he wanted everything at the hotel to be of the highest standard and requested a communicating door between his children's room and his and his wife's room. The defendant's brochure described the hotel as having all facilities for an enjoyable holiday, including mini golf, excellent restaurant, swimming pool, beauty and hairdressing salon. It also described the bedrooms as well furnished, each having a private bath, shower and w.c. The plaintiff and his wife were very disappointed with the hotel. There was no connecting door with the children's room and in any event the room was unusable because of mildew and fungus on the walls; there was no private bath, and the shower and w.c. were dirty; the food was distasteful; there was no mini golf; no swimming pool and no beauty or hairdressing salons. After a fortnight at the hotel the plaintiff and his wife moved to another hotel which was somewhat better but building work was still taking place there. The plaintiff brought an action against the defendants for breach of contract claiming damages in respect of the loss of the holiday for himself, his wife and children. The defendants admitted liability. The judge awarded total damages of £1,100 against which the defendants appealed.

**Held:** Where a person had entered into a contract for the benefit of himself and others who were not parties to the contract, he could sue on the contract for damages for the loss suffered not only by himself but also by the others in consequence of a breach of contract even though he was not a trustee for the others. It followed that the plaintiff was entitled to damages not only for the diminution in the value of the holiday and the discomfort, vexation and disappointment which he himself had suffered by reason of the defendant's breach of contract but also for the discomfort, vexation and disappointment suffered by his wife and children. On that basis the damages awarded by the judge were not excessive and the appeal would be dismissed.

The following *dicta* in particular should be noted:

*Per* Lord Denning MR:

> "The judge did not divide up the £1,100 . . . Counsel for Mr Jackson suggested that the judge gave £600 for the diminution in value and £500 for the mental distress. If I were inclined myself to speculate, I think the suggestion of counsel for Mr Jackson may well be right. The judge took the cost of the holiday at £1,200. The family only had about half the value of it. Divide it by two and you get £600. Then add £500 for the mental distress . . . I think that the figure of £1,100 was about right. It would, I think, have been excessive if it had been awarded only for the damage suffered by Mr Jackson himself. But when extended to his wife and children, I do not think it is excessive. People look forward to a holiday. They expect the promises to be fulfilled. When it fails, they are greatly disappointed and upset. It is difficult to assess in terms of money; but it is the task of the judges to do the best they can".

*(c)  Adcock v Blue Sky Holidays* [*Unreported 13 May 1980*]

**The facts:** The plaintiff booked with the defendants a ski-ing holiday in Italy for himself and friends at a cost of £98 per person plus £42 insurance. The complaints about the holiday, as summarised by the Court of Appeal, were—"The hotel was said to be dirty; the hot water supply was inadequate (to say the least), at times non-existent; the cold water supply was not always available; the central heating did not work properly and was only available for part of the holiday; the rooms were in consequence cold; the blankets and the bedding were inadequate; the beds were themselves uncomfortable; and there was no warm and friendly atmosphere in the place; indeed there were no public rooms in which such an atmosphere could develop". Further, the cistern of the lavatory in the bathroom overflowed, and the bedside lighting was weak. The judge awarded the plaintiff damages of £75, the plaintiff's son £20, the plaintiff's friend £75, the friend's son £20 and the friend's daughter £10. The plaintiff appealed.

**Held:** In the original award not enough attention had been paid to the inconvenience and distress caused to the holiday makers. Adopting a broad approach, damages would be increased from £200 to £500 on the basis of the difference between what was expected and what was obtained. A lump sum was awarded since there was no question of the parties disagreeing about the division of the sum. Accordingly, the appeal was allowed.

The following *dicta* in particular should be noted:

*Per* Eveleigh LJ:

> "The trial judge had applied the correct principle in assessing damages, namely that the plaintiff was 'entitled to compensation for the diminution of the value of the holiday, discomfort and inconvenience and diminution of enjoyment which resulted there-from and for mental distress caused by disappoint-ment' . . . The plaintiff and his party had suffered a lower standard of enjoyment of the holiday than they were entitled to expect and the lower standard of material comforts in fact positively induced not enjoyment but irritation, frustration and depression which all derogated from the holiday atmosphere . . . Although the boys in the party had at all times found the funny side of events, the defendant could not in response to a claim for damages say that the boys themselves showed enough fortitude to put up with it, or indeed to be able to joke about it. They

were entitled to a holiday of a certain standard, a standard very much higher than that which they received; and it is for that which compensation, in my opinion, should be paid".

*Per* Cumming-Bruce LJ:

"I cannot find in those cases (ie *Jarvis* and *Jackson*) anything that really indicates a scale of damages which can readily be applied to the facts of the instant case".

### (d) *Chesneau v Interhome Ltd* [1983] CLY 988

**The facts:** The plaintiff rented from the defendants a house in Grasse, France for three weeks commencing on 13 September 1980 at a total cost of £385, for himself, his wife and three year old child. The defendants, so it was held, represented that the house was in a quiet location near the woods, that it had a garden and swimming pool, that it was approximately thirty-five square metres in floor area, that it had an open gallery with a double bed and that it was not part of a complex. Upon arrival the plaintiffs discovered that the house was one of a complex, the swimming pool was shared by the complex, there was no privacy in the house, which had no bed but a double mattress taking up most of the floor space and the plaintiffs, accordingly, decided not to stay. They contacted the defendants who agreed that the contract should be rescinded and the plaintiffs refunded the costs. The plaintiffs spent £11.40 on telephone calls and found alternative accommodation in St. Tropez two days later at a cost of £209 over and above the original contract price. The plaintiff claimed, on behalf of himself and his family, the sums of £209 and £11.40 and damages for disappointment, stress and vexation under s.2(1) of the Misrepresentation Act 1967.

**Held:** An Assistant Recorder sitting at Wandsworth County Court held that the defendant's representations entitled the plaintiffs to damages under s.2(1) of the Misrepresentation Act 1967 but that, in view of the fact that they had recovered the cost of the holiday for which they had contracted with the defendants, they were entitled to damages for inconvenience only for the two days during which they were making alternative arrangements. He assessed these damages at £30 and also awarded £50 for the plaintiff's loss of opportunity to obtain a villa that suited their requirements.

The plaintiffs appealed. The Court of Appeal awarded them £200 compensation for inconvenience and mental distress, the return of the £209 (the difference between the cost of the original villa and that which they subsequently arranged) and £11.40 for telephone calls.

The following *dicta*, in particular, should be noted:

*Per* Eveleigh LJ:

> "On both sides, but for different reasons or with a different object in view, counsel have argued that damages awarded are, strictly speaking, damages in tort. For myself, I think that that is probably correct. Indeed, they should be assessed in a case like the present on the same principles as damages are assessed in tort ... One has to see the position they were in back in England before they started off and then compare it with the position which they found themselves in as a result of this misrepresentation. They found themselves in the position where they were about to face a disastrous holiday, disastrous from their point of view from that which they had arranged and were entitled to expect ... So the plaintiff was in a position where he would have to say: 'I will go home, regard the holiday as lost and sue for that'. Alternatively, he could have stayed at Grasse, decided to put up with it and sue for whatever damages he might then get on a chance basis. Or, mindful of the fact that he might have been criticised if he did not do so, he could seek to mitigate the overall position by finding somewhere else that would give him the kind of holiday to which he was, as I see it, entitled ... In my judgment, had they not taken the house in Grasse, they would have been entitled to damages in excess of £209 ... So one really is concerned with what they would have received on the general heading, damages such as the courts now award in this kind

of case. It seems to me that, for the distress of the initial period, taking into account also the fact that the holiday they in fact enjoyed was less than they would have had, a figure of £200 would be appropriate to reflect the loss sustained for that. As I say, I think that a greater figure for the general loss of the amenity of the holiday would be attracted for the ensuing three weeks, or just under three weeks, and a figure greater than £209. But, as they have chosen properly to mitigate their loss by the expenditure of that sum of money, I think they are entitled to that amount".

*Per* O'Connor LJ:

"When one is considering the head of damage of inconvenience, discomfort, annoyance and disturbance to what had been planned, in my judgment all those factors can be taken into consideration. For that head the learned judge awarded £30. In my judgment it was a wholly erroneous assessment of damages. It was so far too little that this court is entitled to, and indeed is bound to, interfere and I agree that under that head the award should be increased to £200".

## (e) *Kemp v Intasun Holidays Limited* [1987] 2 FTLR 234

**The facts:** On 2 February 1984 Mrs Kemp and her daughter called at a branch of Thomas Cook in Worcester to choose a summer holiday. There was a conversation between Mrs Kemp and one of the assistants at Thomas Cook. In it Mrs Kemp referred to the fact that her husband suffered from asthma. The finding of the judge in the Worcester County Court about the conversation was:

"Mrs Kemp explained to Thomas Cook that she was sorry her husband could not be there but he was ill. I am satisfied that she said he was suffering an asthmatic and a bronchial attack, as he sometimes did."

The judge also found that Mrs Kemp said that, because of her husband's health, some special insurance was required. But he did not base his conclusions on anything concerning the desirable insurance cover. Following the discussions between Mrs Kemp and Thomas Cook, the plaintiff decided to choose a fourteen day holiday in August 1984 at a hotel called "America I" at Callas de Mallorca at a cost of about £828. The relevant booking form for that holiday, which was included in the defendants' brochure, was taken away by Mrs Kemp as well as a proposal form for an insurance policy. On 6 February Mrs Kemp came back with her daughter and paid the insurance premium of some £29. By 29 February the Kemps had completed and returned the booking form and it was accepted by Intasun.

On 4 August 1984 the family departed on their holiday and for the first thirty hours it proved to be disastrous. They arrived at Palma at about 6.30 on a Sunday morning and were taken in a minibus with other travellers to their hotel, the America I, but found it was full up. The judge awarded £400 for the general inconvenience and disappointment resulting from this.

The plaintiffs were given alternative accommodation in a hotel called Las Chihuahuas which was of substantially lower quality than America I. The judge described the new accommodation as

> "a room in the staff or service quarter of the hotel. This was not a part of the normal hotel accommodation. There was a broken window, filled in with lattice work of bricks, and there was glass on the floor. Mrs Kemp said that the room was filthy, very dirty, very dusty. The toilet had no door, the shower did not work and there was no bath. There were two single beds and a portable bed which they could not make work."

The dirty and dusty condition of this accommodation had a particular effect on Mr Kemp's asthmatic condition. Because of this Mr Kemp, who, as shown by a medical report, suffered from chronic bronchitis and emphysema, had an attack of asthma which caused him and the other members of the family considerable distress. The judge found that Mr Kemp suffered from this throughout the thirty hours that the plaintiffs spent in the alternative accommodation. The judge awarded £800 compensation for this, and the defendants appealed.

**Held:** A tour operator is liable for consequences which flow naturally from his breach of contract, and for any additional consequences which should reasonably have been within his contemplation when entering into the contract. Information which is not part of the booking arrangements but is given to the travel agent in casual conversation is not sufficiently with the tour operator's knowledge to give rise to contractual consequences. Accordingly, the Court of Appeal allowed the defendants' appeal against the award of £800 damages in favour of the plaintiff.

The following *dicta* in particular should be noted:

*Per* Kerr LJ:

> "He (a tour operator) must also accept liability for any other consequences which should have been in the reasonable contemplation of the parties if these flowed naturally from his breach and caused additional foreseeable loss or damage ... For instance, if the consequence of not providing the contractual accommodation is not merely the loss of its enjoyment and so forth, but also the fact that the plaintiffs had to sleep out on the beach, with the result that their health suffered in a natural and ordinarily foreseeable way because they caught colds or even pneumonia, then that would be a natural and foreseeable additional consequence which would equally flow from the tour operator's breach."

*Per* Parker LJ:

> "I cannot accept that a casual conversation in February that the plaintiff was an asthmatic sufferer and because of his health required extra insurance is sufficient to bring it within the contemplation of the parties that, in the event of a breach in August consisting of putting the plaintiff in a disgusting room, an asthmatic attack was not unlikely to occur. I use the words 'not unlikely'

because they were among the words used by their Lordships in *Koufos* v *Czarnikow*."

## (f) Conclusions

The above five cases deal with damages for breach of contract and misrepresentation, and various important points are to be elicited from them:

(i) It is now established law that a holiday maker who proves breach of contract is entitled to recover general damages for diminution in the value of the contract and also for loss of enjoyment, disappointment, mental anguish and inconvenience. This unites the categories of physical and mental distress mentioned previously. This is, of course, in addition to special damages (ie out of pocket expenses which he has incurred as a result of the breach).

(ii) A holiday maker who enters into a contract with a tour operator can sue on it for damages for loss suffered not only by him but also by any others who went on the holiday under cover of the contract.

(iii) None of the cases, despite the extent of the plaintiff's claims, decided that there was total failure of performance of the contract by the defendants.

(iv) None of the cases provide any definite indication of the sort of sum which should be awarded for disappointment etc. There is, though, something of a discrepancy between the *Jarvis* and *Horizon* cases. In the latter, although the decision was not made on this basis, Lord Denning suggested that the £1,100 be split as to £600 for diminution of value of contract and £500 for loss of enjoyment. In *Jarvis* there seems to have been agreement that the diminution of value of the contract was half (approximately £30) so that the damages for disappointment etc were approximately three times that. Perhaps what the cases establish is that, when assessing disappointment, the facilities affected must be carefully considered to establish whether they go to the heart of the holiday. For instance, on a ski-ing holiday a lack of skis is a most material source of disappointment whereas on a holiday in a continuously hot and sunny climate the absence of electric heaters at the hotel is not a major cause for concern.

The courts have given some very broad outlines of the factors to be taken into consideration when evaluating damages. The factors set out below are ones which the writers consider should be taken into account on all occasions, although one or two of these have been specifically rejected by county courts:

(i) What proportion of the holiday was affected by the events complained of? Damages will encompass not only the amount for which an allowance in reduction of the holiday price should be made but also compensation for disappointment etc. To evaluate the allowance referred to above, it is necessary to break down, at least approximately, the overall cost of the holiday so that the cost of the item(s) complained of may be determined and a satisfactory reduction evaluated depending upon the gravity of the breach. This may only provide a nominal sum but it may be increased by damages for disappointment etc.

(ii) What amount of enjoyment did the holiday maker obtain from the holiday? It can be seen that in the *Jarvis* case Mr Jarvis recovered almost twice the cost of his holiday and in the *Adcock* case Mr Adcock and party recovered a sum slightly in excess of the holiday price whereas Mr Jackson in his claim did not recover the holiday price. The reason must be that Mr Jackson, despite the breaches, still obtained enjoyment from his holiday whereas Mr Jarvis did not and, despite the attitude of the minors, neither did Mr Adcock and his party. Aside from flagrant breaches it is unlikely that a holiday maker can allege that no enjoyment whatsoever was obtained from the holiday. An unsatisfactory bedroom in a hotel, for example, does not prevent a holiday maker from enjoying other facilities offered by the hotel or from enjoying normal outdoor activities. As has already been stated, what must be decided is whether or not the matters complained of go to the heart of the holiday.

(iii) Whether or not the holiday maker has made any effort to mitigate his loss? In the event that a bedroom in a hotel is unsatisfactory a holiday maker should not relocate himself in a more expensive hotel of a higher standard and be allowed to reclaim this sum. He should first complain to the tour operator's representative who, in many cases, can arrange satisfactory relocation within the actual hotel or transfer to another hotel at no extra cost. Package holidays have been in existence for some time and tour operators do make it clear that their representatives are available to deal with complaints.

(iv) What was the price of the holiday? It is suggested that the standards to be expected from cut price holidays should not be as high as in full price holidays. The old maxim "you get what you pay for" should be applied. This does seem an equitable consideration to take into account when assessing damages, although the Westminster County Court rejected it in the *Levine* v *Metropolitan Travel* case which is discussed later (see Appendix D).

(v) What was the exact wording in the brochure? If, for example, a hotel is described as "simple and unpretentious" it should not be interpreted as meaning anything other than that the facilities will be fairly basic. It is appreciated that holiday makers expect to enjoy their holiday but their expectations should be realistic. Although tour operators are "peddling dreams", this is merely an unavoidable consequence of the product being sold. It should not be a reason for imposing what are in reality punitive damages.

(vi) Did the holiday maker make any effort to enjoy his holiday? The fact that a holiday maker puts on a brave front in the face of adversity should not constitute a defence to a claim for damages. But courts should be aware that there are some holiday makers who seek to find and magnify faults, perhaps with a view to trying to fund next year's holiday. This should be borne in mind under the heading of mitigation.

(vii) Were there children on the holiday? The county court judge in the *Adcock* case accepted that matters which affect an adult's enjoyment of a holiday will not necessarily affect a child's. If, for example, in breach of contract there is no discotheque this is not something which will cause a child disquiet. Unfortunately, the Court of Appeal in *Adcock* did not go into this point and did not even split up their increased award of £500. It is suggested that this consideration might be taken even further so that if one member of a holiday party enjoyed a holiday despite breaches this should be taken into account when assessing damages.

## 5. County court cases

A major difficulty in advising about damages is that the vast majority of cases are county court cases which are in the main unreported. Different county courts have adopted different criteria. These are, to a certain extent, inconsistent with each other and with the above-mentioned cases, although in law the principles enunciated by the Court of Appeal take precedence over contrary county court decisions.

It is, though, instructive and necessary to consider county court decisions because, as the county court is the most common forum for deciding a dissatisfied holiday maker's claim, they provide practical illustrations of likely awards at first instance. Recent years have seen an increase in the number of county court cases to such an extent that it is impractical, in this book, to comment on each one. Reports of various cases not mentioned elsewhere in the text are contained in Appendix D.

Until the Court of Appeal lays down more definite criteria for evaluating damages, tour operators will have to live with the tendency of county court judges to view matters globally, rather than breaking down the various aspects of the holiday. It is suggested that the factors outlined previously are those which should properly be taken into account and that damages in excess of the holiday price should not be awarded unless the breaches were tantamount to a fundamental breach. Inevitably, only general criteria can be laid down. There should be no effort to provide a scale of sums for certain events. Each case will have circumstances peculiar to it and it is ultimately on these that damages should be assessed, preferably in the light of clearly defined criteria.

# Chapter 6

# Claims

A holiday maker who is dissatisfied with any aspect of his holiday and who fails to obtain satisfaction from the tour operator concerned, must decide whether to pursue matters further and, if so, how. The purpose of this chapter is to consider the two basic alternatives available to him—ABTA arbitration or court proceedings—and to give guidance regarding both making and defending claims.

## 1. Preliminary considerations

In essence a holiday maker will have to consider the same basic criteria in deciding whether to pursue a claim as a travel company will in deciding whether to resist it. These are—

(a) the likelihood of success;

(b) the costs involved in pursuing/defending the claim if successful;

(c) the costs involved in pursuing/defending the claim if unsuccessful.

Apart from forums in which a successful party will not be awarded costs, such as county court arbitration, the normal rule is that a successful party (be he plaintiff or defendant) will recover what are called party and party costs. As a rule of thumb these will be in the region of one-half to two-thirds of his total legal costs. This leaves a successful party with a costs liability to his own legal advisers which in the case of a claimant can all too easily absorb the bulk of the damages which he is awarded. An unsuccessful party will be responsible for not only his own legal costs but the party and party costs of the other side.

In pursuing a claim a holiday maker has certain built-in advantages. In general, the sympathies of the court are likely to be with a dissatisfied holiday maker. Any publicity resulting from a claim is likely to be adverse to the travel company. The costs which travel companies are likely to face in defending most claims will be substantially higher than those faced by holiday makers since the travel companies will, in all probability, require as witnesses persons normally resident abroad. In practice, therefore, the odds are very much in the holiday maker's favour. After all, to allege disappointment and loss of enjoyment he merely has to give evidence himself which can be very difficult for the travel company to shake no matter how minor the default in respect of which proceedings have been issued.

One of the basic points which this book seeks to emphasize is that a holiday maker's contract for a package holiday is with the tour operator who arranges it and, *prima facie,* any liability for defects in the holiday will attach to the tour operator. Thus, a dissatisfied holiday maker should address his complaints to the tour operator, either directly or through the travel agent with whom the booking was made. In cases of obvious default there is merit in using the travel agent's services since he may be able to exert pressure upon the operator to offer satisfactory compensation but the holiday maker should not expect compensation from the agent in respect of matters which are clearly the operator's responsibility. There are occasionally situations in which a holiday maker will consider that the agent misrepresented the facilities available on a particular holiday and/or failed to give satisfactory advice in which case the agent may be solely or primarily responsible.

Consider the following example:

> Mr Jones books a fortnight's holiday for himself and his wife at the Hotel Luxury, Greece at a cost of £800. The operator with whom the contract is made and whose brochure details the facilities available is

144

Utopian Tours Limited, an ABTA member, and the agent through whom the booking is made is Good Advice Limited, also an ABTA member. The Hotel Luxury, a well known hotel in a well known resort, is described in the operator's brochure as having an Olympic size swimming pool. This is of particular importance to Mr Jones since both he and his wife are keen swimmers but do not like swimming in the sea—something which he emphasized to Good Advice who, on the basis of Utopian Tours Limited's brochure, recommended the Hotel Luxury. Upon arrival Mr and Mrs Jones discover that the pool is closed.

In this situation, leaving aside the question of actual liability, which will depend upon the circumstances and date of closure of the pool and whether or not Utopian Tours passed on any information available to it about closure of the pool to Good Advice, Mr and Mrs Jones could have claims against—

(a) Utopian Tours for breach of contract and misrepresentation; and

(b) Good Advice for misrepresentation, breach of duty of care and negligent advice.

## 2. Making a claim

When Mr and Mrs Jones make their claim, they should stress to Utopian Tours and Good Advice that both are being held liable. If each claims that the other is responsible (say, with the operator alleging that errata letters about closure of the pool had been sent to the agent who had failed to warn the Joneses and the agent denying ever having received them), how do the Joneses proceed?

Although both Utopian Tours and Good Advice are ABTA members, it will not be possible for the Joneses to avail themselves of ABTA's arbitration scheme. This is because it does not extend to commercial disputes between its members, and this includes members alleging each other to be responsible. Proceedings in the courts will, thus, be necessary.

## (a) Limitation of claim

Generally, most holiday claims in respect of which court proceedings are issued are brought in the county court. The maximum that can be claimed in county court proceedings is £5,000 which is enough to cover most holiday claims. The normal county court particulars of claim, after recital of material facts and causes of action, claims damages *limited* to £X (which must not exceed £5,000). Care must, however, be taken in the limitation of a claim, as can be seen from *Harvey* v *Tracks Travel* (1984) CLY 1006, the facts of which were as follows:

The plaintiff booked a place on a trans-African expedition tour organised by the defendants at a cost of £870 plus a further £100 towards a food kitty. The trip was scheduled to take fourteen weeks from London to Dar-es-Salaam. The defendants informed the plaintiff that they could arrange a return flight from there for £210, or from Nairobi for approximately £180. The expedition left London on 19 April 1981 and ten days later the truck broke down in Tunis. It took three weeks to repair. On arrival in Nigeria the expedition was unable to purchase food as the defendants had failed to warn the truck driver of extremely high prices with the result that he was not carrying sufficient money. On 8 July 1981 the truck crashed in Zaire and, despite efforts by the tour leader to contact the defendants and request a back-up truck, nothing was done. Miss Harvey and the others were stranded in the bush for some twenty-seven days at the end of which they were running short of food and water, the food kitty had been exhausted and the tour leader was borrowing money from the group members to purchase food. By 4 August 1981 no news had been received and the group decided to hitch-hike to Nairobi. The plaintiff had hitched some 150 kilometres when, on 6 August 1981, she met a relief truck sent by the defendants. She was told by the driver that there was no information as to what should happen to the passengers, that the broken down truck would be towed away, that it should be available in twelve days or so and that she could rejoin it later. She booked a ticket to the nearest town but was unable to return to England as she could not afford the fare of £550 and, accordingly, flew at a cost of some £70 to meet the truck and journey with it to Nairobi. The plaintiff waited till 13 September 1981 by which time the truck had still not arrived. Distressed and frightened she flew to Nairobi and found that tickets to England could not be purchased for less than £487. She obtained this sum from home, returning to the UK on 19 September 1981 whereas she had intended to return at the end of July. She missed eight weeks off work, losing £752 in wages. The defendants' attitude throughout was unhelpful and on return the plaintiff was advised by them "to chalk it up to experience". The plaintiff claimed damages limited to £3,000 and, after obtaining judgment in default, Mr Registrar Lichfield (Westminster County Court) held:

(a) The plaintiff should receive special damages of £1,995, including a full refund of the holiday price as there had been a total failure of consideration; and

(b) General damages should be £1,005.

(c) The Registrar stated that £1,005 represented ordinary general damages for a young girl stranded in Africa for five months, instead of on a fourteen week escorted tour, and that a claim for aggravated damages could have received sympathetic consideration had the claim not been limited.

Returning to our example, the Joneses' claim should be for damages limited to £2,000-3,000, depending upon whether or not any special damages are claimed—say, for the expense of travelling daily to another Olympic sized swimming pool in the area and the cost of using it. The rationale behind this limitation is that the Joneses would claim—

(a) A refund of a portion of the £800 holiday price for the lack of a material facility;

(b) Damages for loss of enjoyment and disappointment. Although technically, these are not to be gauged in relation to the contract price, this does seem to be what happens in practice and it is only in exceptional cases that the compensation per person under this head will exceed the contract price per person; and

(c) Any special damages.

### (b) Small claims court

If the Joneses were prepared to limit their claim to £500 or less, it would come within the county court's automatic reference to arbitration ("the small claims court"). There are several advantages for a holiday maker if he feels able to confine his claim to £500 or less:

(a) The proceedings are much more informal than full county court/High Court proceedings both leading up to and during the hearing of the action. It is, therefore, much easier for a holiday maker to conduct his own claim without seeking legal assistance and incurring the resultant legal costs. In fact, at the pre-trial review the registrar, when giving directions to enable the matter to proceed to hearing, will frequently give an inexperienced party procedural advice.

(b) No orders as to costs are normally made save that a successful plaintiff will recover the costs stated on the Summons (Order 19 rule 6, County Court Rules 1981). This assists a holiday maker conducting his claim in person since the tour operator, even if confident of successfully defending a claim, runs the risk of incurring legal costs in excess of the sum which the plaintiff is claiming. An unfortunate result of this, from a travel company's point of view, is that it renders inapplicable the normal court rules whereby costs are awarded in favour of a defendant, if at an early stage of the proceedings he makes a payment into court which exceeds what is subsequently awarded by the judge (who is not told about the payment until after he has reached his decision). It is, therefore, most difficult for travel companies to protect their costs position and thereby encourage the holiday maker to negotiate a reasonable settlement.

(c) If the registrar certifies that there are costs which have been incurred through the unreasonable conduct of a party in relation to the proceedings that party will be ordered to be responsible to the other parties to the proceedings for those costs (Order 19 rule 6(c)). Such a decision is totally at the registrar's discretion which is only exercised in exceptional circumstances.

(d) The normal rules of evidence are relaxed, to enable a more informal hearing. Although, in theory, this could make it easier for the tour operator to rely upon written statements adduced as evidence under the Civil Evidence Act (this is covered in greater detail at a later stage) rather than produce witnesses, in practice the registrar will be more inclined to accept the evidence given by the holiday maker.

(e) The hearing date for arbitration is likely to be much earlier than that for a full county court trial.

Theoretically, it is possible for any party to proceedings involving claims for £500 or less to make an application to the county court registrar under Order 19 rule 2 of the County Court Rules 1981 for an order rescinding the reference to arbitration on the grounds that:

"(a) a difficult question of law or a question of fact of exceptional complexity is involved; or

(b) a charge of fraud is in issue; or

(c) the parties are agreed that the dispute should be tried in court; or

(d) it would be unreasonable for the claim to proceed to arbitration having regard to its subject matter, the circumstances of the parties or the interests of any other person likely to be affected by the award."

Unless application is made on the grounds of (b) or (c)

above it is unlikely to be successful for two reasons. Firstly, most registrars will by now have heard at least several holiday cases and will not regard it as unusual for them to hear it. Secondly, it is always difficult to advise a registrar who is likely to conduct the arbitration that it is too complicated for him. If the application is unsuccessful it does not bode well for the applicant for the actual arbitration.

### (c) Issue of proceedings

Mr and Mrs Jones determine that they will issue proceedings in the county court. It was, of course, Mr Jones who made the booking and in accordance with *Jackson* v *Horizon Holidays* (see pages 130-131) he is entitled to sue on it on behalf of both himself and his wife. If proceedings are issued against Utopian Tours and Good Advice as first and second defendants, and both intend to defend the proceedings, consideration should be given by each of them to the preparation and service of contribution notices. These are formal pleadings whereby one defendant claims an indemnity from another on the basis that any default was the other's default. If only one of the travel companies has been named as a defendant and if it considers the other to blame, it should issue a third party notice whereby the other is joined as a party to the proceedings. The third party will, though, only be a party to the proceedings to the extent that, if the defendant is held liable, the court will determine whether or not to order that the third party should recompense the defendant. Order 12 of the County Court Rules 1981 and Order 16 of the Rules of the Supreme Court set out the appropriate provisions regarding the issue, service etc., of contribution/third party notices depending upon whether proceedings are in the county or High Court.

Proceedings in respect of complaints about holidays will normally be issued in the county court rather than the High Court since the sums involved do not usually warrant High Court proceedings. However, if a claim is for more than £600, High Court proceedings are possible but the plaintiff, if successful, runs the risk of being penalised by the High Court on costs for not issuing proceedings in the county court. It should also be noted that the county court rules are based upon the rules of the Supreme Court (ie the High Court).

A holiday maker faced with a defendant and a third party should consider seeking the leave of the court to convert the third party into a second defendant in the proceedings. The reason for this is that otherwise, although the holiday maker's claim against the defendant and the defendant's claim against the third party will normally be heard contemporaneously, questions of liability will be decided separately. If, therefore, the court finds in favour of the defendant in respect of the holiday maker's claim against him, the holiday maker will not be in a position to seek any order against the third party in these proceedings. That would only be possible had the holiday maker taken steps prior to the trial to convert the third party into a second defendant.

### (d) Preparation for trial

To prepare for trial Utopian Tours and Good Advice will have to consider the following:

- (i) The witnesses whom they intend to call;
- (ii) The documents in their possession which are not privileged from disclosure and should therefore be placed before the court;
- (iii) Whether or not a payment into court should be made;
- (iv) Whether or not it will be effective to dispense with any oral evidence and rely instead upon statements adduced under the Civil Evidence Act;
- (v) Any plans or photographs which they may wish to place before the court (for instance, if the pool was cracked and generally in disrepair, photographs to evidence this and the extent of disruption); and
- (vi) The bundle of documents to be placed before the court.

It is beyond the purpose and scope of this book to consider

in any detail the technical rules regarding discovery and payments into court but it is worthwhile to make some brief comments. However, the reader should bear in mind that what follows is not an exhaustive set of guidelines but merely an outline of certain pertinent points.

### (e) Payments into court

As has already been stated, most hearings take place in county courts and are unreported. As a consequence there is little consistency in the level of damages awarded. This can make it difficult for the operator to gauge accurately an effective payment into court and for the holiday maker to decide whether to accept a payment into court.

One of the main purposes of a payment into court is to protect a defendant's position on costs. It is based on the defendant's assessment of the maximum amount the plaintiff will be able to recover at trial. It is senseless to seek to pennypinch, but it is possible to make an initial payment into court which is less than that which the defendant considers to be truly accurate and thereafter top it up. But, if this tactic is adopted, it must be remembered that Order 22 Rule 3(1) of the Rules of the Supreme Court states that a payment into court made less than twenty-one days before the trial will not protect the defendant in respect of the costs of the trial. And, the defendant will only obtain costs protection from the top-up payment from the date of its payment into court.

In calculating a payment into court, account should be taken of the interest which would be awarded on any damages which are awarded.

At trial, it is not permitted to inform the trial judge of any payment into court until after judgment has been given. However, in summing up the defendant's advocate will normally reserve a passage to deal with *quantum* in the event that the trial judge finds against the defendant. In addressing the issue of *quantum* the advocate is well advised to put forward figures less than the sum actually paid into court. Trial judges who feel sympathy for a plaintiff may consider that the figures put forward in summing up by the defendant's advocate represent the payment into court and may seek to top these up to protect the plaintiff on costs. Allowing for a "margin of error" may result in whatever damages order is made being covered by the payment into court.

## (f) Discovery

The basic rule is that all relevant documents held by a party must be disclosed except for ones which are privileged from production. Privileged documents include "without prejudice" correspondence, internal memoranda for the dominant purpose of litigation, correspondence between the parties and their legal advisers, instructions to counsel, witness statements etc. It is possible for part of a document to be privileged from disclosure and part not.

Travel companies should bear in mind that, generally speaking, the bulk of their correspondence and internal memoranda written before the issue of proceedings will not be privileged from disclosure. Much of this documentation will emanate from public relations departments and on the spot representatives. Most tour operators have a system whereby their on the spot representatives prepare weekly reports and these will normally be subject to production, as a result of the decision in *Waugh v British Railways Board* [1979] 2 All ER 1169. This case held, *inter alia*, that an internal memorandum was only to be accorded privilege if the dominant purpose for which it was prepared was for submission to a legal adviser for advice and use in litigation. It will only be in exceptional cases that it will be possible to allege that a representative's weekly report was prepared for the dominant purpose of use in litigation.

It is the originals of documents which must be produced and care should be taken to avoid endorsing on documents comments which could prove to be damaging to a party's case.

The authors of letters responding to complaints by dissatisfied holiday makers and of internal company reports should always keep in mind the following:

153

(i) Their words could, in the long run, be read out in open court. Reports, letters etc should, accordingly, be concise, accurate, simple statements of facts. Derogatory or facetious comments should be avoided. Such comments often prejudice the travel company's case and they are likely to be seized upon by reporters at a court hearing with resultant bad publicity.

(ii) The mere endorsement of "without prejudice" at the top of a letter does not automatically preclude disclosure. Only letters which constitute genuine attempts at settlement will be privileged. Statements of purported fact contained in without prejudice letters will not be privileged.

(iii) A series of letters should be consistent in their content. It is always damaging if one letter contradicts what was said in another. Sometimes this cannot be avoided but then it should be done expressly and a virtue made of necessity.

## (g) Evidence

It is the question of oral evidence that can cause travel companies the most difficulty and expense. Usually for a claim to be successfully defended it will be desirable for the operator's on the spot representative and the manager of the hotel featured in the package holiday (presuming that complaint is made about the hotel) to be flown to the UK for the hearing. As well as the expense of having such people attend the hearing, there is the difficulty of taking detailed and satisfactory statements. These can really only be properly obtained by a personal interview (extra expense). Reliance upon statements prepared at a distance, say by the manager of a Greek hotel, can be a risky foundation upon which to defend a claim. Further, the tour operator depends upon the voluntary co-operation of those abroad since the English courts do not have the power to subpoena a witness beyond their jurisdiction to attend the hearing (section

36 of the Supreme Court Act 1981). The holiday maker should also bear in mind these potential costs since, if his claim is unsuccessful, he may be ordered to pay them.

Mention has been made of the use of written statements as evidence under the Civil Evidence Act 1968. In the Joneses' case it might be helpful for Utopian Tours to produce as evidence a statement from the manager of the Hotel Luxury explaining the reasons for the closure of the hotel swimming pool. The relevant provisions of the Civil Evidence Act can be summarised as follows:

(i) Section 2(1) provides that the oral or written out-of-court statements of any person, whether called as a witness in the proceedings or not, shall, "subject to this section and to rules of court", be admissible in chief as evidence of any fact stated therein of which direct oral evidence by him would be admissible.

(ii) The party wishing to adduce a statement as evidence under s.2 must serve a notice upon the other party detailing the matters contained in the statement and indicating the reasons for not calling the maker of the statement. Section 8 of the Act outlines acceptable reasons for not calling the maker of the statement as a witness (he is dead; or overseas; he is physically and/or mentally unfit to attend the hearing; despite reasonable efforts it has not been possible to locate or identify him; or he cannot reasonably be expected to have any recollection of matters pertinent to the accuracy of the statement). Order 38 of the Rules of the Supreme Court incorporates these reasons.

The party upon whom the notice is served may object to the statement if he contends that its maker should attend in person to give evidence. If this is done the court, before trial, can decide the question of admissibility on the application of either party.

(iii) Section 6 covers the matters to which the court

must have regard when considering the weight to be attached to the statement. Was it made contemporaneously with the events to which it refers? Had the maker of the statement any incentive to conceal or misrepresent any facts? This is a consideration which could adversely affect the credibility attached to a statement by a manager of a foreign hotel.

(iv) Section 7 allows evidence to be called which would destroy or harm the credibility of the maker of the statement (ie evidence of bias, previous inconsistent statements etc).

The Act deals with a wide variety of statements and documents which may be admissible in evidence. It is beyond the scope of this book to consider them in detail but both plaintiffs and defendants should bear in mind the possibility of adducing evidence under the Act. However, when advising a travel company, the writers would caution that a statement from a foreign hotelier, when contradicted by oral evidence from the plaintiff holiday maker, is unlikely to be given much weight by the court.

In certain circumstances it may be helpful for a tour operator to call as a witness a member of another country's tourist board who is working in the UK to give evidence about idiosyncratic legislation. In the Joneses' case, for example, the hotel swimming pool may have been closed as a result of unexpected and temporary Government legislation. However, senior members of the tourist board in question are likely to be covered by the Diplomatic Privileges Act 1964. It incorporates various articles of the 1961 Vienna Convention Article 31 of which states that a "Diplomatic Agent" is competent to give evidence but *is not obliged to do so*. Article 1E defines a "Diplomatic Agent" as the head of a commission or member of the diplomatic staff of the mission. The Foreign Office publishes a list of those commonly regarded as being diplomatic agents. In the absence of co-operation by the particular tourist board official, the tour operator will be unable to compel him to give evidence.

In the Joneses' case, Good Advice may wish to allege that

Mr Jones did not stress to their booking clerk the importance of the swimming pool. This would not establish a successful defence in respect of the actual lack of the facility but would be relevant to *quantum* in that, if Good Advice succeed on this point, the materiality of the swimming pool to the enjoyment of the holiday would be greatly reduced. What Good Advice will have to counter in court is evidence from Mr Jones that he did inform Good Advice's booking clerk (John) of the importance of the swimming pool. If John can only say that he cannot remember such a comment being made, it is almost certain that the court will accept Mr Jones's evidence. If, however, Good Advice have forms which were completed contemporaneously with the booking summarising John's conversation with Mr Jones and these contain no reference to the swimming pool, this would go some way towards supporting John's evidence.

## 3. ABTA arbitration scheme

It has been stated earlier in this chapter that Mr Jones cannot use ABTA's arbitration scheme because there is a commercial dispute between Utopian Holidays and Good Advice. Suppose, though, that Mr Jones is only claiming against Utopian Holidays and that there is no dispute between it and Good Advice. It will now be possible for ABTA's arbitration scheme to be used. How does it work?

### (a) Principles of the scheme

The ABTA Conciliation and Arbitration Scheme came into force on 1 April 1975. There are four basic principles of the Scheme:

> (i) Tour Operators are themselves supposed to take all possible steps to resolve complaints.
>
> (ii) In the event of failure to resolve a complaint, the holiday maker can contact ABTA to seek assistance. This will not result in an automatic reference to arbitration but will involve an ABTA Conciliation Officer asking the tour

operator to reconsider its position. In practice, this seldom takes matters any further.

(iii) ABTA's conciliation officer will normally only become involved after correspondence—euphemistically referred to by ABTA as "normal written negotiations"—has passed between the operator and the holiday maker.

(iv) If the involvement of ABTA's conciliation officer does not resolve matters, the holiday maker is invited to make a formal application to the Chartered Institute of Arbitrators for the matter to be settled by an independent arbitrator. If he does apply, the operator must consent to arbitration, and agree to be bound by the decision.

Thus, to put in hand arbitration, Mr Jones will, after corresponding with Utopian Tours, need to enlist ABTA's assistance. If this fails, he can then apply for arbitration and Utopian Tours will be bound to consent.

## (b) Operation of the scheme

Chapter 1 has mentioned briefly disputes the nature or amount of which preclude arbitration. In general terms, ABTA states that the arbitration scheme "is not designed to accommodate disputes in which issues are unusually complicated, the proper resolution of which would be likely to require a formal hearing and oral evidence".

Several other points about the adoption of ABTA's arbitration scheme should be noted. First, application for arbitration must be made within nine months from the end of the holiday. Secondly, the holiday maker must agree to be bound by the arbitrator's decision. The Arbitration Act 1950 does provide for an appeal against an arbitrator's decision or the subsequent issue of proceedings in respect of matters arbitrated but it is beyond the scope of this book to examine these provisions. Thirdly the arbitrator will decide disputes solely upon the documentation placed before him—there will not be an oral hearing.

The basic arbitration stages are as follows:

(i) Mr Jones completes his application form and despatches it to the Institute of Chartered Arbitrators, together with an application fee. The Institute will despatch an application form to Utopian Tours to be completed and returned by them together with their application fee.

(ii) The Institute, after receipt of Utopian Tours' application form will despatch a claim form to Mr Jones. He must complete and return it within twenty-eight days of its receipt together with any supporting documents.

(iii) The claim form will be sent by the Institute to Utopian Tours who must prepare and submit their defence and any supporting documents within twenty-eight days. These will be sent by the Institute to Mr Jones who has fourteen days to submit his comments about the defence.

(iv) An arbitrator will then be appointed by the Institute. If he considers any of the documentation unclear, he can seek further details. Otherwise he prepares his award and submits it to the Institute for despatch to the parties within twenty-one days.

The award which the arbitrator forwards to the Institute comprises two documents. The first is "the Award" which sets out the brief details of the dispute (to enable identification of the matter) and the compensation, if any, which the operator must pay the holiday maker. It also sets out any costs award. The only costs which can be awarded are the application fees—the cost of preparing documents etc must be borne by the parties. If an award in excess of £200 is made, the arbitrator will usually order that the successful party's application fees be paid by the other party. The second document comprises the arbitrator's notes which give an informal indication of the rationale of his award and the matters taken into consideration.

Arbitration under the ABTA scheme is based on an

examination of written statements and not upon an oral hearing of the claim. If Mr Jones considers that he cannot present his case satisfactorily in writing, he should not embark on arbitration unless he has a friend who is equipped to help him.

## 4. The outcome

But what of Mr Jones's claim? Irrespective of the forum in which it is adjudicated, should it succeed? The information set out so far is not sufficient to enable a decision to be made but various scenarios are considered below:

(a) Suppose that the closure of the pool was due to an emergency Greek Government decision taken only a few hours before Mr and Mrs Jones's arrival, and implemented contemporaneously with their arrival at the hotel. Further suppose that there had been no indications in Greece that such legislation was being considered so that neither Utopian Tours nor Good Advice could have had any advance knowledge of closure. In these circumstances, it is submitted that neither Utopian Tours nor Good Advice will incur any liability to the Joneses. What conversations there were about the importance of the pool to Mr and Mrs Jones are irrelevant since their primary importance is to the assessment of damages in the event of liability existing, which it would not where the closure of the pool was an unexpected occurrence over which the travel companies had no control and of which they had no advance knowledge.

(b) Suppose, though, that the Greek Government's decision had been taken a week before the Joneses' arrival and that Utopian Tours' local representative was aware of the situation. Utopian Tours knew, or should have known, of the closure of the pool because their representatives should have reported it to head office straightaway. In any event, it is submitted that for the purposes of civil proceedings, Utopian Tours will be held to have the knowledge of their on-the-spot representatives, although, in view of the *Wings* v *Ellis* decision (see page 88 *et seq.*), this would not be so in the event of a prosecution under the Trade Descriptions Act 1968. This being so, liability will attach to Utopian Tours. They had advance knowledge of the situation and did not inform the Joneses or Good Advice of the closing of the pool so that an alteration of arrangements could be considered.

(c) Utopian Tours may admit liability but dispute *quantum,* and argue that, as the hotel has a beach with fine sand and safe water for swimming, the lack of a swimming pool was only a minor irritant. However, the Joneses allege— and it is accepted by the court—that they told Good Advice how important it was that they be able to make use of the swimming pool. Since the Olympic swimming pool was an item featured in Utopian Tours' brochures, it is submitted that Good Advice were not under a duty to notify Utopian Tours of the importance of the swimming pool to the Joneses, although it would have been better practice had they done so. Mr Jones's conversations with Good Advice prove the importance of the swimming pool to him and his wife, and Utopian Tours must accept an assessment of damages accordingly.

Damages will be awarded under two heads—diminution of contract value and loss of enjoyment (including mental distress). In the writers' opinion, the diminution of contract value in this instance is insubstantial (it being accepted that the only fault with the holiday was the lack of swimming pool)—say £75 per person—but the damages for loss of enjoyment should be considerable—say £280 per person. This represents £20 per person per day which, it is suggested, is equitable compensation for the loss of a facility proven to be important to the holiday maker.

The Joneses' case has provided a concrete background against which to discuss the various means of resolving holiday disputes, problems regarding evidence, and the relevant procedural and tactical considerations. Any claim brought by a holiday maker will have its own special factors but the basic law and general guidelines outlined in this chapter provide the basis for decisions regarding whether and how to claim and whether and how to defend.

# Chapter 7

# The providers of transport and accommodation

## 1. Contractual arrangements

In arranging the various components that make up a package holiday a tour operator enters into contracts with airlines, coach companies, hoteliers and others since it is they who actually provide the transport and accommodation which feature in the package. To discuss in any depth the legal considerations applicable to this range of contracts would require a book on its own. But an outline discussion of the subject is necessary to give readers a fuller understanding of how the package holiday industry operates.

People like hoteliers and coach companies provide services and facilities to holiday makers under contracts between themselves and tour operators. Usually nothing happens which creates a contract between an individual holiday maker and, say, the hotel at which he stays. The position as regards air transport is somewhat different. Although flights are provided under a contract between the tour operator and the airline, the holiday maker is almost invariably issued with a ticket which shows the airline as the issuer. The ticket will often be made out by the tour operator as agent for the airline whose plane it has chartered. But it clearly identifies the airline as the issuer and establishes a contractual, or quasi contractual, relationship between the holiday maker and the airline.

Some brochures say that the tour operator is acting as agent for the carriers and hoteliers whose services feature in the holiday package. In the writers' opinion such statements are of doubtful validity. The word agent has two meanings. The first is a technical legal meaning the essence of which is that the agent is empowered to create binding contracts between his principal and third parties. The second non-technical meaning connotes a firm, or self employed representative, who solicits orders or bookings for his principal and, in some cases, assists in servicing them. The reasons why the authors are so doubtful whether a tour operator can normally be regarded as an agent for the carriers and hoteliers featured in its brochure are as follows:

(a) The contracts which tour operators enter into with carriers and hoteliers are not normally ones which can be described as appointing the operator to be the agent or representative of the carriers and hoteliers concerned. Instead they are contracts under which the tour operator charters a plane or a coach, or buys a block of seats on a particular flight, or reserves a block of hotel rooms for its customers.

(b) The tour operator does not usually receive any commission or other remuneration from the carriers and hoteliers whose services it utilises. It pays them for the services which they provide but does not receive any cash payment from them. Furthermore it sells on what they provide at a profit which is inconsistent with the normal duties of an agent.

(c) The tour operator is not empowered to enter into contracts with holiday makers on behalf of carriers and hoteliers and, with the exception of airlines and shipping companies, carriers and hoteliers do not normally supply holiday makers with tickets, confirmation of booking forms or other contractual documents.

(d) If the operator were the agent of carriers and hoteliers, if it ceased trading they would be obliged to provide their services to holiday makers whose booked holidays had not commenced before the collapse, even though they may not have received any monies from the operator to pay for them. So far as the writers are aware nobody suggests that this is the case.

(e) A tour operator clearly enters into contracts with holiday makers as a principal. It could be argued that the contract is a hybrid one whereby the tour operator agrees to do certain things amongst which is putting the holiday maker into a direct contractual relationship with specified carriers and hoteliers. Occasionally one sees a tour operator's brochure which says something like that. But such brochures imply that the operator is acting as agent for the customer rather than entering into coach and hotel contracts with customers as an agent for coach companies and hoteliers.

(f) The only agency relationship which appears to be mentioned in a tour operator's contracts with carriers and hoteliers is one which appears in most air charter contracts. It stipulates that the charterer (ie the tour operator) enters into the charter agreement with the airline both on its own behalf "and as agent for all persons carried in the aircraft".

(g) If the tour operator is regarded as a representative or booking agent for carriers and hoteliers, it becomes difficult to explain the provisions in most package holiday contracts which enable the operator to cancel the holiday if a minimum level of bookings is not forthcoming, or those which require it to provide alternative accommodation or refunds if the hotel closes down or withdraws some significant facility.

In the writers' view, the reality of most package holiday contracts is that the tour operator does not contract to provide transport and accommodation itself, nor (with the possible exception of air travel) to create contracts between the holiday maker and specified carriers and hoteliers. Instead, it undertakes to make arrangements for carriers and hoteliers to provide such services as fully disclosed independent contractors of the tour operator. As a matter of legal fancy one can construct documents whereby tour operators would emerge as *del credere* agents for carriers and hoteliers or, indeed, as agents for their holiday maker customers. But that would require a radical reconstruction of the documents currently used in the holiday industry.

## 2. Accommodation

### (a) Usual arrangements

The provider of accommodation will normally be a hotelier, villa owner, camp site owner (tents and caravans), or innkeeper and his liabilities and duties to the tour operator will be governed by the terms of the contract between them. A tour operator does not normally book a specific room for the holiday maker as and when the need arises but rather, before the commencement of the season, reserves a number of rooms to be allotted to his customers upon arrival. Whether or not an advance payment is made for such reservations is a matter for negotiation between the parties.

Allowing for the different types of accommodation that exist, the contract between a tour operator and a provider of accommodation (using a hotel as an example) should deal with the following:

(a) The part of the hotel in which the rooms reserved are situated.

(b) The number of rooms and the facilities in them (for example, some may be air conditioned apartments with a balcony, bath, shower and seaview while others may only be air conditioned with a shower).

(c) The period covered by the contract.

(d) The cost of different types of rooms, which may well vary according to the time of the year, and of any additional facilities available on request (eg cots). Also details of any reductions for young children.

(e) Details of meals included in the price quoted by the hotel and of other meals available.

(f) A clear description of all facilities (eg swimming pools, discotheques) provided by the hotel.

(g) An undertaking that the hotel complies with local sanitary, fire and safety regulations and that regular checks to ensure this will be made. Any breach should render it liable at its expense for the immediate relocation of customers of the operator to alternative accommodation of a similar graded standard, failing which the operator should be entitled to terminate the contract straightaway.

(h) An undertaking that the accommodation, food and service will be at least as good as that set out in the hotel's promotional literature and laid down by the relevant local authority for a hotel of its class. If it is not, or if the hotel does not provide the exact accommodation contracted for, it should be obliged to refund to the operator any compensation that the operator consequently has to pay to its customers.

(i) An undertaking by the operator to provide the hotel with a list of clients to be accommodated at least two weeks before their arrival, with a right for the operator to release any then unsold accommodation to the hotelier without being obliged to pay for it.

(j) An undertaking by the hotel to take out an insurance policy against the risk of any customer of the operator suffering death, personal injury, or loss of or damage to property, as a result of negligence on the part of itself, its employees and agents and to indemnify the operator against any claims which may be made against it by its customers as a result of any such negligence.

(k) The hotel should undertake that all the facilities and services supplied by it to any customer of the operator will be of sufficient standard to avoid the risk of injury or death, failing which the operator should be entitled to serve notice requiring the defect to be rectified straightaway, failure to do which will justify immediate termination.

(l) An undertaking by the hotel to keep the grounds and facilities (eg swimming pools) clean and tidy, clean the rooms regularly, and maintain a steady and safe supply of water, gas and electricity.

The above is not meant to be exhaustive. There are many other clauses which are often inserted, such as one imposing an obligation to provide free accommodation for the operator's representatives and one whereby the operator seeks to ensure that the hotel is not charging it more than it charges other operators.

The hotel contract should identify the proprietor of the hotel so that the tour operator will know against whom legal proceedings should be issued if the occasion arises. Under English law firms or individuals who carry on business under a business name, such as the name of a hotel, are obliged to identify themselves on their business stationery and in their contracts but it appears that that is not the case in many holiday resort countries. In theory the failure of many contracts between tour operators and hoteliers to identify the legal person who owns the hotel could give rise to serious legal problems if things go wrong. In practice it seldom does.

Technically speaking, the tour operator should ensure that whoever signs the hotel contract for the hotel is empowered to do so. In practice the contract is normally signed by the ostensible proprietor or manager of the hotel and nobody ever seems to deny that the hotel is legally bound by it.

## (b) Jurisdiction

The question of jurisdiction and the laws which are to govern the agreement require careful consideration. It is more expedient and economic for an English operator to issue proceedings in an English court in respect of an agreement governed by English law and, where this can be achieved, it means that the operator's legal position vis-à-vis the hotelier will be subject to the same laws as the operator's position vis-à-vis the British holiday maker. Whether or not a hotel agrees to this is a matter for negotiation.

Provided that the leave of the English courts can be obtained to issue English proceedings against someone out of the jurisdiction, and provided that the hotel is in a country with which the United Kingdom has an agreement for reciprocal enforcement of judgments, the operator should not encounter excessive difficulty in enforcing a contract which confers jurisdiction on the English courts. If the hotel is in a country with which the United Kingdom does not have such an agreement, the contract with the hotel might as well be subject to the laws and jurisdiction of that country since an English judgment will be unenforceable.

Cases where a hotel contract is subject to, say, Spanish law create an anomalous situation whereby the hotel will not be liable to a tour operator under Spanish law for conditions which satisfy local regulations but fall far below English regulations whereas the operator could be liable to the holiday maker if he becomes aware of the differing standard and of a possible consequent risk to the holiday maker. As explained in Chapter 2, it is considered that a tour operator has a duty to advise his customers of any known risks at hotels and that this duty and its attendant liabilities cannot be avoided merely because conditions at the hotel satisfy local regulations.

The contract between hotel and tour operator should be sufficiently detailed and precise to cover all obvious situations and to avoid any need, in the event of disputes, for the operator to rely on implied terms—such as that the hotel will be fit for human habitation. In all cases where local law will or may apply, or if the hotel is in a country with which the United Kingdom has no reciprocal enforcement of judgments treaty, the operator should take steps to ascertain the local law and, ideally, have the proposed contract approved by a local lawyer.

## 3. Transport

Transport may be by air, sea, rail or road and the

independent contractors who provide it will, therefore, include airlines, shipping companies, coach companies and train companies. Most tour operators' brochures specifically state that the holiday maker is transported subject to the carrier's conditions of carriage and that they are available for inspection. In addition there are various international conventions which determine the liability of those who provide international carriage by air, sea or land.

## (a) Air travel arrangements

Using air travel as an example, it is important to note the range of contracts whereby a tour operator can obtain transport for holiday makers. It can charter a plane from an airline. It can buy a block of seats on a plane—from the airline, or from another operator who has chartered the plane, or from another carrier who has itself bought a block of seats. It can make special arrangements whereby it obtains a provisional allocation of seats to be taken up or released not less than, say, 30 days before the date of the flight in question. It can buy tickets on scheduled flights. Chartering a plane will usually be the most economical alternative in cases where the operator can be confident of filling the whole plane. But if an operator charters a plane and finds that he can only fill 65 per cent of the seats, he may suffer a heavy loss. He will then try to sell some of his spare seats to other operators but this is not always possible. Even where it is, it often involves selling them at a substantial loss.

Airlines naturally expect to receive at least a portion of the contract price well in advance and the balance before departure. Equally naturally, operators desire to postpone the payment of the price for as long as possible. This is not only because of the cash flow advantages of late payment but also, in some cases, because there is a possibility of the airline ceasing to trade before the departure date. An operator will not contract with an airline which it considers at serious risk of failure. But if it refuses to do business with all airlines which could possibly fail, it eliminates a number of attractive cheap flight possibilities. The obvious answer from the operator's point of view is to stipulate that payment will not be made until shortly before the departure date. Whether this can be negotiated in a particular case depends upon prevailing market conditions.

In some cases it may be appropriate to provide that monies held by an operator which are payable in due course to an airline should be held by the operator as trustee for the holiday makers. This should not be necessary where the monies are payable to the airline under a contract between it and the operator because in such cases the operator is not acting as agent for the airline when it collects monies from the holiday maker. Accordingly, all monies which the operator receives from the holiday maker become the operator's money and the amounts payable by it to the airline are debts. In the event that the airline ceases trading before any such debt is paid, its liquidator cannot, it is submitted, trace any money held by the operator and claim that it is impressed with a trust. All he can do is to claim against the operator under the contract between them. But in a situation where the airline is unable to perform its part of the contract, the operator should have a perfectly adequate right of set-off.

The position is complicated by the fact that in due course the operator's customers will be issued with tickets in the airline's name. In the writers' view, this does not produce a situation in which an operator is holding monies collected from holiday makers as agent for the airline. If it is holding them as agent for anybody, it is as agent for the holiday maker. But the better view is that it is holding them as its own monies from which it must pay the debts owed by it to the airline and others who provide services in connection with a holiday.

A possible exception is where an operator is also a sales agent of the airline concerned and buys tickets on a scheduled flight. In such cases there may be grounds for saying that it is selling them to holiday makers in its capacity as a sales agent of the airline. This would appear to be the correct analysis if it reports their sales in its sales agency return and claims to be entitled to commission on them.

171

## (b) Air charter

The situation in which a tour operator charters a plane from an airline will now be considered. In general terms the charter contract is a contract of hire. The operator does not have any proprietary rights in the plane but reserves it for its customers' use. The whole plane is reserved and it is up to the operator whether he fills all the seats. Any failure to do so will not reduce the charter price.

A charter contract may take the form of a lease of the aircraft to the charterer with or without the services of a crew. This type of charter is known as a "bare hull" or dry charter. Under it the charterer becomes for most purposes the temporary owner of the plane. The crew, whether supplied by the owner or the charterer, are the servants of the charterer and under his control.

The more normal type of agreement is the "time and voyage" or "wet" charter. It gives the charterer the right to use the aircraft and its crew for the purpose of carrying passengers or freight upon a specified flight or flights or during a specified period. The crew remain the owner's servants. The charterer may be given certain rights to decide the flights to be undertaken but not the manner in which they are to be performed. Contrary to the position under a bare hull charter the owner is the air traffic operator.

A valuable outline of the various categories of time and voyage charter is provided on page 1047 of Allan Beaver's comprehensive manual of retail travel practice *"Mind Your Own Travel Business"*:

> "*Ad hoc* charters are single or several one-off arrangements. A time charter is where an operator charters an aircraft twenty-four hours of the day for a period of time. The operator is entitled to the exclusive use of the aircraft during the period when it is chartered from the carrier. A series charter means a carrier provides flights between specified points on a regular basis, usually weekly, so that holiday arrangements can be organised back to back. A part charter is the chartering of only part of

the capacity of an aircraft. This can mean that a number of operators have shared a charter. It is more commonly used to describe the situation where an operator has chartered part of the capacity of a scheduled service. This is sometimes also known as a block-off charter".

A time and voyage charter is not as such a contract of carriage (ie a contract to transport particular passengers or goods). However, it will amount to one where it is governed by the Carriage by Air Act 1961 or the Carriage by Air Acts (Application of Provisions) Order 1967. Where this is so, the owner is the contracting carrier and there is a contract of carriage between him and each of the plane's passengers.

Time and voyage contracts normally provide that the charterer enters into the charter contract on its own behalf and as agent for all who travel on the plane pursuant to the charter agreement. This is a strange provision because at the time the charterer enters into the agreement it usually does not even know who the passengers will be.

In the case of international flights a time and voyage charter will provide for the issue of tickets to passengers as required by the Warsaw Convention (see page 177). Sometimes tickets are prepared by the airline and sent to the charterer/tour operator for onward transmission to passengers. Sometimes they are prepared and issued by the charterer/tour operator as agent for the airline.

Time and voyage charters normally provide that the owner will provide a specific plane or planes, or planes of a specified type (eg Boeing 737 in 130 seat configuration), and that they will be fit for the required purpose, properly equipped and maintained, and with a crew competent and sufficient for the duties required of them. Even if there is no express term, the owner will be under a duty to take care to provide a suitable, safe aircraft and a competent pilot *(Fosbrooke-Hobbes* v *Airwork Ltd and British—American Air Services Ltd* [1937] 1 All ER 108).

## (c) Inclusive tour flights

For purposes of illustration let us now consider briefly the type of charter agreement whereby a tour operator contracts with an airline for it to perform all or part of the tour operator's programme of inclusive tour flights ("IT Flights") for a particular season. The time-tables, dates and stopping places constituting the programme are usually set out in a schedule to the contract and the airline undertakes to use its best endeavours to comply with any request by the tour operator to make changes in the programme.

The contract will specify the charter price for each flight. This will normally be composed of route costs (covering landing fees, handling fees, crew allowance and accommodation costs, etc) and an hourly rate charge (covering depreciation or lease charges, payroll costs of the crew, maintenance and overhaul costs etc). The former are usually specified in a schedule whereas the latter result in an hourly rate which is specified in the body of the contract. The airline is normally permitted to increase the route costs element to compensate for increases in the cost of aviation fuel and other specified items. The contract is likely to specify a minimum number of hours to be flown and provide for the tour operator to compensate the airline for any shortfall.

The contract should entitle the airline in appropriate circumstances to substitute another plane from its fleet for the designated plane or type of plane and lay down conditions governing any substitution. It should also schedule the catering requirements which the airline must meet.

Examples of common provisions regarding control of the plane are:

> **"Carrier's servants**
> All ground and operating personnel including cabin staff are authorised to take orders only from the Carrier unless specific written agreement shall have been made between the parties whereby certain defined instructions may be accepted by such personnel from the Charterer.

### Captain's discretion

For safety reasons the Captain of the Aircraft shall have complete discretion concerning the load carried on the Aircraft including the number of passengers and the amount of their baggage and their distribution, as to whether or not any Flight should be undertaken, as to where landings should be made, and as to all other matters relating to the operation of the Aircraft, and the Charterer shall accept all such decisions of such Captain as final and binding."

The contract should include references to the issue of tickets and the Warsaw Convention, and also provisions regarding traffic regulations along the lines of:

"The Charterer will comply and will use its best endeavours to ensure that all passengers will observe and comply with all Traffic Regulations of the Carrier and all applicable laws regulations and directions made by the Civil Aviation Authority or other relevant authority or government including but without prejudice to the generality of the foregoing all Customs Police and Public Health regulations."

Finally, the contract should include a *force majeure* clause and clauses regarding termination, the serving of notices, the applicable law, and various other standard form provisions.

A tour operator can purchase air transport for his customers from other operators — either from one who has chartered the whole plane or from one who has reserved a block of seats. Where it does this, it will contract with the other tour operator involved and not with the airline. However, it will still provide its customers with tickets in the airline's name and will have to incorporate the airline's terms and conditions of passage into its contracts with its holiday makers. This will normally be stipulated in the agreement between the respective tour operators. Any such agreement between tour operators should be conditional upon the purchasing tour operator having a valid ATOL. It should also provide for the purchasing tour operator to be responsible for its own customers and to indemnify the selling tour operator against any claims that may be made against it by them.

### (d) Other travel arrangements

Some coach holidays are provided by operators which own coaches so that there is no need for them to hire coaches. Where this is not so, the operator will normally hire a coach and crew from a coach company. In that event the contract of hire will be similar in some respects to the contract for the chartering of a plane. One difference is that the operator is able to reserve more control over matters such as departure and stoppage times than it can in an airplane charter contract. Another is that it is not normal for holiday makers to be issued with tickets in the name of the coach company. The coach company's standard conditions of carriage are almost invariably incorporated into the tour operator's contracts with its coach tour holiday makers.

It is possible for an operator to share a coach with another operator providing substantially the same holiday. In that event it will enter into contracts with the coach company or the other operator for the purchase of blocks of seats similar to the contracts for the purchase of blocks of airplane seats discussed earlier in this chapter.

Most cruise holidays are provided by shipping companies. Occasionally a tour operator will charter a boat in order to provide a cruise but it is not proposed to discuss that unusual situation. In principal a shipping charter party contract is similar to a contract for chartering a plane and its crew but it contains a number of detailed provisions which are specific to it.

Insofar as rail travel features in a package holiday, it will involve the operator in reserving compartments, or even a whole train, in much the same way as a football club or political party will do for a match or party conference. The rail company's standard conditions of carriage will apply and will be incorporated into the operator's contracts with the relevant holiday makers. Usually the holiday makers will be issued with tickets in the name of the rail company.

## 4. The Warsaw Convention

The Warsaw Convention of 1929 is the foundation stone of the international regulations concerning the liabilities of air carriers to their passengers. It was amended by The Hague Protocol of 1955. The Amended Convention, which has been ratified by a large number of states, was given statutory force by s.1 of the Carriage by Air Act 1961. This states that "the provisions of the Convention known as 'the Warsaw' Convention as amended at the Hague in 1955 . . . shall so far as they relate to the rights and liabilities of carriers, carriers' servants and agents, passengers, consignors, consignees and other persons, and subject to the provisions of this Act, have the force of law in the United Kingdom in relation to any carriage by air to which the Convention applies, irrespective of the nationality of the aircraft performing that carriage".

This establishes that under English law an airline's duties and liabilities are governed to a large extent by the amended Warsaw Convention. The Convention applies to all international carriage of persons, baggage or cargo performed by aircraft for reward (Article 1(1)). International carriage means "any carriage in which . . . the place of departure and the place of destination . . . are situated either within the territories of two High Contracting Parties or within the territory of a Single High Contracting Party, if there is an agreed stopping place within the territory of another State, even if that State is not a High Contracting Party". In simple terms a "High Contracting Party" means a country. Carriage between two points within the territory of a single country without an agreed stopping place within the territory of another country is not international carriage for the purposes of this Convention. This means that flights for package holidays within the United Kingdom are outside the scope of the Warsaw Convention.

## (a) Tickets

Article 3(1) of the Convention provides that in respect of the carriage of passengers a ticket shall be delivered containing:

(a) an indication of the places of departure and destination;

(b) if the places of departure and destination are within the territory of a single High Contracting Party, one or more agreed stopping places being within the territory of another state, an indication of at least one such stopping place;

(c) a notice to the effect that, if the passenger's journey involves an ultimate destination or stop in a country other than the country of departure, the Warsaw Convention may be applicable and that the Convention governs and in most cases limits the liability of carriers for death or personal injury and in respect of loss of or damage to baggage.

A carrier that permits a passenger to embark without a ticket containing the notice required by sub-paragraph (c) will not be allowed to avail himself of the limitations of liability contained in Article 22 (see page 179).

## (b) Liabilities of airlines

Article 17 provides that a carrier is liable for damage sustained in the event of death or wounding of a passenger or any other bodily injury suffered by a passenger if the accident which caused the damage took place on board the aircraft or in the course of any of the operations of embarking or disembarking. Despite its wording, it does not impose strict liability because defences are available for a carrier under Articles 20 and 21.

Article 18(1) provides that the carrier is liable for damage sustained in the event of the destruction or loss of, or damage to, any registered baggage or any cargo, if the occurrence which caused the damage so sustained took place during the carriage by air. Sub-paragraphs (2) and (3) of Article 18 make it clear that "carriage by air" is deemed to mean the period during which baggage is in the carrier's charge. The same defences are open to a carrier as under Article 17. In addition, the passenger's complaint must be made no later than 7 days from the date of receipt of the damaged baggage (Article 26(2)).

Under Article 19 the carrier is liable for damage occasioned by delay in the carriage by air of passengers' baggage or cargo. Article 26(2) provides that complaints in respect of such damage must be made within 21 days of embarkation.

### (c) Limitations of liability

By virtue of Article 20 the carrier is not liable under Articles 17-19 if he proves that he and his servants or agents had taken all necessary measures to avoid the damage or that it was impossible for him or them to take such measures. In *Grain* v *Imperial Airways Ltd* [1937] 1 KB 50, Greer LJ said "this seems to me to amount to a promise not to injure the passenger by avoidable accident, the onus being on the carrier to prove that the accident could not have been avoided by the exercise of reasonable care". Article 21 provides that if the carrier proves that the damage was caused or contributed to by the negligence of the injured person the court may, in accordance with the provisions of its own law, exonerate the carrier wholly or partly from his liability.

Article 22 contains various limitations of liability:

> (i) If a passenger is killed or injured 125,000 Gold Francs (£6,817);
>
> (ii) For loss of or damage to hand baggage 5,000 Gold Francs (£273);
>
> (iii) For loss of or damage to checked baggage 250 Gold Francs (£5.90) per kilogram.

The limit of 125,000 Gold Francs (£6,817) on a carrier's liability for death or personal injury was set at a time when damages awards were much lower than nowadays and when there was a general desire to protect a fledgling industry. But the wealthier developed countries, led by the USA, became increasingly dissatisfied with such a low limit. This resulted in the limitation of liability for death and personal injury being doubled by the 1955 Hague Protocol to 250,000 Gold Francs (£13,633). But this only applies to airlines based in countries which have ratified the Hague Protocol.

One of the countries which has never ratified it is the USA which considers the 250,000 Gold Francs limitation to be far too low. Its insistence on a higher limit for passengers flying to or from the USA led to the 1966 Montreal Inter-Carrier Agreement which applies to all commercial flights which start, finish, or have an intermediate stop, in the USA. It set a limit for death or personal injury of $58,000 exclusive of legal fees or $75,000 inclusive of them.

All this is briefly summarised in the tickets of UK airlines along the following lines:

## "ADVICE TO INTERNATIONAL PASSENGERS ON LIMITATION OF LIABILITY

Passengers on a journey involving an ultimate destination or a stop in a country other than the country of origin are advised that the provisions of a treaty known as the Warsaw Convention may be applicable to the entire journey, including any portion entirely within the country of origin or destination. For such passengers on a journey to, from, or with an agreed stopping place in the United States of America, the Convention and special contracts of carriage embodied in applicable tariffs provide that the liability of certain carriers parties to such special contracts, for death of or personal injury to passengers is limited in most cases to proven damages not to exceed US Dollars 75,000 per passenger, and that this liability up to such limit shall not depend on negligence on the part of the Carrier. For such passengers travelling by a carrier not a party to such contracts or on a journey not to, from, or having an agreed stopping place in the United States of America, liability of the carrier for death of or personal injury to passengers is limited in most cases to approximately US Dollars 10,000 or US Dollars 20,000.

The names of carriers parties to such special contracts are available at all ticket offices of such carriers and may be examined on request. Additional protection can usually be obtained by purchasing insurance from a private Company. Such insurance is not affected by any limitation of the carrier's liability under the Warsaw Convention or such special contracts of carriage. For further information please consult your Airline or Insurance Company Representative.

**Note:** The limit of liability of US Dollars 75,000 above is inclusive of legal fees and costs except that in the case of a claim brought in a state where provision is made for separate award of legal fees and costs, the limit shall be the sum of US Dollars 58,000 exclusive of legal fees and costs."

Readers will have noted that the Warsaw/Hague limits are expressed in Gold Francs. This means the former Poincare French Gold Franc which consisted of 65½ milligrams of gold of millesimal fineness 900. This somewhat archaic unit of value needs to be converted into the national currencies of the various signatories to the Warsaw Convention. In Britain this is dealt with at periodic intervals by the publication of a Carriage by Air (Sterling Equivalents) Order. The one currently in force is Statutory Instrument No. 1778 of 1986.

The Warsaw Convention limitation in respect of death or personal injury is effectively increased in the case of British airlines by Condition H of the CAA's Standard Conditions for Air Transport Licences:

"The licence holder shall enter into a special contract with every passenger to be carried under this licence on or after 1 April 1981, or with a person acting on behalf of such a passenger, for the increase of not less than the Sterling equivalent of 100,000 Special Drawing Rights, exclusive of costs, of the limit of the carrier's liability under Article 17 of the Warsaw Convention of 1929 and under Article 17 of that Convention as amended at the Hague in 1955."

The Sterling value of 100,000 Special Drawing Rights varies from day to day. It is published daily in the Financial Times and at 15 February 1989 was approximately £75,000.

Article 25 of the Warsaw Convention provides that the limits of liability specified in Article 22 shall not apply if it is proved that the damage resulted from an act or omission of the carrier, his servants or agents, done with intent to cause damage or recklessly and with knowledge that damage would probably result.

Article 25 was considered in *Goldman* v *Thai Airways International Ltd* [1983] 1 WLR 1186. In 1977 the plaintiff was travelling on an international flight as a passenger in an aircraft of the defendant airline. On entering an area in which moderate clear air turbulence had been forecast, the pilot did not switch on the sign ordering passengers to fasten their seat belts despite instructions to pilots in the defendant's manual to do so when turbulence could be expected. The aircraft encountered severe turbulence and the plaintiff, who was sitting with his seat belt unfastened, was thrown from his seat. He sustained serious injury to his lower spine. On his claim against the defendant for damages Chapman J gave judgment for £41,852.42 together with interest and costs, holding that, in disregarding the instructions in the manual, the pilot had acted recklessly and with knowledge that damage would probably result. Therefore Article 25 applied and liability was not limited under Article 22.

Subsequently the defendant succeeded on appeal to the Court of Appeal. It held that Article 25 was not to be construed in isolation but in its context and with the qualification that the act or omission had to have been done *both* "recklessly" *and* "with knowledge that danger would probably result." The test was subjective and, therefore, the pilot had only acted recklessly if it was proved that he had omitted to order the passengers to wear seat belts when aware that damage of the kind that did occur would probably result, or indifferent to that likelihood. It was doubtful whether the pilot had been reckless in interpreting the flight operations manual as giving him a discretion to defer switching on the seat belts sign until there was an indication of turbulence but, even if he had been, the evidence did not establish a probability of encountering clear air turbulence of a severity that would cause the kind of injury suffered by the plaintiff. Accordingly, since the pilot could not have had knowledge of the likelihood of the injury, Article 25 did not apply and the defendant's liability was limited under the terms of Article 22.

By virtue of Article 29 a passenger's right to damages under Articles 17-19 is extinguished if an action is not brought within two years reckoned from the date of arrival at the destination, or from the date on which the aircraft ought to have arrived, or from the date on which the carriage stopped.

*(d) Amendments*

Since the amendments made to the Warsaw Convention by the Hague Protocol, there have been other amending conventions to which the United Kingdom has been a party, but, because of their restricted number of signatories they have not yet been brought into force:

> (i) The Guatemala City Protocol of 1971 sought to improve the position of passengers in the event of personal injury or loss by limiting a carrier's defence to Article 17 and by increasing the maximum liability.

> (ii) An international conference in Montreal in 1975 adopted four additional Protocols, again with the aim of imposing greater liability on carriers. It should be noted that the limits of carriers' liabilities, under the Montreal Protocols, are described in terms of Special Drawing Rights (SDRs).

The amended Warsaw Convention has been applied to non-international carriage by the Carriage by Air Acts (Application of Provisions) Order 1967. The Order, which has been amended by statutory instruments in 1969, 1979 and 1981, applies the phrase "non-international" to flights not only within the UK but also between the UK and those countries which are not parties to any of the international conventions. The purpose was to harmonise the regulations for "international" and "non-international" carriage by air. The Order differs from the international conventions in three important respects:

(i) there is no need for a passenger ticket;

(ii) Articles 10-16 of the Convention are excluded; and

(iii) the upper limit on the carrier's liability for the death or wounding of, or bodily injury to, a passenger is 100,000 SDRs (approximately £75,000).

## 5. The Athens Convention

International carriage by sea is also regulated by an international convention, the Athens Convention 1974, the terms of which were made effective in the United Kingdom by s.14 of the Merchant Shipping Act 1979. Schedule 3 of that Act sets out the text of the Convention, the provisions of which are only applicable to "international carriage". By this is meant any carriage in which, according to the contract of carriage, the place of departure and the place of destination are situated in two different states, or in a single state if, according to the contract of carriage or the scheduled itinerary, there is an intermediate port of call in another state.

The Convention covers the carriage of passengers and their luggage by ship but not by hovercraft. Under it the shipping company is liable for damage suffered as a result of the death or personal injury of a passenger and for loss of or damage to luggage, if the incident which caused the damage occurred in the course of the carriage and was due to the fault or neglect of the shipping company or of its servants or agents acting within the scope of their employment. The burden of proving that the incident occurred in the course of carriage, and the extent of the loss or damage, lies with the claimant. If the death of or personal injury to a passenger, or the loss of or damage to cabin luggage, arose in connection with a shipwreck, collision, stranding, explosion or fire or defect in the ship, fault or neglect by the carrier is presumed unless the contrary is proved. In other cases the burden of proving fault or neglect lies with the claimant.

Under the Convention (as amended by the Merchant Shipping (Sterling Equivalents) (Various Enactments) Order 1986 No. 1777) liability for damages for death or personal injury is restricted to 700,000 Gold Francs (approximately £38,000), for loss or damage to cabin luggage 12,500 Gold Francs (approximately £680) and for loss or damage to other luggage 18,000 Gold Francs (approximately £980).

## 6. The Berne and Geneva Conventions

There are also international conventions concerning the carriage of passengers and luggage on land both by rail and road. The 1970 Berne Convention, which incorporated some of the provisions of the 1961 Berne Convention, governs carriage by rail. It is expressly incorporated into English law by the International Transport Conventions Act 1983. The text of the Convention is contained in the Schedule to that Act. The international carriage of passengers and luggage by road is governed by the 1973 Geneva Convention. The United Kingdom has not yet signed or ratified it but the Carriage of Passengers by Road Act 1974 provides for its incorporation into English law when the United Kingdom does ratify and sign.

The Berne Convention is not as far reaching as the Conventions applicable to international carriage of passengers by air and sea since it does not deal with the question of liability of the railway for death and personal injuries, nor with liability for delay. What the Convention says is that such questions must be left to the law of the state in which the incident causing death, injury, loss or damage occurs. It does contain provisions concerning loss or damage to luggage but its application is beyond the scope of this book.

The Geneva Convention provides that a carrier by road is liable for any loss or damage resulting from death or personal injury of a passenger due to an accident which occurs while the passenger is inside the vehicle, or embarking or disembarking. He is also liable for loss of or damage to luggage during the whole time that it is in the vehicle or being loaded or unloaded. However, the carrier will be able to avoid liability if he can show that the circumstances causing the accident are such that he could not have avoided it by exercising greater care. Article 12 of the Convention provides that the law of the country in which the court hearing any claim is situated determines the extent of the injury which gives rise to the claim of compensation and those persons who are entitled to sue for compensation.

The carrier by road's liability for death or personal injury under the Geneva Convention is subject to a maximum of 250,000 Francs (approximately £11,799). Liability for luggage is stated to be a maximum of 500 Francs (approximately £23.60) for each piece of luggage with a limit of 2,000 Francs (approximately £94.90) per passenger.

## 7. Other contractors

This chapter has concentrated on those independent contractors who provide accommodation or transport. Services may also be provided by other persons, such as guides and ski-ing instructors, over whom the tour operator has no direct control. In all such cases appropriate contracts should be entered into albeit sometimes fairly informal.

# Chapter 8

# Insolvency of tour operators and travel agents

## 1. Advance payments

It is a feature of package holiday contracts that the customer pays money to the tour operator long before the holiday begins. Usually the customer pays a 10% deposit at the time when he books his holiday and then pays the balance of his holiday price about eight weeks before departure. If he books within eight weeks from his departure date, he will normally be required to pay the full price when he makes his booking.

This pattern of payment gives rise to special problems in cases where a tour operator ceases trading, at which time he is likely to be holding large sums of money paid by customers whose holidays have not commenced. There is also the problem of holiday makers who are stranded abroad at the time. And then there is the complication that some of the monies paid in respect of the collapsed operator's holidays will be held by travel agents.

In law a contract is not automatically terminated by the bankruptcy or liquidation of one of the parties unless it so provides. Instead, the benefit of the contract passes to the insolvent party's trustee in bankruptcy or liquidator, who is entitled to disclaim contracts which he regards as unprofitable. In some cases the liquidator of an insolvent tour operator has kept uncompleted holiday contracts in being and arranged for them to be performed by another operator. But in this chapter we confine ourselves to the normal situation where that does not happen.

Where a party to a contract makes it clear before the time for his performance of the contract that he will not perform it, this amounts to an anticipatory breach, and one which is so serious that the innocent party is entitled to treat it as a repudiation of the contract. Alternatively the innocent party can stay his hand and wait to see what happens.

When a tour operator ceases trading, it makes it clear (in the absence of any indication to the contrary) that it will not perform its outstanding holiday contracts. In these circumstances a customer who has not then paid the full holiday price would be well advised to accept the operator's repudiation of the contract in which event:

(a) he will not be obliged to pay the unpaid balance of his holiday price;

(b) he will be entitled to claim repayment of all monies previously paid by him; and

(c) he may, in theory, have a claim for loss of bargain or compensation for disappointed expectations.

The ability to claim repayment of monies paid to the operator arises because there has been a total failure of consideration. The position was summarised in paragraph 1098 of Vol 1 of the 23rd edition of *Chitty on Contracts* as follows:

"Where money has been deposited or paid under a contract and, before the payer has received the benefit of any part of what he has bargained for, he rescinds the contract on account of the other party's breach, the consideration is said to have wholly failed and the payer may bring an action for money had and received to recover the money so deposited or paid".

The ability to claim a refund might not be of much value to a disappointed holiday maker, who would probably be one amongst many unsecured creditors of an insolvent company. With luck he might eventually receive a dividend from the liquidator calculated as a percentage of his claim. At the worst he would receive nothing. It was because of this and the problems of stranded holiday makers that the bonding arrangements referred to in

Chapter 1 were introduced. But customers who book holidays not requiring an ATOL with an operator who is not a member of ABTA or the Passenger Shipping Association or the bonded coach operators scheme discussed on page 16 will not be within the scope of such arrangements. If their tour operator ceases trading, they will be confined to proving as unsecured creditors in its liquidation.

## 2. Bonding arrangements

The customer who is best protected by bonding and other arrangements is the one who books a holiday involving air travel the provision of which requires the operator concerned to hold an ATOL. His first line of protection will be the bond which the CAA will require the operator to take out as a condition of his ATOL. If the operator is a member of TOSG, the bond will be in its favour. If it is an ABTA member who is not a member of TOSG, the bond will be in favour of ABTA. The bonds of operators who are members of neither TOSG or ABTA will be in favour of the CAA.

In the event that the bond monies payable as a result of the collapse of an ATOL holder are not sufficient to finance all the refunds which fall to be made to customers who have booked its ATOL holidays, any shortfall will be made good by The Air Travel Trust ("the Trust"). If its assets were insufficient to meet all claims on it, the Government would make good the deficiency, probably by means of a levy on the following year's holiday makers such as was operated in the aftermath of the Court Line collapse.

People who book holidays, such as coach and cruise holidays, the provision of which does not require an ATOL are not quite so well protected. Cruise holidays operated by members of the Passenger Shipping Association are covered by a bond as are coach holidays covered by the scheme discussed on page 16. And if the holiday is provided by an ABTA tour operator, there will be further protection because ABTA requires its members (including members of TOSG) to take out bonds in respect of non-licensable activities (ie holidays for which an ATOL is not required). But they will not enjoy the ultimate protection which is provided by the Trust to holiday makers who book ATOL holidays. If the holiday is provided by an operator who is not a member of ABTA, the Passenger Shipping Association or the Bonded Coach Holidays Section of the Bus and Coach Council, the customer will usually not be protected by any bond and will not be eligible to receive payments from the Trust.

The circumstances in which bonds can be called in and the manner in which claims on them are dealt with are discussed in section 3 below. A full statement of the policies adopted by the CAA, ABTA and the TOSG in administering bonds given in support of ATOLs is given in a joint statement issued by those bodies and the Air Travel Trust entitled "Policies on Administration of Tour Operator's Bonds."

## 3. Collapse of a tour operator

### (a) Stranded holiday makers

Let us now consider what happens when a tour operator ceases trading, concentrating on the position of customers who have booked licensable (ATOL) holidays. Some of these customers will be on holiday when the collapse occurs. In cases where the operator has paid the relevant hotels and airlines in advance, the holiday may continue as planned albeit without the services of the operator's on the spot representative. Where hotels have not been fully paid in advance, whichever of TOSG, ABTA or the CAA is administering the operator's bond will be prepared to pay whatever is still due to the hotelier but this takes time. Some hoteliers are prepared to let the holiday go ahead confident that they will be paid in due course. Others turn nasty and demand immediate payment of the balance of their charges from the stranded holiday maker.

Airlines are usually paid in advance. But TOSG, ABTA or CAA may still have to make and pay for alternative arrangements in cases where, because of the attitude of foreign hoteliers, holiday makers are forced to return early. In addition they may have to do so in cases where holiday flights are provided by the collapsed operator itself or one of its subsidiaries as was the case when Laker Holidays collapsed in 1982.

Catering for stranded holiday makers is a first call on the various bonds and predominantly gives rise to practical rather than legal problems. However, where a stranded holiday maker loses part of his holiday, he will have a claim for a partial refund of what he paid for it and in this respect the ensuing paragraphs may apply to him as well as to holiday makers whose holidays "never get off the ground". The amount of such a partial refund will *prima facie* be related to the proportion of the holiday lost so that, as a starting point, a holiday maker who loses one third of his holiday will be entitled to a refund of one third of what he paid for it. However, a customer who finds himself making long outgoing and return flights for only two days holiday, or whose holiday is abruptly terminated before its high spots occur, should be able to recover more.

These matters are discussed in helpful detail in section 2 of the Policies on Administration of Tour Operator's Bonds issued by the Trust, the CAA, ABTA and the TOSG in July 1987.

### (b) Aborted holidays

We have seen that when an ATOL holder, or a non ATOL holder who is a member of ABTA, ceases trading the relevant bond holder (TOSG, ABTA or the CAA) will call in its bonds and apply the bond monies first in arranging for stranded holiday makers to enjoy the balance of their holidays or be repatriated and then in making refunds to customers who paid for holidays which will never take place. But what should a customer in the latter category do in order to obtain his refund?

If he has booked his holiday through a travel agent who provides a quick money-back guarantee, all that he need do is visit the shop at which he booked his holiday, sign the relevant forms, collect his refund and leave the agent

191

to pursue his claims against the relevant bondholder and, if necessary the Air Travel Trust. The guarantee does not require that the holiday concerned should be provided by the agent as tour operator. Indeed, that would be a meaningless guarantee because the agent would be guaranteeing itself. All that is required is that the holiday should be booked through one of the agent's retail outlets and be one that is within the ambit of the guarantee.

## (c) Credit card payments to operator

Another special situation is where the customer books direct with a tour operator and pays with a credit card. In the case of any credit card other than Access he will find that neither the relevant bondholder nor the Air Travel Reserve Trust will be willing to accept his claim. Instead, they will invoke s.75 of the Consumer Credit Act 1974 and refer him to his credit card company. Broadly speaking, what s.75 does is to render the credit card company jointly liable to the customer for any breach of contract by a supplier who has been paid by credit card. Section 75 is discussed on pages 201-204—in relation to the complex problems which arise where a customer uses a credit card to make payments to a *travel agent* to be passed on to the tour operator whose holiday is being booked. Suffice it to say here that where a credit card (as defined in the Consumer Credit Act) is used to pay a tour operator *direct,* then if the operator ceases trading, the customer should be able to recover the payment from his credit card company. If he only pays part of the price by credit card, it appears that he can recover the whole holiday price from his credit card company, not just the part which he paid by credit card (see page 202).

The reason why customers who pay direct by credit cards other than Access find their claims rejected by TOSG, ABTA, the CAA and the Trust is because these bodies consider that they can and should only make payments to customers who have suffered a loss. A customer who has a valid claim to recover holiday monies from a credit card company has not suffered a loss in respect of them.

Hence his inability to recover them from the relevant bond holder or the Agency.

The position of customers who pay all or part of the holiday price with an Access card is regulated by a special agreement between Access and the various bond administrators. This agreement applies to payments made to travel agents by Access card as well as to ones made direct to a tour operator. As a result of it, bond administrators will accept claims from customers who used Access cards. Accordingly, the approach outlined in section (e) on page 194 will apply to them as well as to customers who pay by cash, cheque or charge card.

*(d)  Recovery of pipeline monies*

Customers of a collapsed tour operator who do not have a valid claim against a credit card company under s.75 clearly have suffered a loss. Their first move should be to contact the travel agent through whom they booked their holiday. In certain special cases they may be able to recover money from him without having to claim against the relevant bond holder or the Trust. For instance, the agent may be holding money paid shortly before the collapse for a booking which has not been confirmed by the collapsed operator. In such a case the relevant booking conditions required by the CAA and recommended by ABTA would make it clear that the monies are held by the agent as agent for the customer and so should be returned to him.

Another special case is where the agent is holding money paid by a customer who has cancelled his holiday *before* the collapse of the operator. A circular issued by ABTA in connection with the collapse of Laker advised that the agent should account for the contractual cancellation charge to the collapsed operator's liquidator and return the balance to the customer. In the writers' view, the ability of an agent to return monies to a customer in such circumstances depends on the wording of the formal agency agreement and on trade practice. If the agreement states that in the event of a cancellation the agent may, after deducting the cancellation charge, return any monies received from the customer and still in the agent's possession, or if that has been the course of dealing between the agent and the operator, it would seem that the agent should be both entitled and obliged to refund such monies to the customer. But if neither the terms of the formal agency agreement nor the course of dealing before the collapse support the return of such monies, the agent may be vulnerable to a claim by the liquidator and so find himself out of pocket.

Another special situation occurs when, at the time of an operator's collapse, a cheque drawn by the agent or the customer in favour of the operator has not been cleared. A customer in this position should immediately stop the cheque. In the somewhat unlikely event of the liquidator suing him on the cheque, the customer should set off his claim against the operator for the loss of his holiday. An agent whose cheque has not been cleared will be tempted to do the same but his position may not be so strong.

Much depends on whether the agent's cheque is paying money which has become the property of the operator (eg money paid in respect of a booking which has been confirmed before the collapse). If it is, then the better view appears to be that if the agent stops the cheque the liquidator will be successful in suing the agent on it. But if the cheque accompanies a booking form which the operator has not accepted before the collapse, then it would seem correct for the agent to stop it on the grounds that:

(i) the money belongs to the customer; and

(ii) the operator has not given the agent any consideration for the cheque.


### (e) Money held by or for the tour operator

The preceding paragraphs have discussed situations in which monies are held by an agent who is, or may be, entitled—or even under an obligation—to return them to the customer. But in most cases monies paid by a customer for a holiday which has not commenced will be held either by the operator, or by the agent in circumstances where it is clear that he holds them as agent for the operator. The latter should always be the case where an agent holds monies after the confirmation of the booking in respect of which they were paid. This is because standard term 9(1) of the ATOL granted by the CAA requires all ATOL holders to notify travel agents that monies held by agents in respect of ATOL holidays are held as agents for the operator from the date of confirmation of the booking. This should be dealt with in the operator's brochure.

When does confirmation of a booking take place? On general principles of contract law, and in the absence of any contrary provision in the operator's booking conditions, it is when the confirmation, which is an acceptance of the offer contained in the holiday maker's booking form, is handed or posted to the holiday maker or his agent. In the past the confirmation of a booking was posted by the operator after the operator received the booking form from the agent.

The confirmation was normally posted to the agent who forwarded it to the customer. In these circumstances it could be argued that the contract was not concluded until the agent, whom the writers regard as the operator's booking agent, posted the confirmation to the customer. But it was generally accepted that posting by the operator to the agent concluded the contract.

Nowadays holiday bookings are often effected electronically. In such cases the booking is confirmed on the travel agent's VDU in the presence of the customer after the customer has completed the booking form and paid his deposit. The customer normally receives a computer print-out confirmation at the time, followed by a conventional confirmation-cum-invoice later. In these cases, any money which the agent collects is held by him for the operator from the moment the booking is made.

Assuming a clearcut case in which monies are held by a tour operator, or by a travel agent as the operator's agent, in respect of an ATOL holiday which "never gets off the ground", what will happen when a holiday maker contacts the agent through whom he booked the holiday? Some agents will immediately refund any monies which they still hold even though in law such monies should be accounted for to the liquidator. Some will go further and refund monies which they have already paid to the operator. As indicated on page 191, agents who provide money-back guarantees will often be under an obligation to do this but some other agents do it for goodwill purposes even though they are under no legal obligation to do so.

In cases where ABTA agents refund monies which have become the property of the operator, they require the customer to sign certain forms supplied by ABTA. These comprise a claim form, a form of assignment whereby the customer assigns the benefit of the customer's claim against the collapsed operator's liquidator, and an authority to the bond administrator to make payments in respect of the claim to the agent rather than to the customer himself. In cases where the agent does not itself make refunds, the customer is asked to sign the same forms—except for the one authorising payments to be made to the agent which is only appropriate in cases where the customer has received a refund from the agent.

The practical outcome will be the same in both cases, namely that the customer will obtain his refund—immediately from agents who adopt a policy of advancing refunds, or some months later from the TOSG, ABTA or the CAA if the agent through whom he booked does not operate such a policy.

The relevant procedures are explained fully in ABTA's Procedures for Financial Failures. And the policies applied by bond administrators in deciding what payments to make out of bond monies are explained in Policies on Administration of Tour Operators Bonds (available from the CAA).

## 4. The Barclays Bank case

The operation of the bonding system was considered in the case of *Barclays Bank & Others* v *TOSG Trust Fund Limited and others* (1984) 2 WLR 650. Although the point of law decided in it can be summarised fairly briefly, it is proposed to explain the facts in some detail because they illustrate in concrete terms the way in which the ATOL bonding system works. The essential facts are clearly set out in the summary contained in the 1984 Weekly Law Reports at page 650:

"In August 1974 the 13th defendant (C Ltd) a holiday tour operator, went into liquidation. The first defendant (TOSG), a company set up to receive and dispense at its complete discretion monies payable under bonds in the event of, *inter alia,* C Ltd being unable to fulfil its obligations to holiday makers, called up bonds given by the plaintiff banks. After repatriating holiday makers stranded abroad, TOSG expended the remaining bond money in repaying in full some of C Ltd's customers who had paid for holidays but not had them. When settling such claims, TOSG required the customers to assign their claims in the liquidation of C Ltd to the 12th defendant ("the Agency") a body established in 1975 to manage and administer a statutory fund for compensating persons losing holidays as a result of the collapse of tour operators. Pursuant to counter-indemnities obtained from C Ltd when the bonds had been executed, the banks proved in the liquidation, *inter alia,* in respect of such part of the bond moneys as had been dispensed by TOSG to the customers who had lost their holidays, and the Agency proved, *inter alia,* in respect of the claims assigned by those customers. The liquidators contended that the two proofs reflected the same debt and that, under the rule against double proof, one or other of them must be reduced accordingly. The banks brought an action for, *inter alia,* a declaration that they were entitled to prove to the exclusion of the Agency for the sum involved, and the Agency counterclaimed for declarations that the liquidators should reject the bank's proof and admit the Agency's proof".

C Ltd was Clarksons, a member of TOSG. By virtue of s.26 of the Civil Aviation Act 1971 and regulation 3 of the Civil Aviation (Air Travel Organiser's Licensing) Regulations 1972 it could not act as an air travel organiser without a licence from the CAA. The CAA granted a licence subject to Clarksons obtaining bonds totalling £2,225,850 from substantial financial institutions.

One of the institutions which agreed to provide a bond in favour of TOSG was Barclays Bank. Clarksons and Barclays entered into a formal counter-indemnity agreement in which Clarksons requested and authorised Barclays to provide a £500,000 bond to TOSG and undertook to indemnify Barclays:

> "against all payments actions . . . which you may make suffer incur or sustain by reason or on account of you (Barclays) having executed the bond".

The bond stated that Barclays was "held and firmly bound unto TOSG in the sum of £500,000 . . ." and it was declared to be void unless during the period of 12 calendar months commencing 1 October 1973 Clarksons should cease trading. The bond imposed certain obligations on TOSG one of them being that:

> "upon payment of the said sum of £500,000 . . . (TOSG) will . . . repay to (Barclays) on demand such part of the said sum as shall not be expended or required by (TOSG) in the performance and execution of its rights duties, powers and discretions as set out in (TOSG's) memorandum and articles of association and that such memorandum and articles will not be altered during the currency of this bond without the prior written consent of (Barclays) (which shall not be unreasonably withheld) first obtained".

During the period of the bond Clarksons ceased trading. Immediately TOSG required Barclays and the other banks involved to pay the aggregate sum of £2,226,000 secured by the various bonds. Subsequently a winding-up order was made against Clarksons as a result of which Barclays' right to repayment under the counter-indemnity given by Clarksons became a right to prove as a creditor in Clarksons' liquidation. TOSG spent £958,000 of the total bond monies in assisting and repatriating stranded Clarksons holiday makers. The balance was devoted to making refunds to customers who in the event never received the Clarksons' holidays for which they had paid.

The role of the Air Travel Reserve Fund Agency ("the Agency") the predecessor of the Air Travel Reserve Trust has already been mentioned, and the mechanics of its operation are described in the following passage from Templeman LJ's judgment in the Barclays Bank case:

> "By an agreement ("the assignment agreement") dated 23 July 1975 and made between TOSG and the Agency, but to which the banks were not parties, it was agreed that TOSG would, subject to the retention of certain reserves and expenses, employ all the moneys remaining in the hands of TOSG and applicable for the purpose of alleviating the consequences of the business failure of Clarksons in repaying in full, so far as the moneys would go, deposits and advance payments made by Clarksons' customers who never, in the event, enjoyed the holidays for which they had paid. The Agency agreed to pay the claims of all Clarksons' customers remaining outstanding after the moneys available to TOSG to reimburse Clarksons' customers were exhausted. TOSG agreed that before paying any customer of Clarksons, TOSG 'will obtain an assignment in favour of the Agency from the payee of his right to prove in the liquidation of Clarksons . . . for the full amount of his claim'. TOSG paid £1,268,000, part of the aggregate sum of £2,226,000 provided by the banks pursuant to their bonds to Clarksons' customers. Each customer who received part of the sum of £1,268,000 lodged a claim with the joint liquidators of Clarksons, and assigned in writing to the Agency "all my . . . rights against (Clarksons) under my . . . claims against (Clarksons) in respect of overseas holidays which I . . . have lodged with the joint liquidators".

The dispute between Barclays and the other banks providing bonds on the one hand and the Agency on the other arose because both claimed in Clarksons' liquidation for the sum of £1,268,000, being the total monies paid by TOSG in making refunds to Clarksons' customers.

The banks' claims were made under the counter-indemnities given by Clarksons to each of them (see *ante*). The Agency claimed on the grounds that the assignments to the Agency obtained by TOSG gave the Agency the right to prove for £1,268,000.

The House of Lords held that:

> "Upon the true and simple construction of the bond and the indemnity, when TOSG paid £1,000 of Barclays' money to a customer whose claim against Clarksons amounted to £1,000, the claim of that customer against Clarksons was extinguished and there became vested in Barclays an indisputable claim against Clarksons for £1,000 under the indemnity. If TOSG paid £200 to a customer whose claim was £1,000, then the customer could thereafter only claim and prove for the balance of £800 and Barclays could claim and prove under its indemnity for £200. By the indemnity Clarksons agreed to repay to the banks every penny that the banks paid under the bond and that TOSG paid to the customers".

In arriving at its decision the House of Lords rejected the argument that the payment of refunds by TOSG entitled it to direct the customers concerned to assign the benefit of their claims to the Agency. This was because TOSG's memorandum of association meant that TOSG were "only authorised agents for the distribution to customers of monies provided by the bonds". The House of Lords held that there were originally two mutually exclusive debts, "namely the debt which Clarksons owed the customers under the contracts and the debt which Clarksons owed the banks under their indemnities". The payments by TOSG reduced the customers' debts by £1,268,000, leaving them with nothing to assign to the Agency, and increased by the like sum the amount owed by Clarksons to the various banks.

## 5. Credit card payments

### (a) Section 75, Consumer Credit Act

A situation which has given rise to considerable disagreement is where a holiday maker uses a credit card to make payments to the *travel agent* through whom he books his holiday. The problem concerns the application of s.75(1) of the Consumer Credit Act 1974 which provides that:

> "If the debtor under a debtor-creditor-supplier agreement falling within section 12(b) or (c) has, in relation to a transaction financed by the agreement, any claim against the supplier in respect of a misrepresentation or breach of contract, he shall have a like claim against the creditor, who, with the supplier, shall accordingly be jointly and severally liable to the debtor".

Section 189 of the 1974 Act defines terms used throughout the Act, some of which must be mentioned to appreciate the significance of s.75. A debtor is defined as "the individual receiving credit under a consumer credit agreement" and a creditor as "the person providing credit under a consumer credit agreement". Consumer credit agreements include *inter alia,* debtor-creditor-supplier agreements (see next paragraph) which can be either restricted use credit agreements or unrestricted use credit agreements. The former are, in general terms, the types of agreement under which credit cards are issued. Thus, the creditor referred to in s.75 can be the issuer of a credit card.

A supplier is someone other than the creditor with whom the debtor comes to an arrangement to purchase goods, services or land. The definition of "debtor-creditor-supplier agreement" contained in s.12 of the 1974 Act is extremely abstract and we quote instead the explanation given in the OFT Booklet *"Regulated and Exempt Agreements"*:

> "Generally, a debtor-creditor-supplier agreement will arise when the creditor is connected in some way with the transaction to be financed by the credit

advanced: for example where the creditor and the supplier of the goods, services or whatever is financed by the credit, are one and the same person. Thus a retailer offering his own credit or a finance house making a hire purchase transaction will be entering into a debtor-creditor-supplier agreement. If the creditor and the supplier are different people, the agreement will be a debtor-creditor-supplier agreement only if there are arrangements between them under which the creditor is prepared to finance the transaction between the supplier and the customer. An example of what would normally be debtor-creditor-supplier credit is a high street shop arranging a personal loan with a finance house for its customers to finance their purchases in the shop. A credit card or trading check for use in certain shops will also usually involve debtor-creditor-supplier credit".

Under s.189 the verb "to finance" means to finance "wholly or partly". Accordingly, it appears not to be necessary in order for s.75 to apply for the creditor to have provided the total funds needed by the debtor to make his purchase from the supplier but merely some of them. In other words, although this may not be accepted by all credit card companies, where a customer uses his credit card to pay the initial deposit but not the subsequent final balance (or *vice versa*) s.75 applies if it would apply if the whole price had been paid by credit card.

## (b) Rights against a credit card company

One of the effects of s.75 is that a customer who purchases goods from a supplier and pays for them by credit card will, in the event that the supplier is liable in law to the customer for misrepresentation or breach of contract, be able to make a claim against the credit card company identical to that which he can make against the supplier. Although the Act permits the creditor to seek an indemnity from the supplier, it does not allow him to seek to exclude this liability to the customer. This is so even where the debtor, by entering into the transaction in question, exceeds his credit limit or in any other way breaks the terms of the credit agreement. However, in such an event, it may be possible for the creditor to counterclaim against the debtor.

There are certain limitations to the credit agreements and types of purchase to which s.75 applies, namely:

(a) The cost of the item being purchased must be more than £100 and not more than £30,000 (including VAT).

(b) The credit agreement must be "regulated" within the meaning of the 1974 Act. This means, amongst other things, that the borrower must not be a corporation and the credit made available must not exceed £15,000.

(c) The credit agreement must not have been made before 1 July 1977.

(d) The number of payments to be made by the debtor in repayment of the whole amount of credit provided in any period must exceed one.

The latter is especially important since it creates a distinction between charge cards, such as American Express, which are *not* subject to the Act and credit cards, such as Access and Barclaycard, which are.

It is possible for a holiday maker to pay direct by credit card to the tour operator providing the holiday. In this event, it is easy to see s.75's application. The holiday maker is the debtor, the tour operator the supplier and the credit card company the creditor. If the tour operator commits a breach of contract or misrepresentation, the holiday maker can direct his claim against either the tour operator or the credit card company or both. The credit card company, provided that the tour operator is liable in law for breach of contract or misrepresentation, will be liable to compensate the holiday maker and cannot seek to avoid liability by claiming that it was not responsible for making the holiday arrangements.

Payments to the travel agents through whom holidays have been booked have however, created difficulties.

Following the collapse of Laker, it was unable to supply holidays which it had contracted to supply and was therefore in breach of contract. Some of Laker's customers, who had paid by credit card the travel agents through whom the holidays were booked, claimed under s.75 against the credit card companies for the refund of the purchase price.

When these claims were made against Barclaycard and Access, they rejected liability on the grounds that the relevant supplier for the purposes of s.75 was not Laker but the travel agent to whom the holiday maker effected payment. They maintained that the collapse of the tour operator, Laker, did not involve any breach of contract by the travel agent so s.75 did not apply. Holiday makers in this position then found that the Air Travel Reserve Fund Agency maintained that the credit card companies were liable under s.75 and that therefore the holiday makers had not suffered any loss in law.

In the event, Barclaycard and Access reached agreement with the Agency regarding the apportionment of responsibility for claims from Laker customers. In the case of Access, the principles of that agreement have been carried forward into a new agreement with the Air Travel Trust. Barclaycard have made alternative insurance arrangements. The practical outcome is that claims by customers who use Access to pay for their holiday are dealt with via the bonding system whereas Barclaycard customers are reimbursed by Barclaycard.

The actions taken by Access and Barclaycard mean that the question of whether a credit card company can be held liable under s.75 where a credit card is used to pay the *travel agent* for a holiday may never be litigated.

## 6. Collapse of a travel agent

The collapse of a tour operator is a traumatic event for customers who have booked holidays with it. The collapse of a travel agent creates far fewer ripples but does generate some legal problems which require consideration. In relation to package holidays these arise where the agent holds monies which have been paid by customers for onward transmission to tour operators.

If the agent holds monies on behalf of a tour operator, there is no problem so far as the customer is concerned. This is because—certainly in cases involving ATOL holidays and probably in other cases—the agent will not be holding a sum on behalf of the operator unless the customer's booking has been accepted by the operator. In that event there is a firm contract between the operator and the customer which is not affected by the collapse of the agent who helped to bring it into being.

There will of course be a problem for the operator because it is owed money by an insolvent company. But that in no way relieves the operator of its obligations to the customers concerned. They have paid their deposit or balance of holiday price to the operator's agent who holds it on the operator's behalf and they are entitled to the full benefit of their contracts with the operator. The operator will have to prove as an unsecured creditor in the agent's liquidation and hope that the agent's net assets will be sufficient to enable the liquidator to pay a substantial dividend. Any shortfall will not be recoverable from the customers.

What is the position where the agent holds monies which belong to the customer? The most likely instance of that is where at the time of the agent's collapse a booking has been taken but not yet accepted by the operator. The operator may be reluctant to accept the booking if he knows that the deposit for it is held by an insolvent agent—and even more reluctant if the booking is a late one in respect of which the customer has paid the whole holiday price to the agent.

The initial presumption is that in this situation the operator is under no obligation to accept the booking and provide the holiday unless the customer sends him another cheque, and that the customer will be left with the thankless task of proving in the agent's liquidation in the hope of recovering some of what he paid to the agent. This would seem to follow from the basic fact that the money held by the agent belongs to the customer. However this may not be the case if, as is submitted in

Chapter 3, the agent when taking bookings, is acting as booking agent for the operator. If that is so, the courts might imply a collateral contract between the operator and the customer whereby, in return for the customer effecting the booking through the operator's agent, the operator warrants that monies can safely be paid to the agent. There are no decided cases regarding this but the explanation of collateral contracts on page 68 suggests that one may exist in the circumstances outlined in this paragraph.

Another case where a collapsed travel agent may be holding money which belongs to the customer is where a customer has cancelled his holiday. But for its collapse the agent would have refunded any monies held by it to the customer after deducting the appropriate cancellation charges. But the insolvency of the agent will limit the customer's rights against it to proving for his debt in the agent's liquidation. However, in the writers' opinion, the customer will also have a good claim against the operator because the customer's right to a partial refund on cancellation is part of the contract between the customer and the operator. This right should not be prejudiced because of a failure to perform on the part of the operator's appointed booking agent. Technically, the customer's claim against the operator will be for the shortfall of what he recovers in the liquidation of the agent but in practice the operator may well be prepared to pay in full and take over the customer's claim against the agent.

If the collapsed agent was a member of ABTA, much of the preceding paragraphs may be primarily of academic interest. This is because the ABTA Travel Agent's Fund (see page 5) will make good losses sustained by members of the travelling public as a result of the collapse of an ABTA travel agent. In addition it will usually make good any such losses sustained by ABTA tour operators.

# Appendix A

# Extracts from the Tour Operator's Code of Conduct and Guidelines for booking conditions

*The following extracts are reproduced with the permission of ABTA*

## CONDUCT BETWEEN TOUR OPERATORS AND MEMBERS OF THE PUBLIC

### 4.1 Minimum Standards of Brochures

Every brochure published by or in the name of any tour operator shall contain clear, comprehensive and accurate information to enable the client to exercise an informed judgment in making his choice, including:

(i) all information necessary to comply with the regulations for the time being of the Civil Aviation Authority and any other governmental or statutory licensing authority;

(ii) the legal identity of the tour operator responsible for publishing the brochure containing the tour, holiday or travel arrangement offered;

(iii) the means of travel (e.g. ship, coach, charter or other aircraft);

(iv) the destination and/or itinerary where applicable;

(v) the date, time and place of departure and return;

(vi) the nature of accommodation and meal facilities offered;

(vii) any additional facilities or special arrangements offered;

(viii) the total price or the means of arriving at the total price, together with a clear statement of the services included therein, and unless the tour operator has guaranteed his prices, it shall also include the base date by reference to which the price in the brochure was calculated, the relevant exchange rate published in the Financial Times World Value of the Pound Table on that date, and the conditions under which such price can be amended;

(ix) the procedure for booking and the contractual conditions under which the booking shall be made, if any;

(x) an accurate summary of the details of any insurance facilities offered.

## 4.2 Statutory Requirements for Brochures

Every brochure published by or in the name of a tour operator shall observe the requirements of the Trade Descriptions Act 1968, the Misrepresentation Act 1967, the Civil Aviation Act 1971 (including any regulations made thereunder) and the Unfair Contract Terms Act 1977, or any amendment or re-enactment thereof in accordance with the first principle of this Code as set out in paragraph 2.2.

## 4.3 Publication and Sale of Brochures

No tour operator shall publish or consent to the publication, or sell, or consent to the sale of, holidays from any brochure which does not conform with the Codes or Regulations of the recognised organisations mentioned in paragraph 2.2 and with all other relevant paragraphs of this Code.

## 4.4 Booking Conditions

(i) Booking conditions, if any, shall define the extent of the responsibilities as well as the limits of the liabilities of tour operators towards clients and shall be so designed that they are easily read and understood.

(ii) Booking conditions shall not include clauses:

(a) purporting to exclude or limit responsibility for misrepresentations made by the tour operator, his servants or his agents;

(b) purporting to exclude or limit responsibility for the tour operator's contractual duty to exercise diligence in making arrangements for his clients or for consequential loss following from breach of his duty; and

(c) stating that complaints will not be considered unless made within a fixed period after the end of a tour or holiday if such a period is of less than 28 days' duration.

(iii) Booking conditions (and/or brochures) shall prominently indicate the circumstances in which and the conditions on which surcharges may be made to clients.

(iv) Where booking conditions (and/or brochures) give a tour operator the right to make surcharges in the event of unfavourable variations in the rates of exchange, such booking conditions (and/or brochures) shall prominently indicate the tour operator's general policy in the event of favourable variations in the rates of exchange.

(v) Booking Conditions shall clearly indicate the tour operator's general policy both in the event of his cancelling and in the event of his altering a tour, holiday or other travel arrangements.

(vi) Booking Conditions referring to arbitration in accordance with paragraph 4.11 of this Code shall not deny to clients the option of taking action in the Courts if they so wish.

(vii) A tour operator shall not print his booking conditions (or insurance details) on the front or on the back of booking forms unless all such conditions (and insurance details) are provided separately to every client on or before confirmation of the booking.

(viii) Booking conditions shall conform with all relevant provisions of this Code.

(ix) Tour operators shall in practice interpret their booking conditions in accordance with the provisions of this Code.

## 4.5 Cancellation of Tours, Holidays or other Travel Arrangements by Tour Operators

(i) A tour operator shall not cancel a tour, holiday or other travel arrangements after the date when payment of the balance of the price becomes due unless it is necessary to do so as a result of hostilities, political unrest or other circumstances amounting to force majeure, or unless the client defaults in payment of such balance.

(ii) If a tour operator, for reasons other than hostilities, political unrest or other circumstances amounting to force majeure, cancels a holiday, tour or other travel arrangements on or before the date when payment of the balance of the price becomes due, he shall inform agents and direct clients as soon as possible, and shall offer clients the choice of an alternative holiday of at least comparable standard if available, or of a prompt and full refund of all money paid. Any such refunds shall be sent to agents within 10 clear days and to direct clients within 14 clear days.

(iii) If a tour operator has to cancel a tour, holiday or other travel arrangements as a result of hostilities, political unrest or other circumstances amounting to force majeure, he shall inform agents and direct clients without delay and shall offer clients the choice of an alternative holiday of at least comparable standard, if available, or a prompt and full refund of all money paid. Any such refunds shall be sent to agents within 10 clear days and to direct clients within 14 clear days.

## 4.6 Alterations to Tours, Holidays and other Travel Arrangements by Tour Operators

(i) If a tour operator makes a material alteration to a tour,

209

holiday or other travel arrangement for which a booking has already been made, he shall inform agents and direct clients without delay and shall give clients the choice of either accepting the alteration which must be of at least comparable standard, if available, or of receiving a prompt and full refund of all money paid. Any such refunds shall be sent to agents within 10 clear days and to direct clients within 14 clear days.

(ii) If a tour operator makes a material alteration to a tour, holiday or other travel arrangement after the date when payment of the balance price becomes due, he shall also ensure that clients receive reasonable compensation which may be in accordance with a scale of payments. The right to receive compensation and any scale of payments shall be clearly stated in the relevant booking conditions.

(iii) A tour operator shall not make a material alteration to a tour holiday or other travel arrangement unless he does so in time to inform agents and direct clients not less than 14 days before the date of commencement of the tour, holiday or other travel arrangements.

(iv) Where a material alteration is necessary due to hostilities, political unrest or other circumstances amounting to force majeure, the above sub-paragraphs shall not apply. A tour operator shall, however, inform agents and direct clients without delay and shall give clients the choice of either accepting the alteration which must be of at least comparable standard, if available, or of receiving a prompt and full refund of all money. Any such refunds shall be sent to agents within 10 clear days and to direct clients within 14 clear days.

(v) For the purpose of the above sub-paragraphs material alterations shall not include:

(a) delays in departures on a tour, holiday or other travel arrangement caused by weather conditions, technical problems to transport, strikes, industrial action or other circumstances beyond the control of the operator;

(b) changes resulting from overbooking by hotels (see paragraph 4.7 below).

## 4.7 Overbooked Hotels

(i) A tour operator shall take all reasonable steps to ensure that tours, holidays or other travel arrangements are not cancelled or altered as a result of overbooking.

(ii) Where tours, holidays or other travel arrangements, are cancelled or altered as a result of overbooking by hotels, a tour operator shall only be deemed to have taken all reasonable steps to prevent the cancellation or alteration if he can show that the overbooking occurred for reasons beyond his control.

(iii) If, despite sub-paragraphs (i) and (ii) above, a hotel is overbooked and a tour operator knows this before the departure of the affected clients, he shall immediately inform those clients and shall offer them the choice of an alternative holiday of at least comparable standard, if available, or a full and prompt refund of all money paid.

(iv) If, despite sub-paragraphs (i) and (ii) above, a hotel is overbooked and a tour operator does not know this before the departure of affected clients, such clients shall on arrival at their destination be offered alternative accommodation and shall also be offered reasonable compensation for 'disturbance' where the location and/or facilities of the alternative accommodation can reasonably be regarded as inferior to that originally booked.

(v) For the purpose of the above sub-paragraphs, hotels include accommodation of other kinds such as apartments, villas, guest houses and camping sites.

## 4.8 Cancellation of Tours, Holidays or other Travel Arrangements by Clients

A tour operator shall clearly state in his booking conditions the amount of, or the basis for calculating, the cancellation fees which the client shall be liable to incur, as well as the terms and conditions under which the client shall be liable to incur such fees.

## 4.9 Complaints and Correspondence from the Association

(i) Complaints shall be dealt with promptly and efficiently and in the event of a dispute with a client every effort shall be made to settle the matter amicably and as quickly as possible.

(ii) All correspondence from the Association about complaints and compliance with the Articles of Association and this Code shall be dealt with promptly and efficiently.

## 4.10 Conciliation

In the event of a breakdown in communication or a serious disagreement between the tour operator and the client, ABTA is prepared to intervene to give help and impartial guidance and to offer the facilities of conciliation.

## 4.11 Arbitration

(i) Tour operators shall include as a term of any contract relating to the sale of their inclusive holidays or tours a provision whereby any dispute arising out of, or in connection with, such sale which is not amicably settled, may be referred to arbitration under a special scheme devised for the travel industry by the Chartered Institute of Arbitrators by arrangement with the Association of British Travel Agents. It shall also be stated that:

(a) the scheme provides for a simple and inexpensive method of arbitration on documents alone with restricted liability of the client in respect of costs;

(b) the scheme does not apply to claims for an amount greater than £1,500 per person or £7,500 per booking form or to claims which are solely or mainly in respect of physical injury or illness or the consequences of such injury or illness;

(c) details of the scheme will be supplied on request.

(ii) Where a client indicates in writing that he wishes to refer an unresolved dispute to arbitration, the tour operator shall complete the necessary formalities promptly and efficiently and shall comply with the terms of the Arbitration Scheme referred to in sub-paragraph (i) above and in particular with all the relevant rules and regulations of the Chartered Institute of Arbitrators for the time being in force. Tour operators should also deal with correspondence from the Association about compliance with these rules and regulations promptly and efficiently.

(*NOTE: A suggested clause for inclusion in booking conditions is set out as an Appendix to this Code*).

## 4.12 Advertising

(i) All advertising by tour operators shall observe the requirements of the Trade Descriptions Act 1968, the Misrepresentation Act 1967 and the Civil Aviation Act 1971 (including any regulations made thereunder) and of any amendment or re-enactment thereof in accordance with the first principle of this Code as set out in paragraph 2.2 and with all other relevant paragraphs of this Code.

(ii) All advertising by tour operators shall comply with the Codes or Regulations of the recognised organisations or associations mentioned in paragraph 2.2 and with all other relevant paragraphs of this Code.

(iii) A tour operator shall not advertise in such a manner as to suggest that other members of the Association may become insolvent.

(iv) A tour operator shall show his ABTA number in all his press advertisements for travel business, but shall not be obliged to do so where these advertisements are in classified run-on form unless such advertisements contain any reference to ABTA.

(v) Before employing a trading name (which for these purposes means a name which is not either the correct corporate name or in the case of an unincorporated business, the name under which ABTA membership is enjoyed) a tour operator shall ensure that he has notified ABTA of such trading name in compliance with ABTA's regulations for such notification.

## 4.13 Transactions and Correspondence

Transactions with clients shall be treated as confidential and correspondence shall be dealt with promptly.

## 4.14 Surcharges – Limit on imposition

A tour operator shall not surcharge a client less than 30 clear days before the date of the commencement of such client's holiday, tour or other travel arrangements. Tour operators shall ensure that at least within 30 clear days before the date of commencement, prices they quote in response to enquiries include any surcharge payable.

## 4.15 Surcharges – ABTA Standards

A tour operator shall ensure that his conduct complies with the principles and rules and procedures contained in 'ABTA Standards on Surcharges' as published by the Association from time to time.

## 4.16 Surcharges Justification and Verification

A surcharge by a tour operator in respect of currency rates, fuel or aviation cost changes or as a result of government action shall in all cases only be made if the tour operator can show that it is necessary for him to do so for reasons beyond his control.

## 4.17 Explanation of Surcharges

A tour operator who makes an additional charge to a client shall give written notice to the client of the additional charge and of its main cost heads and shall also provide, or have available to provide on request, a reasonable written explanation of the reasons for the additional charge by reference to each main cost head.

## 4.18 Airport and Seaport Taxes

Tour Operators shall include airport and seaport taxes in the prices quoted in brochures and advertisements for inclusive holidays in Europe, but shall not be obliged to do so where such holidays are sold in Northern Ireland. For this purpose Europe shall mean Eire, the Channel Islands, the Continent of Europe west of the Ural Mountains, any country or island with a Mediterranean coastline, Madeira, the Azores and the Canary Islands.

### 4.19 Misleading Use of ABTA Symbol

A tour operator shall not, directly or indirectly, cause, permit, assist or encourage a company or firm trading as a tour operator or travel agent which is not a member of the Association to represent itself as a member by the use of the ABTA symbol or by any ABTA number on brochures or other documents or by any other means which may give the false impression to the public that such company or firm is a member of the Association, or in relation to travel business be connected or associated in any way (including through any of its proprietors, shareholders, officers or personnel) with any such company or firm which so misrepresents itself.

. . . . .

# ABTA GUIDELINES FOR BOOKING CONDITIONS

(*Note:* These Guidelines are informal and do not form part of the Tour Operators' Code of Conduct. Nor are they binding on the Code of Conduct Committee or the Tour Operators' Council who, when adjudicating on cases referred to them under the relevant clauses in the Code relating to Infringement and Enforcement, have to consider each case on its merits in the light of all the particular circumstances.)

## INTRODUCTION

    **1.1** It is a matter of fundamental importance that the contracts which ABTA tour operators enter into with their customers should be, and should be seen to be, fair and reasonable.

    **1.2** It is for this reason that the Tour Operators' Code of Conduct contains over thirty clauses and sub-clauses relating to booking conditions.

    **1.3** Most of the relevant provisions in the Code are quite clear on their face. But in some cases questions of interpretation can and do arise. It is in relation to the latter that it is hoped that these Guidelines will be particularly helpful to ABTA tour operators.

## BASIC PRINCIPLES

    **2.1** The basic principles are:

        (i) That brochures shall contain clear, comprehensive and accurate information to enable the client to exercise an informed judgement in making his choice (clause 4.1);

        (ii) that booking conditions shall define the extent of the responsibilities as well as the limits of the liabilities of tour operators towards clients (clause 4.4(i));

        (iii) that booking conditions shall be so designed that they are easily read and understood (clause 4.4(i)).

    **2.2** The following examples are not intended to be comprehensive but merely illustrate the application of those basic principles.

        (i) It must be quite clear to clients what are the conditions

214

which apply to their bookings. This may well be unclear if booking conditions are printed under headings such as 'Holiday Information', 'General Information', 'Facts about your Tour', or 'Your Questions Answered'. It is particularly objectionable if what are in effect booking conditions are included under some such heading on one page of a brochure, while another page contains the main booking conditions under a heading which clearly identifies them as such.

(ii) Put the other way, it is preferable as a general rule that all booking conditions are included in one section of the brochure under a heading which makes it clear that the section contains all the terms of the client's contract with the tour operator.

(iii) This is not to say that tour operators may not, for example, indicate the existence of a price guarantee on a separate page of the brochure (or on the cover) provided that there is a clear cross-reference to the actual terms of the guarantee. Nor does it mean that tour operators may not indicate the terms of guarantees in bold panels as promotional aids. But in no circumstances must the wording of such panels be negated by the booking conditions themselves, so that clients may gain a false impression about the scope of the guarantee.

(iv) The print-face of booking conditions should be large enough to be easily read. But it is not only the size of the print-face which is relevant in this context. Sometimes booking conditions whose print-face would otherwise be quite large enough cannot be easily read because of their colour in relation to the colour of the background. For example, black print-face against a background of dark blue sky can of itself render booking conditions virtually unreadable.

(v) Words in Latin and legal jargon invariably mean that conditions cannot be easily understood and should be avoided.

**2.3** It is a basic principle of the Code that the client should be able to retain a copy of the terms of his contract with the tour operator. This is why clause 4.4(vii) requires that booking conditions (and insurance details) must not be printed on the front or on the back of booking forms (unless they are provided separately to every client on or before confirmation of the booking).

**2.4** It follows from paragraph 2.3 above that a cross-reference to conditions in main brochures is insufficient and all brochures, including those containing 'flight only' programmes, should contain booking conditions for clients to retain without imposing an obligation on them to obtain a main brochure in order to read them.

215

## PRICES

**3.1** There are some clauses in the Tour Operators' Code of Conduct which elaborate on the basic principles referred to above in relation to specific problem areas, of which the main example is the price the client will have to pay for his holiday. This is because the price he will have to pay is obviously a fundamental consideration in his mind when he books his holidays.

**3.2** The Code does not seek to intervene in the pricing policies of ABTA tour operators. This is a matter for their individual commercial discretion. The Code therefore contains no provisions bearing directly on the question of prices.

**3.3** However, the following clauses relate to the way in which prices and possible changes in prices shall be presented in brochures:

(i) Clause 4.1(viii) requires a brochure to contain a clear statement of the date on which the price in the brochure was calculated and of the conditions under which such price can be amended;

(ii) Clause 4.18 requires airport and seaport taxes to be included in the prices of inclusive holidays in Europe, except where such holidays are sold in Northern Ireland.

(iii) Clause 4.4(iii) requires that booking conditions shall prominently indicate the circumstances in which and the conditions of which surcharges may be made to clients;

(iv) Clause 4.4(iv) requires that where booking conditions give the tour operator the right to make surcharges in the event of unfavourable variations in the rate of exchange, they shall also prominently indicate the tour operator's general policy in the event of favourable fluctuations in the rates of exchange; and

(v) Clause 4.17 requires tour operators who impose a surcharge to give clients written notice of the surcharge and of its main cost heads and also to provide (or have available to provide on request) a reasonable written explanation of the reasons for the additional charge by reference to each such cost head.

**3.4** The following are the main problems in this area which have come to light in the course of ABTA's monitoring of brochures.

(i) Booking conditions should not include such phrases as 'the prices in this brochure are calculated at the date of going to press' because clients do not know when a brochure 'went to press'. Clause 4.1(viii) requires a specific date to be mentioned.

(ii) It is a breach of clause 4.1(viii) for a tour operator to

216

impose 'fuel' or 'transportation' or other surcharges if it is not clear to clients that the relevant booking conditions entitle the tour operator so to do. For example, references in booking conditions to surcharges in the event of action by 'Government' or 'Governments and Governmental agencies' would not lead clients to expect to have to pay surcharges because of an increase in the price of commodities such as aviation fuel.

(iii) Where booking conditions say that no surcharges will be imposed after clients have received 'final invoices', invoices should clearly indicate whether or not they are 'final invoices'.

(iv) Booking conditions should not give the impression that surcharges may be imposed in the last 30 days before the commencement of clients' holidays. Otherwise the conditions are in breach of Clause 4.4(viii) read with clause 4.14.

## CANCELLATIONS AND MATERIAL ALTERATIONS

**4.1** In the case of cancellations or material alterations, clauses 4.5 and 4.6 of the Code require tour operators to offer clients a choice of an alternative comparable holiday (if available) or their money back. This must be a genuine choice. Tour operators should not offer an alternative holiday first and then, only if the client complains, agree to a refund.

**4.2** Booking conditions should not give the impression (for example, by the use of such expressions as 'at the tour operator's discretion') that tour operators may cancel arrangements after the date when payment of balance becomes due for reasons other than force majeure or non-payment by the client, as such a condition would be in breach of Clause 4.4(viii) and Clause 4.5(i).

**4.3** For the purpose of Clause 4.5, the Code of Conduct Committee will regard a tour, holiday or other travel arrangement as having been CANCELLED if it is changed in such a way that the revised arrangements amount to the substitution of an entirely different tour etc. Much will depend on the particular circumstances of each case, but the Committee will normally regard the following as examples of changes amounting to CANCELLATIONS which therefore cannot be made after the date when payments of the balance price becomes due and if made before that date entitle clients to an alternative comparable holiday or a full refund of all money paid:

(i) a change of resort to one in a different country or one in the same country but an unreasonable distance from the original resort or one of a different type;

(ii) a change in accommodation to that of an entirely different type;

217

     (iii) a change of flight time of more than 24 hours;

    (iv) a change of airport to one which is substantially less accessible to the client;

    (v) a change of itinerary omitting a main advertised place or event;

    (vi) increased cost other than surcharges levied in accordance with the Code.

**4.4** For the purpose of Clause 4.6, the Code of Conduct Committee will regard a tour, holiday or other travel arrangement as having been MATERIALLY ALTERED if it is changed in such a way that the revised arrangements, although not amounting to a cancellation (see paragraph 4.3 above), nevertheless involves a significant change to the tour etc. originally booked. Much will depend on the particular circumstances of each case, but the Committee will normally regard the following as examples of changes amounting to MATERIAL ALTERATIONS which therefore cannot be made during the last 14 days before departure and, which, if made after the date when payment of the balance price becomes due, entitle clients to an alternative comparable holiday or to a full and prompt refund of all money paid and, in either case, to receive compensation which may be in accordance with a scale of payments. (The right to receive compensation and any scale of payments must be clearly stated in the relevant booking conditions):

    (i) a significant change of resort;

    (ii) a change of accommodation to that of a lower category and/or price;

    (iii) a change of flight time imposing substantial inconvenience on clients or involving a reduction in time spent at the resort which is significant in relation to the length of the holiday;

    (iv) a change of airport which is inconvenient to the client.

**4.5** It is difficult to define precisely the expression in Clauses 4.5 and 4.6 of the Code 'or other circumstances amounting to force majeure'. Broadly speaking, the Committee will define this as referring to circumstances such as natural disasters (e.g. epidemics) and it will certainly exclude from the definition decisions to cancel or materially alter tours, holidays and other travel arrangements made for commercial reasons such as failure to obtain desirable load factors.

# ARBITRATION

**5.1** Clause 4.11(i) of the Code requires booking conditions to include reference to the Arbitration Scheme for the Travel Industry.

**5.2** It is important that the relevant booking condition should include all the matters specifically referred to in sub-clauses (a), (b), and (c) of clause 4.11(i). For example, the condition should not omit to mention that arbitration on documents is inexpensive and that there is restricted liability on clients in respect of costs. Otherwise clients who might have wished to refer a dispute to arbitration may be discouraged from so doing.

**5.3** It is fundamental that clients should not be deprived of their right to take action in the Courts if they so wish. Clause 4.4(vi) of the Code specifically prohibits booking conditions from denying this right to clients. It follows that a booking condition which says that disputes 'shall' be referred to arbitration or otherwise requires disputes to be referred to arbitration is a breach of this clause.

**5.4** The Appendix to the Code contains a suggested arbitration clause for inclusion in booking conditions.

## MISCELLANEOUS

**6.1** Deposits must not be referred to as 'non-refundable', because in certain circumstances the Code requires all money paid by clients to be refunded.

**6.2** It is not possible in law for a tour operator to exclude responsibility for the performance of his contract with his clients by stating in his booking conditions that he contracts only as an agent for carriers, hoteliers and other suppliers if in fact he is selling a package as principal. This is normally the case and ABTA's clear legal advice is that in such circumstances a clause of this sort is no less than a mis-statement of fact which contravenes clauses 4.4(i) and 4.4(ii)(b) of the Code.

**6.3** Booking conditions must not impose a limitation (for instance, the amount of the holiday cost) on or exclude a tour operator's liability for his failure to exercise diligence in making arrangements for his clients. Such a limitation or exclusion is prohibited by clause 4.4(ii)(b) of the Code.

**6.4** Under the Unfair Contract Terms Act 1977, a booking condition excluding or restricting liability for death or personal injury resulting from negligence is void. Such a condition is therefore in breach of clause 4.2 of the Code.

**6.5** Booking conditions to the effect that 'luggage is at all times at the owner's risk' are in breach of clause 4.4(ii)(b) of the Code because they have the effect of excluding the tour operator's responsibility to exercise diligence.

**6.6** Brochures offering travel arrangements which include tickets for future special events must be suitably qualified if the availability of tickets cannot be guaranteed. Otherwise the brochure is misleading in contravention of clauses 4.1 and 4.3 of the Code.

## CONCLUSION

**7.1** The ABTA Secretariat is pleased to give informal advice to ABTA tour operators about the application of the Tour Operators' Code of Conduct to booking conditions.

**7.2** However, tour operators who take advantage of this facility may not indicate that their booking conditions are approved by ABTA or the Office of Fair Trading.

**7.3** Nor can tour operators seek to avoid their own prime responsibility for ensuring that booking conditions comply fully with all the applicable clauses of the Code.

# Appendix B

# Air Travel Organisers' Licence Schedule of Standard Terms

## Standard Term 1

  (i)  The licence holder shall quote clearly and legibly:—

    (a) the licence number stated at the head of the licence and his name on all publicity material in which he holds himself out as a person who does or may make available accommodation for the carriage of persons on flights and which is published between the date on which the licence is issued and the date on which it expires

    (b) his name and licence number on every booking form or other document forming or evidencing the formation of a contract for the carriage of persons on flights which he issues during the currency of his licence.

  (ii)  Where the licence holder has authorised an agent to act on his behalf he shall ensure that the agent states that he is acting as agent for the licence holder and quotes clearly and legibly the licence holder's name and licence number on all publicity material in which the agent holds himself out as a person who does or may make available accommodation for the carriage of persons on flights as agent for the licence holder and on any booking form or other document forming or evidencing the formation of a contract for the carriage of persons on flights which the agent issues on behalf of the licence holder.

  (iii) For the purposes of Standard Term 1 where the licence holder is a company the licence holder's name shall be the registered name of the company.

## Standard Term 2 A

The licence holder shall keep in force for the period stated in the licence a Bond of the amount so stated, being a Bond entered into by a person approved for that purpose by the Authority, which Bond shall be deposited with the Authority and shall, where the licence holder is a limited company, be in the terms set out in Part I of

Schedule 3 published in the Civil Aviation Authority Official Record Series 3 — Part I Air Travel Organisers' Licensing, and where the licence holder is not a limited company, be in the terms set out in Part II of the said Schedule 3.

## Standard Term 2 B

The licence holder shall throughout the period of the licence comply with the bonding requirements of the Association of British Travel Agents Limited or of the Tour Operators' Study Group from time to time in force, and in pursuance thereof shall obtain and keep in force a bond or other security of the amount stated in the licence;

> provided that, if at any time those bonding requirements are not such as to ensure that in the event of the bond or other security being realised the said amount (after deduction of the costs of administration) will be used for the benefit of persons who have paid for but have not received accommodation for carriage by air to be provided by the licence holder under the authority of the licence (except insofar as the said amount exceeds what is required for this purpose), the holder shall comply with Standard Term 2 A.

## Standard Term 3

1   Not later than one month after the end of each period ending 31 March, 30 June, 30 September and 31 December during which the licence is in force, the licence holder shall furnish to the Authority in a manner set out in Annex A hereto a statement of the number of passengers carried on flights during that period whose accommodation on the flight was made available to them by him pursuant to the licence, showing the number of such passengers carried by each airline.

For the purposes of Standard Term 3 a flight shall be deemed to have taken place on the date on which it ends.

2   Not later than one month after the end of each period ending 31 March, 30 June, 30 September and 31 December during which the licence is in force, the licence holder shall furnish to the Authority in a manner set out in Annex B hereto a certificate of his turnover during the period.

3   The licence holder shall annually furnish to the Authority in a manner set out in Annex C hereto a report by auditors appointed by the licence holder on his turnover during each period ending 31 March, 30 June, 30 September and 31 December during which the licence is in force. For the purposes of Standard Term 3 the auditors who furnish the report shall be the same auditors as those who sign the licence holder's audited accounts for the year in question or

such other auditors as may be approved by the Authority for the purpose.

## Standard Term 4 A

The licence holder shall furnish to the Authority a copy of any brochure in which he or any agent acting on his behalf quotes the prices at which he is prepared to make available accommodation for the carriage of persons on flights or to provide an inclusive tour which includes carriage by air and a copy of any booking form relating to any such brochure. A copy shall be furnished as soon as the brochure has been published.

## Standard Term 4 B

The licence holder shall furnish to the Authority a copy of any brochure, leaflet, or other printed matter in which he or any agent acting on his behalf quotes the prices at which he is prepared to make available accommodation for the carriage of persons on flights or to provide an inclusive tour which includes carriage by air and a copy of any booking form relating to any such brochure, leaflet or other printed matter. A copy shall be furnished as soon as the brochure, leaflet or other printed matter has been published.

## Standard Term 5

The licence holder shall inform the Authority within 21 days of the occurrence of any change in the following information provided in his application for an Air Travel Organiser's Licence:

    (a)  the business address or address of registered office

    (b)  the status of the licence holder (eg by his becoming a limited company or change of name)

    (c)  the parent, holding, associated or subsidiary company or companies

    (d)  the directors, company secretary or managerial staff

    (e)  the partners

    (f)  the authorised or issued share capital

    (g)  the names and addresses of any shareholders owning 15% or more of the shares in the company.

    (h)  the auditors

    (i)  any trading name or names.

## Standard Term 6

The licence holder shall

    (a)  in the case of a body corporate incorporated under the Companies Act 1985 furnish the Authority with a copy of the Annual Statement of Accounts and Directors Report at the same time as the Statement of Accounts and Directors

Report are published to the shareholders in the company or as soon as possible thereafter, and

(b) in all other cases furnish certified statements of annual accounts to the Authority at the end of the licence holder's financial year or as soon as possible thereafter and in no case later than four months thereafter.

### Standard Term 7

The licence holder shall not sub-charter accommodation on a flight except to a person who holds an Air Travel Organiser's Licence authorising him to make available accommodation for the carriage of persons on that flight.

### Standard Term 8

Passengers shall be informed (by means of advertisement or otherwise) before entering into a contract for carriage on any flight made pursuant to the licence of:

(a) the name of the operator of the aircraft on which the passenger is to be carried, the type of aircraft which he intends to operate, and the airport of destination at which it is intended to set down the passengers or

(b) the fact that the licence holder is not in a position to state the operator, the aircraft type or the destination.

Where passengers are informed of the operator, aircraft type or destination they shall at the same time be informed whether they can or cannot cancel their contract without penalty in the event of any subsequent change of operator, aircraft type or destination.

### Standard Term 9

1. The licence holder shall not enter into a contract through the intervention of an agent, being a contract for accommodation to be made available pursuant to the licence, unless he has made it clear in writing to the agent and to the customer that any money paid by the customer to the agent under or in contemplation of the contract is held by the agent as agent for the licence holder from the date on which confirmation of the customer's booking is despatched by the licence holder until the date on which the agent pays the money to the licence holder.

2. The licence holder shall not enter into a contract through the intervention of an agent, being a contract for accommodation to be made available pursuant to the licence, unless he has made it clear in writing to the agent and, so far as is practicable, to the customer, whether or not any money paid by the customer to the agent under or in contemplation of contract is held by the agent as agent for the licence holder from the date on which the money is paid by the

customer to the agent until the date on which confirmation of the customer's booking is despatched by the licence holder.

## Standard Term 10

Where passengers are carried pursuant to this licence for the common purpose of attending a football match, each passenger shall have been provided with a valid ticket of admission to the match and before the date of any such flight the licence holder shall provide the Authority with details of the operator of the flight concerned, of its point and time of departure, of the football match to be attended, and the numbers of passengers to be carried for this purpose.

## Standard Term 11

The licence holder shall not make available accommodation for the carriage of persons on flights whether forming part of any inclusive tour or not unless he has ensured that, within 14 days of his receiving notification of the booking and in any event before the flight, the customer has received a document containing the following information which shall be provided on the form set out in Annex D hereto, or by way of another form giving the same information which has been approved by the Authority:—

  (a)  confirmation of the name of the customer and of the number of passengers included in that booking with in each case details of:—

      (i) the date and flight numbers of the outward and return flights on which the licence holder has undertaken to provide accommodation for the carriage of passengers and the airports of arrival and departure; if the flight numbers are not known at the time the document is issued, this should be indicated on the document;

      (ii) any additional goods, services or other benefits (eg surface accommodation, car hire) which the licence holder has undertaken to provide;

      (iii) the total amount payable in respect of the passengers included in the booking and, if appropriate, an indication that surcharges may be payable;

      (iv) the name of the agent (if applicable).

  (b)  the name and principal place of business or the registered office of the licence holder, and

  (c)  the number of the Air Travel Organiser's Licence issued to the licence holder.

## Standard Term 12

The licence holder (and no other person on his behalf) shall retain either copies of every document issued pursuant to Standard Term 11 and every other document forming or evidencing the formation of a contract to make available accommodation on a flight pursuant to this licence (including booking forms and similar documents and any documents accepting bookings) or an electronic record of the information contained in such documents for a period of three months from the date of the latest flight to be provided under the contract and the licence holder shall furnish to the Authority any or all of such contracts and forms by which bookings are confirmed or copies thereof or a print out of information kept by electronic means within fifteen days of the same being demanded by the Authority.

# Appendix C

# Extract from ABTA Standards on Surcharges

### 3. Rules for Informing Clients and Potential Clients of the Conditions Relating to the Price of their Holidays

It is a fundamental rule that holiday brochures must make clear the surcharge conditions which apply to holidays. To help to achieve this, there is a choice of paragraphs for prominent inclusion in brochures. The choice of one or other from the standard wordings below is mandatory. Care is also required to ensure that brochure flashes and advertising copy do not conflict with the substance of the conditions. This means that there are only limited circumstances where the word "guarantee" or the expression "No surcharges" may be used.

Members should bear in mind that Part III of the Consumer Protection Act is due to take effect in March 1989 and in consequence there is a heavier requirement to ensure that price indications (including statements about how prices are calculated) are not misleading. The form of brochure wording given in the Standards should assist members in meeting the new required level in this area.

    a)   Full Price Guarantee

        "The price of your holiday is fully guaranteed and will not be subject to any surcharges."

        A full price guarantee is the only situation where terms such as "No Surcharges" or "Guaranteed No Surcharges" or "Full Price Guarantee" or similar phrases may be used.

    b)   Partial Price Guarantees

        (i) Price guaranteed except for governmental action.

            "We guarantee that the price of your holiday will not be subject to any surcharge except for those resulting from governmental action. Even in this case, we will absorb an amount equivalent to 2% of the holiday price which excludes insurance premiums and any amendment charges. Only amounts in excess of this 2% will be surcharged, but where a surcharge is payable there will be an administration charge of *p together with an amount

*the amount must be inserted together with the words "per person" where applicable.

to cover agents' commission. If this means paying more than 10% on the holiday price, you will be entitled to cancel your holiday with a full refund of all money paid except for any premium paid to us for holiday insurance and amendment charges. Should you decide to cancel because of this, you must exercise your right to do so within 14 days from the issue date printed on the invoice."

(ii) Guarantee, with no currency surcharges, but with other items which may be surcharged.

"Whatever happens to the value of the Pound, the price of your holiday will not be subject to any currency surcharges. The price of your holiday is, however, subject to surcharges on the following items: (a full list of surchargeable items must be included in this sentence, eg governmental action, aircraft fuel, overflying charges, and airport charges). Even in this case, we will absorb an amount equivalent to 2% of the holiday price which excludes insurance premiums and any amendment charges. Only amounts in excess of this 2% will be surcharged but where a surcharge is payable there will be an administration charge of *p together with an amount to cover agents' commission.

If this means paying more than 10% on the holiday price, you will be entitled to cancel your holiday with a full refund of all money paid except for any premium paid to us for holiday insurance and amendment charges. Should you decide to cancel because of this, you must exercise your right to do so within 14 days from the issue date printed on the invoice.

Members must not use brochure flashes or similar with expressions such as "No Surcharges" because surcharges can arise. ABTA considers that brochure flashes should read "Price guarantee except for (specify exclusions ... eg governmental action)".

c) —Currency not guaranteed and other elements may also be surcharged.

"The price of your holiday is subject to surcharges on the following items: governmental action†, currency†, aircraft fuel†, overflying charges†, airport charges† and increases in scheduled airfares†. Even in this case, we will absorb an amount equivalent to 2% of the holiday price which excludes insurance premiums and any amendment charges. Only amounts in excess of this 2% will be surcharged but where a surcharge is payable

---

*the amount must be inserted together with the words "per person" where applicable.
†A full list of surchargeable items must be included in this sentence.

there will be an administration charge of *p together with an amount to cover agents' commission. If this means paying more than 10% on the holiday price, you will be entitled to cancel your holiday with a full refund of all money paid except for any premium paid to us for holiday insurance and amendment charges. Should you decide to cancel because of this, you must exercise your right to do so within 14 days from the issue date printed on the invoice."

Brochure flashes must not contain words linking prices and guarantees.

## 6. Sanctions

The sanctions for breaches will be those prescribed by the existing Code of Conduct. Where sensitive commercial information is involved the operator has the choice of either releasing the information to the Code of Conduct Committee or empowering the Monitoring Committee to make a judgement.

*the amount must be inserted together with the words "per person" where applicable.

# Appendix D

# County court cases

The cases reported below are not discussed in the body of this book.

*Askew* v *Intasun North*

(Ashby-de-la-Zouch County Court – [1980] CLY 637)

The plaintiff, who had booked a holiday in Puerto de la Cruz for himself and his wife, was told on arrival that he would not be staying at the hotel which he had booked but in a hotel of a different type. The defendants knew this before the plaintiff's departure but made no effort to inform the plaintiff. The change caused the plaintiff's wife considerable distress.

It was held that the holiday was a complete disaster and that the family derived no benefit, although they did try to make the best of it. Damages of £943.23 (the cost of the holiday) plus £80 for car hire were awarded for breach of contract, and damages of £300 for "assault on feelings".

*Levine* v *Metropolitan Travel*

(Westminster County Court – [1980] CLY 638)

The plaintiffs paid £323.50 for a seven-day package holiday in Tel Aviv. The hotel was found to be totally unsatisfactory and the defendants admitted liability.

The judge rejected the submission that the holiday was a cheap one and that the value to be expected was therefore less. The proper test was to see the value of the loss sustained which was assessed at £200. In addition, damages for "assault on feelings" in the total sum of £200 (£100 per plaintiff) were awarded.

*Bragg* v *Yugotours*

(Westminster County Court − [1982] CLY 777)

The plaintiff paid £326.80 for a two-week holiday for herself and her daughter in Yugoslavia. On arrival at the hotel, the Yugotour representative was "unforgivably rude" and "did everything possible to ruin the plaintiff's holiday". The plaintiff was initially allocated a room with fungus and slime on the walls and was then moved to a room with damp bedding, shabby decor, exposed wires and a defective toilet. For the second night the plaintiff was moved to a single room with a camp bed for her daughter. Beetles later emerged from the floor. On the third day the plaintiff was moved to an alternative hotel without a sandy beach or children's facilities, and the plaintiff and her daughter contracted chills from damp bedding. The plaintiff asked to return home but was told that this was impossible. Yugotours offered to return the cost of the holiday plus £80 compensation.

It was held that there had been serious breaches of contract but that the plaintiff had not lost the whole value of the holiday. She was awarded £550 to cover diminution of the value of the contract and compensation for loss of enjoyment.

*Hunt* v *Hourmont*

(North and Port Talbot County Court − [1983] CLY 983)

The plaintiff booked and paid for a seven-day, two-centre holiday for a school party, comprising forty-three pupils and five teachers. Each pupil paid £98. The plaintiff complained that in Paris the food provided was uninteresting and insufficient in quantity and that the coach which was supposed to be available for evening use was not available one evening and on another could only be used for a short time. At the second centre, the plaintiff alleged that the party could not stay at the hotel which they had booked. The substitute was, it was alleged, dirty, cold and had inadequate heating. The toilets were so dirty that the female teachers had to clean and disinfect them before they could be used; the bedrooms were damp and musty with peeling papers and mould on the walls; the beds and bedding were so damp that the party slept fully clothed on the beds, not in them; the food was served almost cold, was of poor quality and insufficient in quantity. The pupils therefore bought food elsewhere and the party leader spent considerable time telephoning the defendant's representative and complaining to the hotel proprietor who told them that they should leave if they did not like it.

It was held that it would be an exaggeration to describe the holiday as a complete disaster but it was held that the second centre was inadequate in every conceivable respect. Pupils were awarded damages of £60 each for diminution in value and loss of enjoyment. The teachers were awarded £110 for extra worry and responsibility, and the leading teacher was awarded £210 because of extra worry, responsibility, work and unpleasantness in dealing with complaints.

*Rhodes* v *Sunspot Tours*

(Preston County Court – [1983] CLY 984)

The plaintiff paid the defendants £777 for a holiday in a Maltese self-catering apartment for himself, his wife and three children. Upon arrival at 2 am, the apartment key could not be found and they were housed in a hotel, the arrangements for which were unsatisfactory. The following day they were shown into the apartment but found that it had not been cleaned, and that the toilet had broken away from the wall creating an unwholesome smell. A bed mattress was stained with blood and urine and the cot mattress was torn. An independent witness described the flat as "grotty, grimy and horrible". After five days the plaintiff was offered an alternative apartment. Upon an inspection, green mould was found in the fridge. The plaintiff stayed in the first flat for the remainder of the holiday but ate out for all meals including breakfast, due to the unclean kitchen. The plaintiff's wife was very upset by the experience and she and the plaintiff each lost about twelve pounds in weight during the fortnight.

It was held that:

(i)    the defendants were in breach of contract providing a "disastrous" holiday; and

(ii)   the plaintiff reasonably refused the alternative accommodation offered, since by then an "atmosphere of mistrust" existed between the plaintiff and the defendant; and

(iii)  damages of £1,000 included the total waste of the price of the holiday, the discomfort and distress of the first night and the upset to all the family for the balance of the holiday.

*Bagley* v *Intourist Moscow*

(Westminster County Court – [1984] CLY 1024)

The defendants agreed to act as travel agents for the plaintiff and make the necessary arrangements for him to go by rail and sea from London to Eastern Siberia and thence by air to Japan. The plaintiff signed the booking form incorporating some terms and conditions but not expressly specifying what the defendants' obligations were under the contract.

The defendants informed the plaintiff, in the brochure containing the booking form, of the entry requirements for all countries except Japan. The plaintiff did not know he needed a visa to enter Japan, did not obtain one and was refused entry. He was confined to a hotel for six days and then deported by air to the UK. He paid £154 for hotel expenses in Japan and settled litigation over his return fare for a total of £488. He lost the opportunity to spend a few weeks in Japan and to travel back to the UK overland via India.

It was held that:

(i) there was an implied term that the defendants were obliged to inform the plaintiff of entry requirements for Japan or to warn the plaintiff that they were not able so to advise him. It was a relevant factor that the plaintiff was a private individual without expert knowledge; and

(ii) general damages of £1,500 were awarded, the plaintiff having wasted £324 for the journey out and £488 on the journey back; and

(iii) loss of the benefit of the overland journey back was irrecoverable as being outside the contemplation of the party as the defendant had not been informed of it; and

(iv) special damages of £154 were awarded but the return air fare was not awarded since the plaintiff would always have had to travel back.

*Taylor* v *International Travel Services*

(West London County Court – [1984] CLY 1023)

The plaintiff paid the defendants £1,306.52 for a three-week holiday for himself, his wife and their child in a self-contained villa of exceptional quality in an exclusive estate in Marbella, Spain. The price was stated to include flight and car hire. Three days before they were due to leave, the defendants cancelled the booking, stating that the villa had been double-booked by its owners. The defendants returned the money, as an alternative villa was not available. The defendants had, however, failed to arrange flights or car hire which prevented the plaintiff from renting an alternative villa in Marbella. The plaintiff found an alternative villa for two weeks in Spain in a less attractive location for £1,206 inclusive. Prior to payment to the defendants, the plaintiff had informed the defendants that the plaintiff's wife, a professional singer, had been invited to perform at a concert during the first week of the holiday which she wished to accept as the booking was not confirmed. The defendants assured the plaintiff that arrangements for the villa had been confirmed and in reliance of this misrepresentation the plaintiff's wife declined the concert engagements. The plaintiff claimed damages including the lost concert fees.

Judgment was entered in default and the defendants did not, in fact, appear at the hearing for the assessment of damages before the Registrar. The Registrar held as follows on the assessment of damages hearing:

(i) the plaintiff could recover special damages of £787.50 for the concert fee which the plaintiff's wife had lost as a result of the defendants' representation; and

(ii) the plaintiff would recover general damages in the sum of

233

£1,150. The plaintiff was entitled to £250 in respect of the cost of travelling to Manchester instead of Gatwick, parking and associated inconvenience as well as the loss of pay for one week's additional holiday justifiably taken by the plaintiff. For loss of enjoyment of the wasted first week of the holiday, the plaintiff was entitled to recover double the average weekly cost of the promised quality villa at a lost bargain price of £900. For loss of enjoyment over the last two weeks the plaintiff was entitled to 50 per cent of the cost of the alternative holiday averaged out over three weeks which was £400; and

(iii) the claim for loss of enjoyment of the plaintiff's infant child was ignored.

## Abbatt v *Sunquest Holidays*

(Canterbury County Court − [1984] CLY 1025)

The plaintiff booked and paid for a fourteen-day package holiday in Romania, the price for two adults and two young children in a hotel suite being £769. The defendants' brochure represented, *inter alia*, that there was a fine beach at the resort and that there was a swimming pool, nanny service and meals provided on a full board basis at the hotel. Additionally, it represented that the resort and hotel were ideal for children. Upon arrival at the hotel, the plaintiff discovered the suite to be cramped with broken tiles and a broken shower. The swimming pool contained dirty, untreated water and was unsuitable for children, and the nanny service had not been available for two years. Meals were of a very poor choice and quality and were long in duration as a result of which the children ate little. Untreated sewage had been deposited on the beach which needed clearing before the children could play. The effect of the condition of the resort and the hotel was that the family returned to England after six days.

It was held that:

(i) the plaintiff was entitled to expect a reasonable standard of facilities. There were substantial and relevant breaches of representations; and

(ii) there was no defined formula for assessing damages, and damages of £1,000 were awarded for diminution in value and loss of enjoyment.

## Harris v *Torchgrove Limited*

(Manchester District Registry − [1985] CLY 944)

The plaintiff booked a holiday for himself, his wife and three teenage children in an apartment in France, selecting an apartment from the defendants' brochure. It was stated to be in "a quieter part of town". The total cost for four weeks was £1,400. When the plaintiff and family arrived, they were taken to a different apartment which was over a restaurant. It generated much noise and smell and adjoined a fruit-machine parlour. The apartment only had accommodation for four although on the second day of the holiday, a portable bed was supplied.

It was held that the defendants were liable, and damages totalling £2,157.83 were awarded against them. This sum included damages for loss of enjoyment, special damages and interest.

In the course of the judgment, it was said:

> "A tour operator sells a dream. If he sells a dream he must make it come true. This is fragile; therefore it imposes a great obligation on him to take care."

### *Scott & Scott* v *Blue Sky Holidays*

(Willesden County Court – [1985] CLY 943)

The plaintiffs paid the defendants £512 for a seven-night holiday at a four-star hotel in Tenerife. Upon arrival they were placed in a cramped and noisy room without twin beds (as required). They complained and were transferred to another room, but not until the following afternoon. The evening meals were luke warm and greasy. After the first of the evening meals, the plaintiffs ate out for the rest of the holiday, spending £41.

It was held that:

(i) the holiday had not been an unmitigated disaster but complaints regarding the food and the first night's accommodation were well cited and the plaintiffs were entitled to expect better conditions at an internationally classified four-star hotel; and

(ii) damages are at large and not to be determined by reference to the sums spent on the holiday; and

(iii) the plaintiffs' failure to seek to mitigate their loss by complaining to the defendants' representative at the hotel operated to reduce what would otherwise have been "substantial" damages to £400.

### *Powell* v *Arrowsmith Holidays*

(Liverpool County Court – [1985] CLY 945)

The plaintiff was three months pregnant. She booked a holiday for herself and her husband for fourteen days in a Spanish hotel. It was a written term in the contract that they would be provided with twin beds, a bath, separate toilet and a balcony. They requested a room on the ground or first floor because of the plaintiff's pregnancy. On the day before departure the defendants attempted to vary the contract because of overbooking on behalf of the hoteliers. They offered the plaintiff's husband an apartment. He refused. No alternative accommodation was offered. The plaintiff and her husband flew out the next morning. They were kept waiting for five to six hours. The plaintiff was extremely upset. They were given eventually a single cramped room with two single beds and a shower. After the fifth night they were given a double room on the fourth floor. The defendants argued (i) that the plaintiff had accepted variation of the contract via her husband, (ii) that the terms in the standard booking form excluded breaches of overbooking by hoteliers and their failure to provide alternative accommodation, and (iii) that there were no breaches of contract. After four hours of evidence the defendants withdrew their defence and submitted to judgment. General damages for inconvenience etc were assessed at £750.

### *Tucker* v *O.T.A. Travel*

(Salisbury County Court – [1986] CLY 383)

The plaintiff booked a holiday for himself, his wife and four-year-old daughter in a three-star hotel in Majorca, having chosen it from the defendants' brochure. The hotel was described as very reliable with a reputation for good service and cuisine, tasteful decor and a friendly atmosphere. The plaintiff chose the defendants' holiday because the brochure indicated that flights were scheduled ones, daytime and direct to the airport of destination. His daughter was shy and insecure and would be difficult if travelling at night. The plane was overbooked and he was offered a non-direct flight with no guarantees that he would make his connection at the other end. The plaintiff refused this offer and re-booked the first direct flight available. He attempted to telex the hotel, and returned home losing two days of his holiday. The plaintiff flew out two days later to find the hotel overbooked. He had to spend two nights in an apartment with a defective toilet, peeling wallpaper, beds with no springs and a dirty, rusty wash-basin. The defendants argued that (i) the contract with the plaintiff was only to use their best endeavours to arrange the flight and hotel, and that (ii) if there was a breach due to the overbooking, the plaintiff had failed to mitigate his loss by not accepting the alternative flight.

It was held that:

(i) the contract with the plaintiff was to provide the flight and hotel accommodation; and

(ii) the plaintiff had not failed to mitigate his loss as the defendants had not proved that he had failed to be reasonable within the meaning of the law; and

(iii) the plaintiff was entitled to out-of-pocket expenses of £100 and a sum attributable to a notional rebate in respect of four days' lost hotel accommodation (£129.29) and £300 for general damages for inconvenience, which would have been more had the plaintiff not exaggerated the problems. Total award: £529.29.

*Carter* v *Thomson Travel*

(Oldham County Court − [1986] CLY 976)

The plaintiff paid the defendants £859 for a two-week holiday for herself, her husband and three children in a self-contained exclusive villa in Majorca. It was discovered on arrival that the villa had been built very recently and the plumber was still carrying out repairs in the bathroom. The inside of the villa was damp and cold — the plaster work had not dried out prior to the plaintiff's arrival. The family's clothing and bedding became damp and they slept in sweatshirts and socks. The swimming pool could not be used and the plaintiff felt unable to allow her children to play around the villa because a vicious dog on a long chain from a nearby farm was able to encroach upon the property. The villa was burgled on the tenth day as a result of which the plaintiff's family moved to a hotel.

It was held that the facilities at the villa fell below what a reasonable person could anticipate. For diminution in the value of the holiday, special damages of £259 were awarded, and for mental distress, inconvenience and disappointment general damages of £1,000 were awarded.

*Jacobs* v *Thomson Travel*

(Bloomsbury County Court − [1986] CLY 975)

In January 1985 the plaintiff purchased a holiday for himself, his wife, mother and son at a five-star hotel in Israel from the defendants for £2,455. The holiday was for seven days in April 1985. The plaintiff wished to spend passover at the hotel, but did not advise the defendants of this. The day before departure, the defendants told the plaintiff that he could not stay at the five-star hotel contracted for and offered him an inferior hotel at the same resort. The plaintiff refused the offer, the holiday was cancelled and the defendants returned the price to the plaintiff. The plaintiff claimed damages for inconvenience and disappointment, including that suffered because the family had to spend passover at home.

It was held that:

(i) the plaintiff was entitled to general damages for disappointment etc and was not obliged to accept an alternative holiday. In assessing compensation for the disappointment, the court took into account that the plaintiff and his family had another holiday in Israel in May 1985 and frequently took foreign holidays; and

(ii) the plaintiff was not entitled to extra damages because it was passover since that was too remote in view of the fact that the plaintiff had not told the defendants that he was religious and the passage was important; and

(iii) general damages were assessed at £250 and special damages in respect of loss of earnings and telephone calls at £210.

*McLeod* v *Hunter*

(Westminster County Court — [1987] CLY 1162)

The plaintiff booked a holiday with the defendant in May 1986 for a luxury villa in St Jean Cap Ferrat. He paid £1,030 for accommodation for the week commencing 2 August. The villa was described as being "a quality villa" with spectacular views. It had an elegant interior with accommodation for eight. The plaintiff intended the stay as the highpoint and rest-over after a touring holiday with his wife and three children. Immediately before the family set off, the defendant cancelled the booked accommodation, and the plaintiff agreed to take an alternative which the defendant assured him would be found. This turned out to be sub-standard. It was an apartment rather than a house; it was cramped and very uncomfortable. It did not provide the luxurious rest which the plaintiff had bargained for. On arrival, it was too late to change elsewhere.

It was held that:

(i) damages for diminution in value of the holiday provided: £439; and

(ii) general damages for inconvenience and disappointment: £500; and

(iii) interest at 12.5 per cent from 9 August 1986 to 8 January 1987.

*Baldwin* v *Tameside Travel*

(Manchester County Court — [1987] CLY 1148)

The plaintiff booked a flight to Tenerife for himself, two other adults and three children. The plaintiff had assured his children the flight would be on a Tristar aircraft. The plaintiff considered the Tristar superior to the Boeing 727. On 20 March 1985, the plaintiff duly booked the seats at a total cost of £1,161. The booking form referred to the flight being with British Airtours. A few days before departure, the plaintiff received the tickets and discovered they were in respect of a Dan Air Boeing 727. Furthermore, the departure time was at 7.30am (instead of 10.10am). The plaintiff gave evidence that with young children this caused considerable inconvenience. The plaintiff boarded the aircraft but found his family was split up in the seating arrangements. The plaintiff sued for special damages of £147, being his loss caused by being given a flight he could have obtained for £147 cheaper from another travel agent. He claimed further general damages for inconvenience.

The judge found that as the booking form referred to a British Air-tours aircraft and the plaintiff was put on a Dan Air Boeing, this was in breach of contract. The plaintiff was awarded £147 in special damages and £150 in general damages for stress and inconvenience.

## *Hartley* v *Intasun Holidays*

(Ellesmere Port County Court – [1987] CLY 1149)

The plaintiff booked a package holiday with the defendants in Majorca at a price of £270. The plaintiff, through his own error, arrived at Manchester airport a day late and missed his flight. A representative of the defendants at Manchester airport indicated that it would be possible to accommodate him on a flight later that day to Ibiza from where he could obtain a local flight to Majorca, and the representative telexed the resort to request them to keep his hotel room available. On arrival at the resort, the plaintiff found that the hotelier had re-let his room, and the plaintiff was accommodated in inferior accommodation in a different resort. The plaintiff claimed damages against the defendants for failure to supply the accommodation which had been booked.

It was held that the change of departure date by the plaintiff constituted a cancellation by him of his holiday, which attracted 100 per cent cancellation charges and this was in accordance with the defendants' booking conditions. The defendants were entitled to retain the whole purchase price and do nothing to make alternative arrangements for the plaintiff. They should not be penalised in damages for making an attempt, without charge, to patch up some form of holiday for the plaintiff. Claim dismissed.

## *Sage* v *Bladon Lines Travel Limited*

(Wandsworth County Court 3 November 1987)

In November 1984, the plaintiff, on behalf of himself and three other families, booked a package holiday with the defendants to commence on 22 December, including accommodation at the Chalet Lamastra. The total cost of the holiday was £4,863, and the holiday was to include food and the services of two chalet girls. The plaintiff alleged that the chalet girls did not keep the kitchen in the chalet clean, that the steps to the chalet were not cleared properly, that there were insufficient chairs for the party to sit on, that there were no chest of drawers or mirrors in the bathroom and livingroom, that the chalet was inaccessible by coach and that the oven did not work for some of the holiday. Further, there were particular problems concerning heating on New Year's eve.

The judge said:

> "I have made findings of fact in some detail. I am left with the final matter, to decide, in view of all these facts, whether the

defendants did not provide services and accommodation to a reasonable standard in accordance with all the circumstances and particulars in the brochure. One or two matters trouble me, ie the number of towels, which were not in accordance with the manual. It troubles me that the rep and the two chalet girls were new to the job and that Mr. Sage and party were their first customers. I cannot help remarking that the plaintiffs had a raw deal but substantially they got what the brochure said. If one looks at the brochure, there is no promise that they provide chalet girls with experience, it only refers to their training. Chalet girls do not do the work for many seasons; it is a hard life.

I am troubled with the question of whether the travel company promises fundamental things will be provided, ie that they guarantee the working of a heating system in a cold climate. I am afraid, in seeking to find a breach of duty on the part of the defendants, I look in vain. I take no pleasure in coming to that conclusion, because the plaintiff and his party had a raw deal. They were disappointed by their holiday, but I bear in mind that nothing could be done in the circumstances. I make the highest criticism that Anita did not ring on New Year's Day and that there was a lack of communication.

I am bound to find that there is not misrepresentation ... I therefore must dismiss the claim."

### Toubi v Intasun Holidays Limited

((1988) 4 CL 94)

The plaintiff booked a holiday with the defendants, six months in advance. She chose a four-star hotel and flight timings convenient for her daughter's health. Some three days before the plaintiff's departure, the defendants learnt that the hotel was overbooked and could not accommodate the plaintiff. The plaintiff rejected the alternative of a three-star hotel which the defendants offered. Since the defendants could not arrange an alternative four-star hotel they refunded the plaintiff's cost of the holiday. The plaintiff sued for damages for distress, loss of enjoyment etc.

It was held that the contract between the plaintiff and the defendants was subject to booking conditions which covered this subject. The defendants had been let down themselves by the hotel and had done their best to offer alternatives. The defendants, however, were not in breach of contract and, accordingly, the plaintiff's claim failed.

### Jones & Jones v Villa Ramos (Algarve)

((1988) 2 CL 78b)

The plaintiffs booked with the defendants a holiday in the Algarve for

May 1987. The defendants' brochure described the apartment complex as having "a very large pool facility with bar, restaurant, sun lounging equipment and kiddies' pool". On arrival, the plaintiffs were told that due to a dispute they would not be allowed to use any of the facilities. This stance was maintained despite an offer by the plaintiffs to pay for the use of the facilities. The plaintiffs were forced to travel by hired car to beaches to swim but the weather did not always make such swimming possible or safe. The plaintiffs accepted that the apartment itself was entirely satisfactory.

It was held that the defendants were liable for breach of contract. The plaintiffs were awarded £750 for diminution in the value of the holiday provided, £1,000 for general damages for inconvenience and disappointment and interest at 12 per cent.

*Wilson* v *Pegasus Holidays (London)*
*(T/A Pegasus Student Travel)*

((1988) 8 CL 129)

The plaintiff, a teacher, booked a one-week skiing holiday in Italy, acting as agent for thirty-one pupils. Each pupil paid £249. The plaintiff and another teacher went free as party leaders. The children were aged 12–13. The plaintiff, one month before departure, discovered that her booking was not confirmed. She was told by the defendants that she could have her money back or accept a holiday at a different resort in a different hotel. The defendants' representative made representations to the plaintiff about the alternative holiday based on "very little" investigation which turned out to be material misrepresentations. The hotel was described in the defendants' brochure as offering a "superb standard of accommodation". In fact it had inadequate toilet and bathing facilities, exposed electric wiring and was in very poor decorative order. The skiing slopes were some distance from the hotel and the bus service was erratic. Consequently, skiing time was lost and young children were forced to walk to the slopes carrying their ski equipment.

It was held that the defects in the holiday amounted to breaches of implied terms in the contract as well as founding a claim in misrepresentation. Each child was awarded £125 for loss of enjoyment and diminution in the value of the holiday. The plaintiff as the party leader was awarded £400 because of extra stress, worry and responsibility and, for the same reasons, the other teacher was awarded £200.

*Duthie* v *Thomson Holidays*

((1988) 6 CL 78a)

The plaintiff booked with the defendants a fourteen-day package holiday including hostel accommodation. On arrival, the defendants alleged that the plaintiff had booked for flight only, but subsequently provided one night's accommodation. The following night the plaintiff had to sleep rough on the beach and she spent the remaining nights either in a cheap hotel or sleeping in the open on camp sites. The plaintiff claimed damages for breach of contract.

It was held that there had been breach of contract by the defendants. The plaintiff was awarded £250 for general damages for mental distress, inconvenience and loss of enjoyment, and £44 for special damages in respect of the cost of camp sites and hotel charges.

[NOTE: Charter flight passengers to Greece are required to have an accommodation arrangement — it is a Greek requirement. Many brochures which are intended to sell charter flight seats only, to circumvent this requirement, state that hostel accommodation is also arranged. Tour operators, and most customers, know that there is no intention on either side to seek to make use of any accommodation "arrangements". This case is an example of a holiday maker either not knowing or not playing by "the rules of the game"!]

# Index